WOMENSWORK
FIVE NEW PLAYS
FROM THE
WOMEN'S PROJECT

Edited by
Julia Miles

THEATRE BOOK PUBLISHERS

WOMENSWORK: Five New Plays from The Women's Project

Library of Congress Cataloging-in-publication data:

WomensWork: five new plays from The Women's Project.

    Bibliography: p.
    Contents: Abingdon Square / by Maria Irene Fornes — Ma Rose / by Cassandra Medley — Etta Jenks / by Marlane Meyer — Five in the killing zone / by Lavonne Mueller — [etc.]
    1. American drama — Women authors. 2. American drama — 20th century. I. Miles, Julia. II. Women's Projects (New York, N.Y.).
    PS628.W6W68 1989   812'.540809287   89-15196
    ISBN 1-55783-029-0

APPLAUSE THEATRE BOOK PUBLISHERS, INC.
211 W. 71st Street
New York, NY 10023
212/595-4735

First Applause Printing, 1989.

CONTENTS

INTRODUCTION

In 1978 I asked, "Where are the women playwrights?" Eleven years later I think most people who know about theatre would answer, "Alive and well and writing increasingly challenging, provocative drama."

These playwrights are adding their strong, intelligent, passionate voices to the theatre at a time of identity crisis. The old question of theatre as art or theatre as commerce or theatre as a combination of both haunts us even as we go on making theatre the best we can.

In 1978 when I began The Women's Project at the American Place Theatre approximately 7% of non-profit plays produced were written by women. In 1989 the percentage has approximately tripled. Not enough. Statistically 20,000 people see a Broadway play each night. Only 1,000 of those see a play written by a woman — Wendy Wasserstein's *Heidi Chronicles*. Not enough.

And yet this spring, 1989, I have been traveling around the country seeing plays written by women and reading plays by women and it has given me great encouragement and hope because what I've found in this somewhat conservative theatrical climate is heartening. Playwrights such as Lynne Alvarez, Darrah Cloud, Constance Congdon, Alex Finlayson, Laura Harrington, Heather McDonald, Anna Deveare Smith, Gina Wendkos, and playwrights included in this anthology, among others, take chances with difficult subjects and often break the perimeters of the strict realistic form.

And the truth and strength and individualism of their voices is making a difference and will continue to do so until the percentages of men and women playwrights are equally distributed. At that time we'll shout hooray and celebrate.

The plays included here all tell different stories but they do share a common interest in viewing personal narratives against large public backdrops: *Abingdon Square*'s tragic love triangle with World War I in the background; *Etta Jenks*' sad pursuit of an empty dream set within the pornography industry; the family struggle in *Ma Rose* among mother, daughter, and grandmother seen erupting during a civil rights march; the grief and reconciliation of women surviving their husband's deaths after a steel mill explosion in *Mill Fire*; and the failure of technology during a particularly grisly assignment in Vietnam in *Five in the Killing Zone*. Each does the most important thing a play can do — it moves and delights and makes us see our world just a little more clearly.

ABINGDON SQUARE by Maria Irene Fornes. I've been a fan of Irene's for twenty odd years. She has changed and enhanced American theatre by her consistently pure and unique theatrical vision, her influential teaching, and decisive directing style. In *Abingdon Square*, Irene explores the extreme passions that erupt from the marriage between a young girl and an older man. The play is a rich and incisive study of a young woman's late sexual awakening, set in pre-World War I Greenwich Village. Mel Gussow in *The New York Times* found the atmosphere Jamesian in the way the play captured "the mood of a lost way of life." Erica Monk in *The Village Voice* wrote that "Fornes sticks to the conventions of the period she's writing about. Such a story can easily turn banal and silly; what Fornes does is force us to see it new, with the uniqeness and emotional weight it would have if it happened to our own relatives." Certainly, this study of a woman's awakening to passion and loss grows all the more provocative because of its historical backdrop — the emergence of America into the harsh reality of the 20th century with the first of the terrible world wars.

ETTA JENKS is by Marlane Meyer, a young California woman recently moved to New York. The play is on the surface, a hip, raunchy investigation into the seamy world of pornography. Beneath its surface brittleness and quick-paced cinematic structure, however, the play has a sure metaphysical core that contains a deep belief in the power of miracles — and transcendence. Mel Gussow in *The New York Times* described the play as an "ancient story ... turned into a sardonic, eye opening plunge into a contemporary netherworld." The effect of *Etta Jenks* was "a pungency" with "a bitter aftertaste." Gussow called Meyer "a playwright with an uncompromising voice" and Sullivan in *The L. A. Times* compared her to David Mamet. I'm sure he meant it as a compliment, but Marlane has her own special voice.

MA ROSE by Cassandra Medley. Cassandra wrote the funny, touching sketch, Ms. Mae, in our successful musical review, *A ... My Name Is Alice* and came into her own when she expanded a one act version of *Ma Rose* into a full-length play. She takes her audience into the intimate circle of a black Midwestern family as they play emotional tug of war over care of their aging and senile family matriarch. In the course of the drama, Cassandra depicts conflict between a new-generation, successful, upwardly mobile young black woman and her tradition-bound family. Jerry Talmer of *The New York Post* said after the opening of *Ma Rose*, "We have a playwright, and a play, to welcome ... With these words I began to hear the voice of another black lioness grandmother, Mama Younger of Lorraine Hansberry's 'A Raisin in the Sun,' and my heart felt as charged as back then in 1959, before the freedom marches."

MILL FIRE by Sally Nemeth. Set in Alabama in the late 1970's, Sally transforms an all too ordinary story of a catastrophe into a play that reaches classic, tragic stature. Using the circumstances of a mill explosion, the play traces the ways people survive unaccountable, random disaster. Her protagonist, the spirited, sensual Marlene, is an unconventional widow whose fight against the inevitable acceptance of loss is poignant and yet, heroic. *Variety* called the play "a searing consideration of the cruelty of accidental death." Certainly, *Mill Fire* reminds us of the ephemeralness of our lives but its strength lies, in part, in the non-linear and very theatrical style of its telling.

FIVE IN THE KILLING ZONE by Lavonne Mueller. Lavonne has had six first productions by The Women's Project and Productions and her courage in taking chances always astonishes me. Frank Rich writing in *The New York Times* said of her that Lavonne had "a sensibility to be cherished ... with an arresting, scabrous vision of the American way of death." *Killing Zone* is one of her plays examining the male experience in war. Five soldiers stationed in a free fire zone in Vietnam have the inglorious job of identifying body parts to find a man who can be named the Unknown Soldier. As their technological resources fail, the men find an unorthodox solution to their macabre search that affirms their humanity. Their choice proves they are men first and soldiers second.

These plays put an end to the old question, "What should a woman write about?" Everything she knows or dreams about. All of it. Amen.

ABINGDON SQUARE

by

Maria Irene Fornes

ABOUT THE PLAY

An earlier version of *Abingdon Square* was given a workshop production at Seattle Repertory Theatre in 1984. Following a staged reading at New York's American Place Theatre in April, *Abindgon Square* opened there on October 8, 1987, produced by The Women's Project and Productions Inc. and directed by the author. The text published here is a revision completed by the author in December 1987.

CHARACTERS

Marion, from age 15 to 24.
Juster, Marion's husband, from age 50 to 59
Michael, Juster's son, the same age as Marion.
Frank, Marion's lover, one year older than Marion.
Mary, Marion's cousin, the same age as Marion.
Minnie, Marion's great-aunt, from age 58 to 67.
A Glazier, a very strong tender man.
Thomas, Marion's son, eight months old.

TIME AND PLACE

ACT ONE: 1908-1912.
In a house on 10th Street, New York City.

ACT TWO: 1915-1917.
In the house on 10th Street, Mary's place, an apartment on Abingdon Square, a beer parlor, and Minnie's house.

SETTINGS

The living room of a house on 10th Street. *To the right is a double door which leads to a sitting room, the foyer and the main door. On the back wall there are two large French doors. On the right there are double doors that lead to other rooms. Up center, a few feet from the back wall are a sofa and two armchairs. On each side of the sofa there is a tall stand with a vase. Down left there are a chess table and two side chairs; down right there is a small desk. There is a chair on the upstage side of the desk and another on the right side.*

The attic. *A platform about two feet high on the left side of the stage. On the upstage side of the platform there is a wall with a small door.*

Mary's living room. *An embroidered shawl is placed on the sofa. The area surrounding the center is dimly lit.*

The living room of an apartment on Abingdon Square. *A back wall is placed behind the sofa. On the wall there is a fireplace; above the fireplace there is a large mirror.*

The beer parlor. *A square plain wood table and two chairs in a pool of red light, center stage.*

Minnie's living room. *A chair center stage in a pool of light.*

Juster's bedroom. *A platform about two feet high on the right side of the stage. On the upstage side of the platform there is a wall with a small door. Parallel to the back wall there is a narrow bed.*

ACT ONE

SCENE 1: *10th Street. August 1908. It is dusk.* JUSTER *sits in the garden facing up left. He sings Handel's "Where'er You Walk."* MARION *hides between the two windows and listens.*

JUSTER: [*Singing.*]

Where'er you walk,
Cool gales shall fan the glades.

[*She moves to the left window and looks at him.*]

Trees, where you sit,
Shall crowd into a shade.
Trees, where you sit,
Shall crowd into a shade.

MARION: Pst!

[JUSTER *leans over to see who has called.* MARION *moves her hand towards him.*]

SCENE 2: *Two weeks later. It is a sunny afternoon.* MARION *enters running from the left.* MICHAEL *is chasing her. They run around the room laughing and screaming. He grabs her and takes a piece of chocolate from her hand. He unwraps the chocolate and puts it in his mouth. She chases him. She grabs him and they fall. He covers his mouth. She tries to pull his hand away.*

MARION: Give it to me.

[*He swallows the chocolate, lets her remove his hand, and opens his mouth.*]

MICHAEL: It's gone. I swallowed it.

MARION: You're bad! [*She holds him tightly.*] I love you Mike! I love you.

MICHAEL: Me, too! I love you too!

MARION: I don't love you as a mother does, though. I love you as a sister loves a brother. I must be a mother to you. You should have a mother. You need a mother. How could a boy like you grow up without a mother.

MICHAEL: I'd rather have you. You're more to me than any mother could ever be. You're my sister, my daughter, my cousin, my friend. You are my friend! My grandmother!

MARION: You're joking and I'm serious.

MICHAEL: I'm serious. You are to me the best person I'll ever know.

MARION: [*Standing.*] You need a guide, a teacher in life.

MICHAEL: I don't need a guide. I need a friend.

MARION: You need someone who'll tell you what to do.

MICHAEL: I don't. I'm doing fine. I'm a good boy. A mother would say to me, "You're doing fine m'boy. You give me no trouble and you don't need a mother." When I need help I'll go to you and you'll help me.

[*As the following speech progresses* MARION *speaks rapidly as if in an emotional trance.*]

MARION: You're sweet. You are the sweetest creature on earth. I wish I were sweet like you. I wish I had sweetness in my heart the way you do. Soon I will, officially, be your mother, and I say this in earnest, I hope I can make myself worthy of both you and your father. He brought solace to me when I knew nothing but grief. I experienced joy only when he was with me. His kindness brought me back to life. I am grateful to him and I love him. I would have died had he not come to save me. I love him more than my own life and I owe it to him. And I love you because you are his son, and you have a sweetness the same as his. I hope I can make myself worthy of the love you have both bestowed upon me and I hope to be worthy of the honor of being asked to be one of this household which is blessed — with a noble and pure spirit. I'm honored to be invited to share this with you and I hope that I succeed in being as noble of spirit as those who invite me to share it with them. I know I sound very formal, and that my words seem studied. But there is no other way I can express what I feel. In this house light comes through the windows as if it delights in entering. I feel the same. I delight in entering here. I delight in walking through these rooms and I'm sad when I leave. I cannot wait for the day when my eyes open from a night's sleep and I find myself inside these walls. Being here I feel as if I'm blessed. — If life dealt me a cruel blow when my parents died, now it offers me the kindest reward. I hope I never give either of you cause for regret. I hope you, as well as he, will always tell me if I have done something wrong — or if I have done less than what you expect, or if you have any reason for disappointment. Would you promise me you will?

MICHAEL: I promise.

SCENE 3: *Shortly after.* MINNIE *and* JUSTER *are entering from the foyer.* MARION *stands left.*

MINNIE: [*As she goes to sit, to* MARION.] Sit down, dear.

[MINNIE *sits right.* JUSTER *sits left.* MARION *sits on the sofa.*]

MINNIE: I was just talking to Juster about the question of your obligations. The questions you posed to me, and whether you will continue your studies, or what obligations you will have. And we thought you should ask the questions directly to him. — He doesn't seem to know the answer. — Go ahead, dear.

MARION: I wanted to know about my obligations here. I believe that when one marries one has obligations and I asked Aunt Minnie what those obligations would be. And she said she was not sure. But that she thought maybe I will be running the house. — Is that so? And I told her that I have never run a house and I don't know if it's something I could learn to do.

I told her that I should tell you that I have never run a house. It may be that you don't feel that I am suited to do it.

JUSTER: I'm embarrassed to say that I have no idea how to run the house. When I was born my mother ran the house. Then, when I married, my wife Martha ran it. Then, when she became ill, Jenny, our housekeeper, took over the running of the house. And when my wife Martha died, Jenny continued running the house till now. I never did.

MARION: And what does running a house consist of?

JUSTER: I don't know, Marion. — Minnie, don't you know?

MINNIE: Yes, I do. I run my own house, Juster. But I don't know if you run your house the same way I run mine.

JUSTER: You should talk to Jenny, Marion, and decide what it is you want to do.

MARION: Thank you, I will. — Will my cousin Mary continue giving me instructions? I would like to know if that is something I will continue doing — if she will continue tutoring me.

JUSTER: Indeed Marion, nothing in your life should change unless you want it to.

MARION: Because of all the years I was not able to go to school I feel I don't yet comprehend a great many things.

SCENE 4: *Two months later. October 1908. It is dusk.* JUSTER *stands center left.* MICHAEL *stands up left.* MARY *stands up right.* MARION *and* MINNIE *embrace center.* MARION *holds a white veil and a missal.* MINNIE *sobs.*

MARION: My dear aunt. I am happy. Believe me, I am happy. I will be very happy.

[MINNIE *sobs.* MARION *holds her. A few seconds pass.*]

MARION: Don't cry, my dear.

[MINNIE *sobs.* MARION *holds her. A few seconds pass.*]

MARION: My dear aunt, don't cry.

[MINNIE *goes on sobbing.* MARION *releases her slowly and takes a step away from her.* MARION *lowers her head.* MARY *puts her arm around* MINNIE *and exits with her.* MINNIE *mumbles and cries while she exits.*]

MARION: Why is she so unhappy?

JUSTER: Weddings make people cry, Marion.

[MARION *looks at him.* JUSTER *takes her hand and brings it to his lips. She kisses his cheek.*]

SCENE 5: *Six months later. April 1909. It is late afternoon.* MARION *sits at the desk. She writes in a notebook. There is an open textbook in front of her.* MARY *sits left. They speak in a conspiratorial manner.*

MARY: That's what I hear.

MARION: Who told you!

MARY: My cousin. He knows his family—and him. He also knows him. — The man is married. And the wife's sister came to visit. She lives in New Paltz and her sister, the wife, is also from New Paltz. They're both from New Paltz. Her sister — the sister of the wife — came to visit and she stayed for months. The three of them slept together. Together in the same bed. The man and the wife and the wife's sister slept together in the same bed.

MARION: The three of them?

MARY: Yes! The three of them in the same bed.

MARION: Why did they do that?

MARY: To make love!

MARION: How?

MARY: I don't know. I imagine he first makes love to one and then the other.

[*Both squeal, terrified and thrilled.*]

MARION: That's perverse!

MARY: It is! That's why I'm telling you.

MARION: It's horrendous!

MARY: I know.

MARION: How did you find out?

MARY: He told me.

MARION: He!

MARY: My cousin.

MARION: How did he know?

MARY: Everyone knows.

MARION: How?

MARY: Noises in the bedroom. The servant heard them.

MARION: It couldn't be true.

MARY: Oh yes, if you see them you would know.

MARION: How?

MARY: The way they behave.

MARION: How?

MARY: Sinister, Marion, and sexual.

MARION: The wife is not jealous?

MARY: No.

MARION: He's with both of them?

MARY: Yes!

MARION: In the street?

MARY: Yes. He looks at one and then the other — passionately.

MARION: He's shameless.

MARY: They all are.

MARION: It's he who does it.

MARY: Not only he. They also look at him.

MARION: With passion?

MARY: Yes.

MARION: In front of the other?

MARY: They don't mind.

MARION: They don't?

MARY: Apparently not.

MARION: The wife's to blame then.

MARY: Yes, it's her fault, not his.

MARION: It's his fault, too.

MARY: The sister is pretty. Who can blame him?

MARION: Is she?

MARY: She's lovely. If she lets him — what is he to do?

MARION: He can say no.

MARY: If the wife doesn't mind why should he?

MARION: Because it's sinful. It's a sin. He's sinning. He will go to hell. God won't forgive him. It's his soul. He is responsible for his own soul. He can't just say, "They don't mind." He should mind. It is his own soul he has to think of. He'll go to hell.

MARY: I know. — They'll all go to hell.

MARION: And so will we.

MARY: Why!

MARION: For talking about it!

MARY: No, we won't!

MARION: Yes! We will! We must do penance!

MARY: We didn't do anything!

MARION: Yes, we did!

MARY: What!

MARION: We talked about it and we thought about it.

MARY: Did you!

MARION: I did, Mary! I thought about it. I imagined it! I did!

MARY: Marion, how could you?

MARION: Didn't you?

MARY: No!

MARION: Oh, God! I've sinned!

MARY: Oh, Marion! Repent.

MARION: I repent! Oh God! I repent! Oh God! How could I! Oh God! [*She falls on her knees. She is out of breath.*] Oh, God! Forgive me! [*She begins to calm down.*]

MARY: What did you think?

MARION: I imagined them in bed.

MARY: What did you imagine?

MARION: I can't tell you.

MARY: What?

MARION: He makes love to one while the other is there, very close. She looks and she listens. She watches their bodies move. She's very close.

MARY: How close?

MARION: Touching. She must.

MARY: That's awful.

MARION: She must.

MARY: Oh, Marion. And then?

MARION: He kisses her, too.

MARY: No!

MARION: He holds them both. And knows them both.

[MARY *gasps.*]

MARY: Oh, Marion. [*She goes on her knees.*] Now I have sinned, too. Will God forgive us?

[*They embrace.*]

SCENE 6: *One month later. May 1909. It is evening.* JUSTER *sits up left reading.* MICHAEL *sits cross-legged on the floor in front of the sofa. He reads a book.* MARION *sits at the desk. She writes in a diary.*

JUSTER: [*Reading.**] If you wish to see it for yourself, take a pencil and push the pointed end into the open mouth of the flower and downward toward the ovary and the honey, just as a bee would thrust in its tongue. If it is a young flower you have chosen you will see the two anthers bend down as if they knew what they were doing, and touch the pencil about two inches from the point leaving a smudge of golden pollen on it. A day later, the stigma will have lengthened and, if you would, then push your pencil in again. You will find that it

*From *My Garden in Autumn and Winter* by E.A. Bowles

now hangs far enough to touch the pencil in the same place where the pollen was laid, while the empty anthers have shriveled. — Thus on its first day of opening the anthers rub their pollen on the back of visiting bees; and on the next the stigma hangs down far enough to receive pollen from a younger flower. — If you wish to see the mechanism by which the anthers are bent down, cut away the hood until you lay bare the stamens as far as the point where they are joined to the corolla. Here you will notice that they have slender white flying buttresses that keep them in place. Just in front, standing out into the passageway down the tube of the flower, are two white levers growing out from the filaments and blocking the mouth of the tube. Push your pencil in again and you can see what happens. It strikes against these levers and pushes them down with it. As the buttresses hold the filaments in place, their upper portion is bent over from that point until the anthers touch the pencil.

SCENE 7: *The attic. Five months later. October 1909. It is morning.* MARION *stands on her toes with her arms outstretched, looking upward. She wears a white camisole and underskirt. Her whole body shakes with strain. She perspires heavily. On the floor there is a blanket and a large open book. She rapidly recites the following passage from Dante's "Purgatorio."* MINNIE's *words should not interrupt* MARION's *speech.*

MARION: *He girt me in such manner as had pleased
　　　Him who instructed; and O strange to tell!
　　　As he selected every humble plant,
　　　Wherever one was pluck'd another there
　　　Resembling, straightway in its place arose.
　　　Canto II: They behold a vessel under conduct of an angel.
　　　Now had the sun to that horizon reach'd,
　　　That covers, with the most exalted point
　　　Of its meridian circle, Salem's walls;
　　　And night, that opposite to him her orb
　　　Rounds, from the stream of Ganges issued forth,
　　　Holding the scales, that from her hands are dropt
　　　When she reigns highest: so that where I was
　　　Aurora's white and vermeil-tinctured cheek

*From the 19th-century translation by Henry Frances Cary

To orange turn'd as she in age increased.
Meanwhile we linger'd by the water's brink,
Like men, who, musing on their road, in thought
Journey, while motionless the body rests.
When lo! as, near upon the hour of dawn,
Through the thick vapors Mars with fiery beam
Glares down in west, over the ocean floor;

MINNIE: [*Offstage.*] Marion …

MARION: So seem'd, what once again I hope to view,
A light, so swiftly coming through the sea,
No winged course might equal its career.
From which when for a space I had withdrawn
Mine eyes, to make inquiry of my guide,
Again I look'd, and saw it grown in size

MINNIE: [*Offstage.*] Marion…

MARION:
And brightness: then on either side appear'd
Something, but what I knew not, of bright hue,
And by degrees from underneath it came
Another. My preceptor silent yet
Stood, while the brightness, that we first discern'd,
Open'd the form of wings: then when he knew

MINNIE: [*Offstage.*] Marion, are you there?

MARION: The pilot, cried aloud, "Down, down; bend low
Thy knees; behold God's angel: fold thy hands:
Now shalt thou see true ministers indeed."

[*She faints.*]

MINNIE: [*Offstage.*] Marion … [*A moment passes.*] Marion …

MARION: [*Coming to.*] … Yes. Don't come up … I'll be right
down.

[MINNIE *enters.*]

MINNIE: Are you all right?

MARION: … Yes.

MINNIE: [*Kneeling and holding* MARION *in her arms*] What are
you doing?

MARION: I'm studying.

MINNIE: ... You're drenched ...

MARION: I know...

MINNIE: Why don't you study where it's cool?

MARION: I have to do it here.

MINNIE: You look so white. [*Drying* MARION's *perspiration*.] Look at how you are drenched. Why do you do this?

MARION: I wasn't aware of the heat.

MINNIE: Now you are cold. You are as cold as ice.

[MARION *moves to the left. She leans against the wall and covers herself with the blanket.*]

MARION: I feel sometimes that I am drowning in vagueness — that I have no character. I feel I don't know who I am. Mother deemed a person worthless if he didn't know his mind, if he didn't know who he was and what he wanted and why he wanted it, and if he didn't say what he wanted and speak clearly and firmly. She always said, "A person must know what he ought to believe, what he ought to desire, what he ought to do." — I write letters to her. — I know she's dead. But I still write to her. I write to her when I am confused about something. I write and I write until my thoughts become clear. I want my thoughts to be clear so she'll smile at me. I come to this room to study. I stand on my toes with my arms extended and I memorize the words till I collapse. I do this to strengthen my mind and my body. I am trying to conquer this vagueness I have inside of me. This lack of character. This numbness. This weakness — I have inside of me.

SCENE 8: *A day later. Dusk.* JUSTER *walks from left to right in the garden. He wears a shirt with the sleeves rolled up. He carries a small tree, whose roots are wrapped in canvas, under his arm.*

SCENE 9: *Five months later. March 1910. It is late afternoon. There is a phonograph on the table.* MICHAEL *is placing the needle on a record. It plays a rag.* MARION *and* MICHAEL *dance.*

MICHAEL: That's it. You're doing well. That's good. Ta rah. Pa rah.

MARION: Teach me the words. Teach me how to sing it.

MICHAEL: Ta rah. Pa rah. Ta rah. Pa rah.

[*They sing these words to the whole song. The record comes to an end.*]

MARION: Again ... let's do it again. [*He starts the record again.*] Hold me, Mike and sing into my ear as they do in the dance halls.

[MICHAEL *does.* JUSTER *appears in the vestibule. He hangs his hat on the hatrack. He takes off his coat and hangs it in the closet. He comes into the living room and watches them dance.* MARION *sees* JUSTER *and waves to him. He waves to her.*]

MARION: Look at me, I'm dancing. Look at this. [*They do a special step.* JUSTER *smiles.*]

MICHAEL: And this. [*He demonstrates another step.*]

JUSTER: That's wonderful.

MICHAEL: Come, learn how to do it, Father.

JUSTER: [*Smiling.*] Oh, I don't think I could.

MICHAEL: Yes, yes, you could. I'll teach you. I just taught Marion.

MARION: Oh, yes, it's easy. You just listen and the music and the words will tell you how to move. I learned. I am sure you could learn, too. I never thought I could learn and I did.

[MARION *dances toward* JUSTER. MICHAEL *puts* JUSTER's *arms around* MARION *in dancing position.*]

MICHAEL: Do it.

[JUSTER *tries to move.*]

JUSTER: Oh, I don't think I can. I never was light on my feet.

MICHAEL: Yes, you are, Father. You could do it. You could dance beautifully. You already have the stance.

JUSTER: Oh, I don't think I can.

MARION: Try again. Just listen to the music.

JUSTER: No, no. I'm sure I can't. You dance. I'll watch you. I like to watch you.

[*He leads* MARION *by the hand toward* MICHAEL, *then sits and watches.*]

I like to watch you do it.

[JUSTER *claps while they dance.*]

SCENE 10: *Four months later. July 1910. It is late afternoon.* MARION *sits at the desk. She is writing in a diary.* MICHAEL *appears in the doorway to the left. He holds flowers in his hand. He tiptoes up behind her and covers her eyes.*

MARION: [*Pressing the diary against her chest.*]: Oh!

MICHAEL: [*Taking his hand away.*] I didn't mean to scare you. — It's only me. — I brought you flowers.

[MARION *sighs. She closes her diary.*]

MICHAEL: Don't worry. I didn't read any of it.

MARION: It's a diary. [MICHAEL *sits.*] I was describing an event.

MICHAEL: What event? Is it a secret?

MARION: It's a secret. A meeting.

MICHAEL: What sort of meeting?

MARION: Something imagined. In my mind.

MICHAEL: Diaries are to write things that are true.

MARION: This diary is to write things that are not true. Things that are imagined. Each day I write things that are imagined.

MICHAEL: Could I read it?

MARION: No.

MICHAEL: Why not? If it's imagined.

MARION: It would embarrass me.

MICHAEL: Is it romantic?

MARION: Yes. It is the story of a love affair.

MICHAEL: Whose?

MARION: A young man's named F.

MICHAEL: With whom?

MARION: With a young girl.

MICHAEL: Who is she?

MARION: Me!

MICHAEL: You!

MARION: Yes!

[*He gasps.*]

MICHAEL: You! [*Touching the diary.*] In this? How thrilling!

MARION: Yes.

MICHAEL: Do you write each day?

MARION: Yes.

MICHAEL: Since when?

MARION: Since August.

MICHAEL: Do you see him each day?

MARION: No.

MICHAEL: Why?

MARION: Because I can't

MICHAEL: Why not?

MARION: Because I'm married!

MICHAEL: Oh, yes?

MARION: Of course. A married woman cannot see her lover often.

[*She opens her mouth in amazement. They laugh.*]

MICHAEL: Where do you meet?

MARION: In the street. In a parlor.

MICHAEL: Does he come here?

MARION: No!

MICHAEL: And then?

MARION: We talk.

MICHAEL: Have you kissed?

MARION: No!

MICHAEL: Will you kiss him?

MARION: I think so. In the future.

MICHAEL: Is he real?

MARION: He is real, as real as someone who exists. I know every part of him. I know his fingernails — every lock of his hair.

MICHAEL: What does F stand for?

MARION: I haven't found out yet. — Francis of course. What other name starts with an F?

MICHAEL: Franklin.

MARION: No. His name is not Franklin.

MICHAEL: Of course not. Floyd.

MARION: No.

MICHAEL: Felix.

MARION: No. Don't ask such questions.

MICHAEL: I'm sorry. I'm intruding. I'm sorry.

MARION: I'll tell you what you want but be discreet. You have to know how to enter another person's life.

MICHAEL: I know. I'm sorry. [*There is a pause.*] What does he look like? May I ask that?

MARION: He's handsome. He has a delicate face and delicate hands. His eyes are dark and his hair is dark. And his skin is white. He looks like a poet. He looks the way poets look. Soulful.

MICHAEL: Where did you first meet him?

MARION: In a shop.

MICHAEL: Where does he live?

MARION: I don't know yet. I don't know him that well.

MICHAEL: How long have you known him?

MARION: Three months.

MICHAEL: How often do you meet?

MARION: Once a week.

MICHAEL: Why not more often?

MARION: You have to be careful.

[*They laugh.*]

MICHAEL: You're mad.

[*She laughs.*]

MARION: I know.

SCENE 11: *Three months later. October 1910. It is morning.* MARION *enters right, carrying a hooded cloak. She walks left furtively and looks around. She puts on the cloak, lifting the hood over her head, covering her face. She looks around again and exits right hurriedly.*

SCENE 12: *Three months later. January 1911. It is evening. It is* JUSTER'*s birthday.* MARION *sits in the chair to the right,* MINNIE *and* MARY *stand by her side.* MICHAEL *sits on the floor to* MARION'*s right. He holds a banjo.* JUSTER *sits in the chair to the left.*

MARION: My dear husband, in honor of your birthday, we who are your devoted friends, son and wife, have prepared a small offering — an entertainment. May this, your birthday, be as happy an occasion for you as it is for us.

[MARION *extends her hand toward* MICHAEL, *who starts playing.*]

MARION, MINNIE, MARY and MICHAEL: [*Singing.*]
*True love never does run smooth,
At least that's what I'm told,
If that is true then our love surely must be good as gold.
How we battle every day and when I want a kiss,
I have to start explaining
And it sounds about like this:

"Dearie, please don't be angry
'Cause I was only teasing you.
I wouldn't even let you think of leavin' —
Don't you know I love you true.

Just because I took a look at somebody else

*"Angry" by Dudley Mecum, Jules Cassard, Henry Brunies and Merrit Brunies.

That's no reason you should put poor me on the shelf.
Dearie, please don't be angry
'Cause I was only teasing you."

[*They repeat the song.* MARION *and* MARY *do a dance they have choreographed.*]

MARION: Dear husband, now it's your turn to sing.

[*They all gesture toward* JUSTER.]

JUSTER: [*Singing.*]
"Dearie, please don't be angry
'Cause I was only teasing you.
I wouldn't even let you think of leavin' —
Don't you know I love you true.

Just because I took a look at somebody else
That's no reason you should put poor me on the shelf.
Dearie, please don't be angry
'Cause I was only teasing you."

[MARION *kisses* JUSTER *on the cheek.*]

SCENE 13: *One month later. February 1911. It is evening.* MARION *sits in the left chair.* MICHAEL *lies on the floor. They are both still, stiff and somber.*

MARION: It was he. There was no doubt in my mind. I saw him and I knew it was he.

MICHAEL: Did he see you?

MARION: No, I hid behind the stacks.

MICHAEL: Then?

MARION: I took a book and buried my head in it. I was afraid. I thought if he saw me he would know and I would die. He didn't. I saw him leave. For a moment I was relieved he hadn't seen me and I stayed behind the stacks. But then I was afraid I'd lose him. I went to the front and I watched him walk away through the glass windows. Then, I followed him ... a while ... but then I lost him because I didn't want to get too near him. — I went back there each day. To the bookstore and to the place where I had lost him. A few days later I saw him again and I followed him. Each time I saw him I followed him. I stood in corners and in doorways until I saw him pass. Then I followed him. I was cautious but he became aware of me. One day he turned a corner and I hurried behind him. He was there, around the corner, waiting for me. I screamed and he laughed. He grabbed me by the arm. And I ran. I ran desperately. I saw an open entranceway to a basement and I ran in. I hid there till it was dark. Not till then did I dare come out. When I saw that he wasn't there I came home. — I haven't been outside since then. I'll never go out again, not even to the corner. I don't want to see him. I don't want him to see me. I'm ashamed of myself. I'm as worthless person. I don't know how I could have done what I did. I have to do penance.

SCENE 14: *Two months later. April 1911. It is afternoon.* MARION *stands on the right window looking out.* JUSTER *is outside. There is a sound of shoveling as* JUSTER *speaks.*

JUSTER: Have you seen the tree? It's already budding. It's the first to sprout. It's so eager for spring. Have you noticed how it's grown? It's less than two seasons that I planted it and look how tall it is now. When I put it in the ground it was no more than six feet tall. Now it's at least twelve. The spread of the branches was no more than five feet and look at it now. [*Pause.*] Marion, — what are you looking at? It's this one I'm talking about.

[*She turns her head to the left where he stands.*]

MARION: I know which one you mean.

JUSTER: Doesn't it look strong?

MARION: I suppose it does.

SCENE 15: *Nine months later. February 1912. It is evening.* MICHAEL *and* JUSTER *play chess.* MICHAEL *sits down center. He studies the board.* JUSTER *stands behind* MICHAEL *and also studies the board.* MARION *stands up left.* JUSTER *turns to look at her.*

JUSTER: You look beautiful. You look like a painting. [*She smiles with faint sadness.*] Play, Michael. Make up your mind.

MICHAEL: I don't know what move to make.

JUSTER: Make whatever move seems best to you.

MICHAEL: I get confused. I don't see one move being better than the next.

JUSTER: What do you think, Marion?

MARION: What do I think?

JUSTER: Yes, what should Mike do? Should he scrutinize the board and imagine each move and its consequences, or should he just play and see what happens? I imagine both are good ways of learning. [*As he walks to center.*] One way, I think, is a more Oriental way of learning — through meditation. The other is more Western. Reckless. We are reckless, we Westerners. Orientals meditate until they have arrived at a conclusion. Then they act. We Westerners act. Then, we look to see if what we did makes any sense. Which do you think is the best way to act?

MARION: I don't know. I think I'm like an Oriental. I don't think I take chances. I don't take any risks. I don't make any moves at all.

MICHAEL: [*As he moves a piece.*] Check.

[JUSTER *looks at the board.*]

MARION: Does that mean you won?

MICHAEL: No. It's exciting to check though. It's exciting to make a move and be reckless and create an upheaval and for a moment to think that it's mate.

MARION: And if it isn't mate? Do you lose?

MICHAEL: I don't know.

JUSTER: [*Making a move.*] For now he just loses a bishop.

MARION: Maybe it's best to be like an Oriental.

MICHAEL: I don't know. When you reflect you have to know what you are reflecting about. When you move without reflecting — [*As he moves a piece.*] — you just move! Just do it!

[MARION *lifts her skirt to see her toes and takes six steps looking at her feet.*]

SCENE 16:   *Seven months later. September 1912. It is late afternoon.*
There are some letters on the chess table. MARION *sits in a chair facing*
the window. FRANK *stands in the garden outside the window.*
MARION's *manner of speaking reveals sexual excitement.*

MARION: You're trespassing. — Where you are standing is
private property. It's a private garden and when strangers
come into it we let the dogs out.

FRANK: Let them tear me up. I'll stay here and look at you.

[MARION *moves between the two windows.* FRANK *walks to her.*
She moves to the stage left chair and sits. FRANK *follows her and*
sits at her feet. She starts to go. He grabs her ankle.]

MARION: Let go.

FRANK: I'm chained to you. I'm your shackle.

MARION: You are?

FRANK: [*Pulling her foot toward him.*] Come.

MARION: [*Pulling back.*] No. — Let go.

FRANK: Never. [*She jerks her foot.*] Never. [*She jerks her foot.*]
Never. [*She jerks her foot.*] Never.

[*She laughs.*]

MARION: What if someone sees you?

FRANK: I'll be arrested.

MARION: Let go of my foot. [*She touches his face. She is scared by*
her own action and withdraws her hand.]

FRANK: I know every move you make. I've been watching you.
— You spy on me. I spy on you.

MARION: Let go. Someone will see you.

FRANK: There's no one here but us.

MARION: How do you know?

FRANK: He won't be home for hours.

MARION: Who?

FRANK: Your father.

[MARION *is startled by his remark and becomes somber. She walks to the chair next to the desk and sits.*]

MARION: He's not my father.

FRANK: Who is he?

MARION: He's my husband. [*They are silent a moment.*] He is my husband and I don't want to see you ever again. I am married and you should not be here. [*Short pause.*] Leave now, please. [FRANK *is motionless for a moment. Then, he walks away. She is calm and absent as if something had just died inside her.* JUSTER *enters right.*]

JUSTER: Good evening, dear.

MARION: Good evening.

[JUSTER *walks left, picks up the mail and looks through it. He looks at her.*]

JUSTER: Are you all right ... ? You look pale.

MARION: Do I look pale?

[*He comes closer to her.*]

JUSTER: I think you do.

MARION: I'm fine.

[*He kisses her and walks left. He speaks without turning.*]

JUSTER: Is Michael home?

MARION: He's in his room.

JUSTER: Will dinner be at six?

MARION: I believe so. [JUSTER *exits left.*] ... I'm sorry ...

[FRANK *appears again.*]

FRANK: Did you speak to me?

MARION: I'm sorry.

FRANK: You've broken my heart.

MARION: I saw you and I lost mine. And I also lost my mind. That's why I followed you. I had lost my mind. — I thought of nothing but you. Each day I looked for you in the streets. And if not, I dreamt of you. A few days ago I looked outside this window and I thought I saw you moving among the trees. I thought I was hallucinating. This happened a few times. Were you there? Was that you?

FRANK: Yes.

MARION: What madness. It's my fault. I know it's my fault. I've been married since I was fifteen and I've never done anything like this. I love my husband and I'll always be faithful to him. I won't hurt him. He doesn't deserve this. Please, leave or I'll start crying and they will hear me and they will come and find me like this.

[*After a moment* FRANK *runs off.* MARION *goes to the couch and sits. She sobs. The lights fade. They come up again. The room is dimly lit.* JUSTER *enters.*]

JUSTER: Have you been here all this time?

MARION: I was looking at the clouds. It seems it's going to rain.

[*He looks out.*]

JUSTER: I don't think so. Night is falling. That's why it's getting dark — Dinner is served, dear. Will you come?

MARION: Yes ...

JUSTER: Are you all right?

MARION: ... No ... I'm not feeling very well.

JUSTER: Should you have dinner?

MARION: ... I think not ...

JUSTER: Would you like to stay here?

MARION: I'll go up to my room.

JUSTER: May I help you up?

MARION: I'll be up in a moment ...

[*He sits next to her.*]

What is today's date?

JUSTER: September twentieth.

MARION: Of course. It's the end of summer. The trees are beginning to turn.

JUSTER: Yes..

[*She leans on his chest. He puts his arms around her.*]

MARION: Your hands are cold.

JUSTER: There is a change in the air.

[*He strokes her hair.*]

ACT TWO

SCENE 17: *10th Street. Two years, four months later. January 1915. There is a telephone on the desk. It is early afternoon. The day is over-cast.* MARION *stands by the window to the left. She looks out. She is motionless. An adagio is heard.*

SCENE 18: *10th Street. Three months later. April 1915. It is late morning. The vase on the right stand is missing. A* GLAZIER *is standing on a ladder in the up left corner. He wears belted overalls. He hammers points on the upper part of the window.* MARION *enters right. She carries the vase with flowers. She stops to look at him. He continues working. She walks to the right stand. She looks at him again. She is transfixed. He turns to look at her. Their eyes lock. She cannot turn away.*

GLAZIER: Could I have a drink of water?

MARION: Yes.

[*She does not move. He comes halfway down the ladder and waits. He goes close to her, still looking at her. He puts the vase to his mouth and drinks the water through the flowers. She stares. He laughs.*]

GLAZIER: May I?

[*He laughs again. She stares at him. She is possessed. He picks her up and takes her upstage. They disappear behind the sofa. She emits a faint sound. The lights fade.*]

SCENE 19: *10th Street. Five months later. September 1915. It is evening.* MICHAEL *sits next to the desk facing up.* MARION *sits on the sofa. She looks pale and absent. She stares at the floor.* JUSTER *stands behind the sofa.*

JUSTER: I never thought I would have another child. I never thought Marion and I would have a child. I am so much older than she. I am beside myself with joy. Marion is a little worried. She is fearful. — You are the first to know. I have suggested she ask Aunt Minnie to come and stay with us. Marion needs a woman's companionship. But she hasn't decided if she'll ask her. Maybe you could persuade her. — She has missed you very much. I haven't heard any laughter in this house since you left. Marion has missed you. I hope you consider going to school in New York this year. Marion is desolate, Michael. Would you consider returning home?

[JUSTER *looks at* MARION. *He then looks at* MICHAEL *helplessly.* MICHAEL *looks at* MARION. *He is pained.*]

MICHAEL: I will think about it, Father.

SCENE 20: *10th Street. One year later. September 1916. It is late morning. Center stage, there is a playpen with a teddy bear sitting in it.* MARION *enters from left. She carries* THOMAS, *eight months old. She takes the teddy bear.* FRANK *appears outside the window.*

FRANK: Hello.

MARION: ...Frank...

FRANK: My name is not Frank.

MARION: It isn't? [*He shakes his head.*] What is your name?

FRANK: Jonathan.

MARION: Jonathan?

FRANK: Yes.

MARION: Your name is not Frank? [*She laughs.*] That's not possible.

FRANK: My name is Jonathan. I was named after my father.

[*She laughs.*]

MARION: I'm so happy.

FRANK: Why?

MARION: I'm so glad to see you. [*She sighs.*] Where have you been?

FRANK: I was away.

MARION: Where were you?

FRANK: In Michigan.

MARION: What were you doing in Michigan?

FRANK: Working with my uncle. — Have you thought of me?

MARION: Oh, yes.

FRANK: What have you thought?

MARION: That I love you.

FRANK: What a pleasant surprise. May I come in?

MARION: [*Laughing.*] No.

FRANK: Come outside then.

MARION: Not now.

FRANK: When?

MARION: Tomorrow.

FRANK: At what time?

MARION: At one.

FRANK: Where?

MARION: In the square.

FRANK: Abingdon?

FRANK: Yes.

FRANK: [*Moving his had toward her.*] See you then.

MARION: [*Her fingers touching his.*] See you.

SCENE 21: *10th Street. Five months later. February 1917. It is evening.* MARION *sits to the left of the chess table.* MICHAEL *sits down right.*

MARION: He often speaks of closing the house and moving south, where the weather is temperate. He likes using that word. Temperate. It's quite clear why he does. He means moral balance. Evenness of character. He means that he knows what I do when I leave the house. That he knows about Frank and me. He's saying that he'll seek moderation at any cost. That he's ready to divorce me and put an end to our family life. I'm ready for it. I'm ready to face him with it. He's just making it easier for me. [MICHAEL *looks down.*] What's the matter?

MICHAEL: When I'm with him, I care about nothing but him. [*They look at each other for a moment.*] I love him. He's my father and I love him. And I don't want to see him suffer. When I'm with you I forget that he's my father and I take your side. He's my father and I love him and I respect him. And I feel terrible that I've been disloyal to him. And I feel worse to see that he's still gentle and kind to both you and me. I'm sorry because I love you too, and I know that you too need me. But I can't bear being divided, and I have to choose him. I'm leaving, Marion. I can't remain here any longer knowing what I know and feeling as I do about it. It's too painful and I'm demeaned by my betrayal of him. There are times when I want to tell him the whole truth. And if I don't, it's because I love you too and I feel there's no wrong in what you're doing. I really don't. I think you're right in what you're doing. You're young and you're in love and it's a person's right to love. I think so. Frank is handsome and I think he is honest. I mean, I think he loves you. He's not very strong, but he's young. No one is strong when he is young. I'm not. Only I'm still playing with soldiers and he has entered into the grown-up world. If I were in his place it would terrify me to be the lover of a married woman. Good-bye, my sister. I must leave. I am constantly forced to act in a cowardly manner. I cannot be loyal to both, and I cannot choose one over the other, and I feel a coward when I look at you, and I feel a coward when I look at him. I am tearing out my heart and leaving it here, as half of it is yours, and the other half is his. I hope I won't hurt you by leaving — beyond missing me, which I know you will. I mean beyond that. I mean that I hope my leaving has no consequences beyond our missing each other. Take care. [*He starts to go, then turns.*] What if you're discovered? Will he leave school, take on such responsibility? Will he get a job and marry you?

MARION: ... I don't know. I haven't thought about that ...

JUSTER: [*Offstage right, in a disconnected manner.*] Are you leaving? [*A short pause.*] Are you staying for dinner?

MICHAEL: I have some studying to do.

JUSTER: [*Offstage.*] Stay. We should be eating soon. You could leave after dinner. We should have dinner soon. [*He enters and walks to center without looking at them. He seems absent. He stops and looks at the floor as he speaks.*] How are you, my dear?

MARION: ... Good evening ...

JUSTER: You both look somber. I hope nothing's wrong.

MARION: ... No, nothing's wrong.

JUSTER: [*Walking left as he speaks.*] I've had a bad day myself. Sit down, Michael. I'll be back in a moment. [*The volume of his voice does not change as he leaves the room.*] I'll be back in a moment. [*There is the sound of water running as he washes his hands.*] It was difficult at work today. Everyone seems to be constantly shirking responsibility. That seems to be the main problem in the world today. It's not possible to get things done properly, both in the house and at work. Will the person whose duty it is to prepare dinner be here on time to prepare it? Will that person be at the market early enough to ensure that the ingredients he gets are fresh and not wilted and sour? [*He enters drying his hands with a hand towel.*] Will my office staff appear to work properly dressed and properly shaven? It seems as if each day the lesson has to be taught again. The same lesson. Each day we have to restore mankind to a civilized state. Each night the savage takes over. We're entering the war. I'm sure we are. — In no time we will be in the middle of a war. Yes, you wash your face! Yes, you comb your hair. — Yes, you wear clothes that are not soiled. Why can't people understand that if something is worth doing it's worth doing right! [*He sits down and puts the towel on his lap. He takes one of his shoes off.*] I take care of my feet. My socks are in a good state of repair. When they wear out I pass them on to someone who needs them. [*Taking off his other shoe.*] Others mend their socks. I don't. I don't mind wearing mended clothes. My underwear is mended. So are my shirts, but not my socks. [*With both feet on the floor.*] I have always wanted to give my feet maximum comfort. It is they who support the whole body yet they are fragile. Feet are small and fragile for the load they carry. I wear stockings that fit so they won't fold and create discomfort to my feet. If I treat my feet with respect, my brain functions with respect. It functions with more clarity and so does my stomach. I digest better. In the morning at the office, I look at my mail. Then I call my assistant. I discuss some matters with him. Then I call my secretary. She comes in with her stenographer's pad and sits down on the chair to my right. I collect my thoughts for a few moments. Then I stand on my feet, walk to the window at my left, and from there, standing on my feet with my stomach properly digesting my breakfast and my brain as clear as the morning dew, I dictate my letters.

MARION: I will go see if dinner is ready. [*She exits left.*]

JUSTER: What is wrong with Marion? She's not herself.

MICHAEL: Nothing. Nothing I know of.

JUSTER: What is wrong with you? What is the matter with you?

MICHAEL: Nothing, Father.

JUSTER: Have you thought it over?

MICHAEL: What?

JUSTER: Are you coming home?

MICHAEL: Not yet.

JUSTER: Fine. You do as you must, Michael. [*There is a puase.*] It is hard to know whom to trust, whom to show your heart to.

MARION: [*Offstage.*] Dinner is ready.

JUSTER: Come, Michael.

[MICHAEL *walks up to* JUSTER *and waits for him.*]

JUSTER: Let's have dinner.

SCENE 22:   *10th Street. Two weeks later. March 1917. It is late afternoon.* MARION *and* FRANK *are embracing in the space behind the sofa. She speaks with urgency.*

MARION: I have been warned that this is a dream. That tomorrow you won't love me. I've been told I must prepare myself. That when you leave me my life will end. That my pain will be eternal. Hold me. Hold me in your arms. [*He does.*] Something terrible is happening. Something terrible happens each day. You're not touched by it — but I am impure. I lie each day. I am rotten and deceitful. Except to you, each time I speak I tell a lie. Lies come out of my mouth. I am impure. How I wish I could spend my days with you and not have to lie. [*There is a pause.*] Frank, wouldn't you like it if we spent all our time together, day and night? If we traveled together? If we walked on the street together, holding hands? If we spent the whole evening together sleeping in each other's arms? How would you like that? [*There is a silence.*] Frank ...

FRANK: We have to be careful.

SCENE 23: *10th Street. Two weeks later. Afternoon.* MARION *stands center left.* JUSTER *stands to her left. He holds a receipt in his hand.* JUSTER's *briefcase is on the floor next to the desk.*

JUSTER: Do you know what this is? [*She lowers her eyes.*] This is a rent receipt! A receipt for the rental of a place on Abingdon Square. It's made out to you, do you know what this is? Do you know what this receipt is?

MARION: I've rented that place. I needed a place of my own. To be private. I needed to have my own place.

JUSTER: What for?

MARION: A place of my own.

JUSTER: A place to meet your lover? [*Taking her hand and crumpling the receipt against the palm.*] Take it! Take it! Take it! [*He goes to the desk and sits. As he speaks he opens the drawers, holds the briefcase on his lap, takes out papers and puts them in the briefcase nervously.*] What are your plans?

MARION: In regard to what?

JUSTER: In regard to your life!

MARION: I've not made any plans.

JUSTER: Well, do. I'd like to know what you intend to do. How long would you need to decide? I would like to know what you plan to do as soon as possible. [*He starts putting papers, checkbooks and ledgers in the briefcase as he speaks.*] I expect you to leave as soon as possible. I expect you to move your things — what you can, today. A few things. What you may need for immediate use. The rest I'll have sent to your own place. If you have a place of your own you should move there. [*She starts to speak. He continues.*] Thomas will stay with me. Don't think you will take him with you. Don't bother to look for him. He's not in the house. I have taken him to a place where you won't find him and no one but I knows where he is. So don't bother to look for him. Don't try to find him. I am leaving now. I'll return later tonight. When I return I expect you'll be gone. Jenny will help you pack and she will take you and whatever things you want to take to that place or any other place you wish. If you don't leave, you'll never see Thomas again. You're an adulterous wife and I'll sue you for divorce. A court will grant me sole custody of the child. Do you have anything to say?

[*There is a moment's silence.*]

MARION: I will not leave unless I take Thomas with me.

JUSTER: If you're still here when I return, you'll never see him again.

[MICHAEL *enters right.*]

JUSTER: Marion is leaving tonight and she'll never enter this house again. She's not wanted here. She has debased this house. She will not be forgiven and her name will never be mentioned here again. And if you think of her ever again you'll never enter this house.

MICHAEL: Father, may I intercede?

JUSTER: In regard to what!

MICHAEL: Father —

JUSTER: [*Interrupting.*] No. I will not hear what you have to say. I don't want your advice. Marion will leave. You may escort her wherever it is she is going if you wish.

SCENE 24:   MARY's *place. One month later. April 1917. It is evening. MARY sits on the sofa.* JUSTER *sits left. He wears a hat and coat and holds his briefcase on his lap.*

JUSTER: I never saw myself as deserving of her love. She was preciously beautiful, modest. She was thoughtful and respectful. There was no vanity in her. — When her mother died I don't believe she cried once but her spirit left her. She seemed absent. That was the way she grieved. — She was obedient. She did what was asked of her, but she had lost her sense of judgment and her desire to choose one thing over the other. She accepted what others chose for her. She sat for hours staring into space. I took her for walks. I took her to the park. We took boat rides on the lake. Our meetings became more frequent. We became natural companions. I loved her company, and I found myself always thinking of her. She was sad and still when I wasn't there. When she saw me, she smiled and came to life. Her aunt told me this, too. That she only smiled when she saw me. I foolishly believed that his meant she loved me. I proposed marriage and she accepted. Her aunt, too, thought it natural when I asked for her hand in marriage. She gave us her blessings. There was no exuberant joy in our wedding, but there was the most profound tenderness. I was very happy and I thought Marion was also. There were times when she was taciturn, but I thought she was still grieving for her mother. She was a child and she needed a mother more than a husband. But a husband is all she had. I could not be a mother to her. Four years later Marion had a child. I was overwhelmed with joy, but Marion was not. She became more taciturn than ever. [*There is a pause.*] I began to feel she hated me. And she does hate me, and she has made me hate her. You see her. I know you see her. [*Pause.*] War has been declared, Mary, and I'm afraid that Michael will be drafted. He too will be taken away from me.

SCENE 25: *Abingdon Square. Two weeks later. May 1917. It is evening.* MARION *stands left.* MARY *sits right. They drink vermouth and smoke.*

MARION: I am in a state of despair! Thanks to Frank. How could I not be. Have you ever lived with someone who speaks one way and acts another! — Someone for whom words mean nothing? — Or if they mean anything, they mean something different from what they mean to you? My life is a puzzle. —

I don't know where I stand. I am constantly asking: What do you mean? — What is it you mean? — What does that mean to you? — Why did you say that? — Why did you do that? Have you?

MARY: Me?

[MARION *sits left.*]

MARION: When I sinned against life because I was dead I was not punished. Now that life has entered me I am destroyed and I destroy everything around me. May God save me. I have always trusted in his goodness and his divine understanding. May God have mercy on me. — I have never denied him.

SCENE 26: *A beer parlor. Two weeks later. Evening.* JUSTER *sits left.* MICHAEL *sits right. There is a glass of beer in front of each. Juster speaks rapidly.*

JUSTER: I have tried. I offered her some money. She didn't accept it. I knew she wouldn't. She stared at me and said nothing. We were in a public place. She stared and I waited for her to answer. After a while I knew she had no intention of answering. I said to her, "Do you have anything to say?" She still said nothing but I felt the hatred in her eyes. I said, "I suppose you are not accepting my offer?" She said nothing. I said, "For God's sake, say you don't accept it and if you don't let's get on to something else." Her hatred is such, it burns. Paper would burn if it were held up to her glance. When I reached the door I saw her back reflected in the glass. She was so still that there was no life in her. She was still like a dead person. I regretted having offered her the money. I had no reason to think she would accept it. What do they live on. [*Short pause.*] Have you seen her?

MICHAEL: No.

JUSTER: She's gone berserk. She's gone wild like a mad woman. She's insane. You haven't seen her?

MICHAEL: No.

JUSTER: You haven't been in touch at all? Letters?

MICHAEL: No.

JUSTER: Last week I followed her to a dance parlor. [MICHAEL *looks at him.*] Yes, Michael. You have not been here and you don't realize what's going on. Marion's behavior is irrational. She's not sane. — I followed her and she went in a dance parlor. It was still light outside, and yet people were already dancing. I followed her in and I took a table by the window. A man wearing a soldier's uniform greeted her. They started dancing. And moved to a dark corner. She knew I was there looking at her and that's why she did what she did. They kissed and caressed lewdly. I've never seen such behavior in public. — Never did I think I would see someone ... I so cherished behave like that. She knew I was there. She knew I followed her there, and yet she did what she did. [*He takes a drink.*] One day, last week, she came to my office. I was standing by the window. I did not notice her at first. Then I heard her say, "Does this happen every afternoon?" — She had been standing at the door. And I said, "Does what happen every afternoon?" She said, "Do you stand at the window every afternoon?" I said, "Yes." And she said, "What do you look at?" I said, "I look out. I don't look at anything in particular. I look out because that's how I concentrate on what I have to do." "And what is it you have to do?" "Right now I'm in the middle of dictating my letters." Then she stood behind my secretary and leaned over to look at her writing pad. Then she said, "What is that? A secret code?" Shorthand! Then she said, "This is a love letter." Then, she came to where I was and looked out the window and said, "Do you use binoculars?" I told her that I could see quite well without binoculars and she said, "From where you are, can you see the house on Abingdon Square?" She thought I was spying on her. She's mad. She's capable of anything. [*He looks absently at the street. He takes a revolver from his pocket and puts it on the table.*] I carry this with me at all times. I don't know if I will shoot her or if I will shoot myself. I know that one of us will die soon.

MICHAEL: ... Father ... I must try to stop you.

[JUSTER *puts the revolver in his pocket. He takes a purse out of his pocket, takes money out and puts it on the table. He stands and starts to walk away. He stops.*]

JUSTER: Would you take care of the bill, Michael?

MICHAEL: ... Yes ... [JUSTER *starts to exit*.] Father ... I've enlisted.

[JUSTER *stops, looks at* MICHAEL *for a moment, turns away slowly and exits.*]

SCENE 27: *Abingdon Square. Two weeks later. June 1917.* MARION *stands up left.* MARY *sits right.*

MARY: Juster?

MARION: Yes, Juster. I hate him. I will shoot him. I imagine I shoot him and I feel a great satisfaction. A satisfaction equal to flushing a toilet, seeing the water flush out and vanish forever. I am crude. I know I'm crude. I know I'm uncivilized. I know I am a part of a civilized race but I am uncivilized. Thomas is not his!

MARY: Marion!

MARION: He's not.

MARY: Is he Frank's?

MARION: No.

MARY: Whose is he?

MARION: A stranger's ... A stranger. Just someone. Someone who came in the house one day and never again. I never saw him again. — Just a man. A stranger. No one. — I have a bad destiny, Mary. I have an evil destiny. It constantly thwarts me. — Nothing comes to me at the right time or in the right way.

SCENE 28: MINNIE's *living room. One week later. It is evening.* MINNIE *sits on a chair, center stage.* MARION *is on her knees facing* MINNIE.

MARION: I need my child. I need my child, Minnie. I need that child in my arms and I don't see a way I could ever have him again. He has been irrevocably taken from me. There is nothing I could do that would bring him back to me. I have

begged him to let me see him. I have gone on my knees, I
have offered myself to him. I have offered my life to him. He
won't listen. He won't forgive me. I'm at his mercy. I wish for
his death. I stalk the house. I stand on the corner and I watch
the house. I imagine the child inside playing in his room.
When spring comes I may be able to see him in the garden. I
know he's not there, but that's how I can feel him near me.
Looking at the house.

MINNIE: Why won't he let you see him?

MARION: He's gone mad! He's insane, Minnie.

MINNIE: Juster?

MARION: Yes! He's insane! He wants to destroy me. But I'll
destroy him first.

MINNIE: Marion, I don't understand you. I forget things. I'm
too old. I don't remember what you're talking about. It's no
longer in my mind. The flesh is sore and swollen. [*Touching
the side of her head.*] — This part of it is stretched and redder
than the rest, as if it's hotter. As if it had a fever. As if it had
hair. — It throbs.

Scene 29: *10th Street. A few days later. It is late morning.* JUSTER *sits
at the desk. He speaks to* MICHAEL *on the phone. After a few moments*
MARION *appears outside the left window looking in.*

JUSTER: She follows me. She's insane. She's jealous, Michael.
She is jealous of me. Her jealousy is irrational. As irrational as
everything else she does.

[MARION *steps on a twig.*]

JUSTER: [*To* MARION.] What are you doing?

MARION: Who is here with you?

JUSTER: I'm alone.

[*She hears a sound and turns to the left.*]

MARION: What was that? Someone's in the back.

[*She exits left. He speaks on the phone.*]

JUSTER: She's outside. Doing who knows what in the garden.
She just looked through the window and demanded to know

who's here with me. — There is no one here with me. Not even Jenny is here. I have sent her away. She's out of her mind.

[MARION *enters right.*]

MARION: Who are you with?

JUSTER: I am with no one.

MARION: Who are you talking to?

JUSTER: I'm talking on the telephone. [*She picks up the phone, listens for a moment and hangs up.*]

MARION: I had forgotten how I loved this house. I love this house. [*Pause.*] I have been ill. I have had fevers. [*Pause.*] I'll tell you a riddle. See if you can solve it:
If a person owns an object, where is it?
It's under his arm.
If a person loves an object, where is it?
It's in his arms.
If a mother's baby is not in her arms, where is it?

[*Pause.*] Where is it? Where is Thomas? Where have you taken him? Is there someone in your life? Someone influencing you? How can you do this? How can you put me through this? What do you gain?

SCENE 30: *Abingdon Square. Two weeks later. July 1917. It is evening. The stage is dark. There is the sound of a gunshot. The lights come up.* JUSTER *stands downstage facing up. He wears an overcoat and a bowler hat. His right arm hangs, holding a revolver.* MARION *is up center. She faces him. Her arms are halfway raised and her mouth and eyes are open in a state of shock.* MARY *enters running from the left.* MARION *turns to look at* MARY. *Both* JUSTER *and* MARION *go through the motions he describes.*

JUSTER: I came in. I said nothing. I took the gun out and aimed at her. She stared at me. Her courage is true. She stared at death without flinching. My eye fell on the mirror behind her. I saw my reflection in it. I am much older than she. Much older. I looked very old and she looked very young. I felt ashamed to love her so. I thought, let her young lover kill her if she must die. I turned the gun to my head. She moved toward me calmly. She put her hand on mine and brought it down away from my head. She said, Please. I was moved by her kindness. I turned to look at her. And again I was filled with rage. My finger pulled the trigger.

[*He shoots again.* MARION *runs upstage and returns to her position at the start of the scene.*]

JUSTER: That was the blast you heard. The gun was pointing at the floor. Everyone here is perfectly all right.

[JUSTER *begins to choke. He turns front slowly. He starts to walk backwards gasping for air. He falls unconscious on the sofa. His eyes are wide open.* ⋅

SCENE 31: *10th Street. A month later. August 1917. It is dusk.* MARION *sits right of the couch.* FRANK *stands behind the couch to the left.*

FRANK: And if he doesn't come to, will you spend the rest of your life taking care of him?

MARION: When I reach out to touch him I don't know if I'm reaching outside of me or into me. — If he doesn't come out of the coma … ? I feed him. I bathe him. I change him. I wait for the day when I can speak to him. To speak to him at least once.

FRANK: I wanted to ask you if there is anything I can do.

MARION: … No …. Thank you, Frank.

[FRANK *sits on the right side of the couch.*]

FRANK: I may be leaving once again, Marion.

MARION: Oh … ?

FRANK: Yes, I may be moving on.

MARION: I know, Frank, I know you must go.

[*They sit silently for a while.*]

SCENE 32:   JUSTER's *bedroom. A day later. It is evening.* JUSTER *lies in his bed unconscious. His head is stage right. He is in a coma. He is unshaven.* MARION *stands on the upstage side of the bed.* JUSTER *begins to come to. His speech is impaired.*

JUSTER: ... It looks much nicer here than in the parlor

MARION: What does?

JUSTER: ... It feels bad.

MARION: What feels bad?

JUSTER: ... It is happier here ...

MARION: What?

JUSTER: It's happier. Don't you know it.

MARION: What?

   [*His eyes open. They are bloodshot and swollen.*]

JUSTER: Who's here?

MARION: It's me.

JUSTER: Who?

MARION: Marion.

JUSTER: Marion.

MARION: Yes.

JUSTER: Why are you here?

MARION: Because you're ill.

JUSTER: What's wrong with me?

MARION: You had a stroke.

JUSTER: What have you done to me!

MARION: Nothing.

JUSTER: Yes, you have.

MARION: What have I done?

JUSTER: You've done harm to me.

MARION: No.

   [*He looks at her suspiciously.*]

JUSTER: What have you done to me? Get out!

MARION: I've fed you.

JUSTER: What have you fed me?

[*She is silent.*]

JUSTER: Poison!

MARION: No.

JUSTER: I hate you! You're repulsive to me! [*Pause.*] You've touched me!

MARION: Yes.

JUSTER: Do you enjoy seeing me like this! [*Pause.*] Where's Michael? [*Pause.*] Has he been here?

MARION: I sent for him.

JUSTER: I want to see him.

MARION: He's trying to get here.

JUSTER: Why can't he come?

MARION: He calls every day.

JUSTER: [*Starting to get out of bed.*] I want to get up. I want to be downstairs when he calls.

MARION: He won't call till later.

JUSTER: [*Still trying to get up.*] I'll call him.

MARION: He can't be reached.

JUSTER: Am I dying?

MARION: I don't know.

JUSTER: I don't want you here. [*She takes a step back.*] Get out! Get out! [*She starts to leave, then stops.*] Get out!

MARION: ... May I come back later? [*He does not answer.*] I understand.

[*She exits. He lifts himself to a sitting position, stands and stumbles to the living room.*]

JUSTER: ... Marion .... Marion! [*He starts to fall.*] ... Marion ... Marion ... Marion ...

[MARION *runs in. She holds* JUSTER *in her arms.*]

JUSTER: I love you.

MARION: ... I love you, too.

[*She sobs.* MICHAEL *enters, walks slowly to them, and stands behind them. He wears an army uniform. There is bright light behind them.*]

MARION: Michael ... ! Michael ... ! He mustn't die! He mustn't die! Don't die ... ! Don't die ... !

THE END

MA
ROSE

by

Cassandra Medley

To Lula Earley and Marc-Steven Dear

CHARACTERS
    Ma Rose, an elderly black woman in her 90s
    Vera-Rose, Ma Rose's daughter, a light-skinned black
    woman 55-60
    Rosa, Vera's daughter, dark-skinned, mid-30s, very
    fashionable businesswoman
    Wayman, Ma Rose's son, 65
    Ethel, Wayman's wife, 55-60

SETTING
A small midwestern town, various scenes interchange between MA
ROSE's *house and* WAYMAN's *house.*

Act One, Scene 1 *takes place in the church basement of a city, 200
miles from* MA ROSE's *small town.*

TIME
Early December, 1980.

The play moves back and forth in ROSA's *memory. The set should have
a warm quality and yet be sparse with minimal pieces suggesting the
over-all effect of sound and lighting.*

ACT ONE

SCENE 1

At rise there is a spotlight on ROSA — *a black woman in her mid-
thirties,* ROSA *is dressed in a business suit, with her coat over her arm;
she carries a suitcase in one hand and a briefcase in the other. She stares
out silently reflecting for a moment, then softly we hear the voice of* MA
ROSE *singing a capella.*

MA ROSE: ... I'm so glad ... trouble don't last always ... I'm so
    glad ...

ROSA: [*Calling out softly into the shadows.*] Ma Rose?! Nana???

    [*Lights up to reveal the basement of a church, perhaps suggested by
    a simple, hanging crucifix.*]

    [VERA, *an anxious-looking black woman in her early sixties, is seen dressed in a choir robe, stock still and facing the audience. She is staring out with a dazed expression of worry and tension on her face.*]

[*It is mid-morning on a Sunday. We hear the foot-stomping, hand-clapping sound of a gospel choir singing "Pass Me Not Oh Gentle Savior" coming from the upstairs.* ROSA, *as in memory, crosses tentatively through the shadows towards* VERA.]

ROSA: [*Calling out softly.*] Ma? ... Mom ... ?

[VERA *stretches out her arms, clasps* ROSA *to her and collapses on* ROSA's *shoulder as* ROSA *holds her tight.*]

ROSA: [*Patting* VERA *softly on the back.*] Sh-h-h-h-h-h-h ... now ... now ... yes ... I know ... I know ... yes ... yes ... so good to see you — been so long — too long —

VERA: I am not prepared for this.

ROSA: [*Holding* VERA *close and tenderly.*] Sh-h-h-h now — now [*Pause.*] Have you spoken any more to Uncle since you called me?

VERA: Like I told you, he say her "mind ain't right," that's what he say.

ROSA: Gawd. "Mind ... "?

VERA: "Ain't right." That's what he told me.

ROSA: [*Shaking her head resolutely.*] No —

VERA: "Mind. Ain't. Right." That's what he say.

ROSA: Well now — look. I bet you anything we get there and find she's tired out, that's *all*. Not to say anything 'gainst Uncle, but now you know how that is, "mind ain't right" — I mean, what does that *mean*, huh? Think about it. Could mean anything — or nothing —

VERA: "Mind ain't right" means "mind ain't right" —right?! [*Pauses.*] I mean if something ain't right with your mind — then — it ain't "right" —

ROSA: Mommie, now all we know for *sure* is that Ma Rose needs our help.

[*The sound of the foot-stomping above their heads is louder, song "He's Sweet I Know" is heard faintly.*]

VERA: [*Responding to the sound.*] Sing the song, people! [*Clapping.*] Sing the song — [*To* ROSA.] Rosa, I got up there in the choir this morning and look like I just couldn't get Ma Rose's singing and clapping outta my head — and 'fore I knew nothing they was bringing me downstairs here — had clear collapsed.

ROSA: Why *sure* — course you did — well, I'm here now — thank goodness I'm here —

VERA: … "mind ain't right … "

[ROSA *helps* VERA *to remove her robe.* VERA *straightens her dress underneath and smoothes her hair.*]

ROSA: You let *me* worry 'bout Ma Rose. I'll get this all straightened out — here now, where's your boots?

[ROSA *finds a pair of boots, kneels down, removes* VERA'*s shoes and begins to help her put on the boots.*]

Ease down … that's a good girl …

VERA: Thank goodness you here … yes I got you — you I got — yes yes — [*She strokes* ROSA'*s hair.*] Girl — *tell* me something *good* — help me take my mind off — What you know good? — What's been happening — ?

ROSA: Here's your hat. Gloves? Not in your coat pocket —

VERA: I know you must got something good to report. You always got *something*…

ROSA: [*Smiling, teasing.*] Matter of fact—I don't think you gonna be *too* disappointed …

[ROSA *picks up her bags, and as an afterthought pulls a newspaper from her briefcase.*]

VERA: [VERA *stops and glances at the paper. Her face lights up.*] Ah-ha! Promotion number — how many does *this* make — ?!

ROSA: [*Smiling at* VERA.] Read it in the car. *There's* that smile I want! There's that smile!

VERA: [*Glancing over the paper.*] Oh yes, this what you supposed to be doing. Moving on up! Leaving no tracks behind. That's what I expect. *Show* 'em you as good as anybody! *Better*! Awright!!

ROSA: [*Showing* VERA.] New business cards … [*Holding out an additional sheet of paper.*] … Check out this salary …

VERA: [*Looking up at* ROSA *in awe.*] Why I've never known a Negro face to face who made that kinda money in my life.

ROSA: [*Pauses satisfied.*] Okay — ready? [*Smiling.*] Here we go, gloves ... hat ... purse ... suitcase in the trunk? Don't forget your Bible.

VERA: [*Still glancing at the newspaper.*] And don't smile for nobody on your pictures ... Look too hang-dog if you ask me ... Smile more! That's not the kinda pictures I wanna be passing out.

ROSA: [*Sighs quietly.*] [*As she pulls on her gloves and walks towards the door.*] Watch your step coming out.

[VERA *suddenly sits down, staring straight ahead, evidently afraid to leave.*]

ROSA: [*Turning to realize* VERA *is not following her.*] [*Softly.*] Yes — yes — yes — I know it's hard — but just let me handle it — [*She comes over and kneels at* VERA'*s feet.*] Look. When it comes to this lady here [*Pointing at herself.*] she don't *rest* till everything's smoothed out, straightened out and all put back together —

VERA: [*Feigning determined interest in the newspaper.*] So what *is* this now?

ROSA: Ma, it can wait. Let's get in the car.

VERA: Well, if it can wait, then *why* mention it? You *know* I can't stand that ...

ROSA: I'm this year's Chair for the "New York Chapter of the National Coalition of Executive Minority Women."

VERA: [*Delighted.*] Wonderful! Ain't you something else!

ROSA: ... women from all types of corporations and businesses. Black women ... Hispanics ... Asians ... I am *so* excited!

VERA: I bet.

ROSA: [*Gently taking* VERA *by the arm to raise her.*] Come on. Walk on my arm. I'll help you. [*Pauses.*] Wait till you hear 'bout my seminars. I'm conducting seminars now ...

VERA: Yes?

ROSA: "Meeting the Challenges of Corporate Management" — That's why I was in Atlanta last week. Next week it's Salt

Lake City. [*Starting to walk* VERA *out.*] You'd be surprised how many of us advance to positions and *still* in spite of doing well, hold onto that old baggage of feeling inferior ... you would be surprised.

VERA: That a fact?

ROSA: ... and then also the fact is that, too often the so-called "title" is just a front for a false kind of "pretense" of power for the person of color, and the minority person is very often hired as a convenient corporate symbol for a company and that's a heavy load to carry —

VERA: [*Still not allowing* ROSA *to move her very far.*] Come up for air. Come up for air ... [*Pause.*] And I guess there's still not no new steady gentleman "in the picture"?

[ROSA's *smile tightens. She remains silent.*]

VERA: So who's disappointed you this time? Who turned out to be "not good enough" for you on *this* go-round?

ROSA: [*Smiling with effort.*] You know, it would have been much easier on me to fly down and meet you at Uncle's directly.

VERA: [*Smiling with effort.*] No, you fly here *first* like I told you.

ROSA: [*Smiling with effort.*] Well, here I am.

VERA: [*Smiling.*] You fly *here*, hear? We'll drive down to Uncle's together, like I *say*.

ROSA: All right, Mother, calm down.

VERA: *You* calm down.

[*Silence.* ROSA *just smiles at* VERA, *her smile a frozen mask of suppressed rage.*]

VERA: [*Smiling.*] I get little enough time to see you as it is. You never call nobody. Don't write nobody to tell nobody if you *still* breathing. Don't send nobody no postcards ...

[*Silence.* ROSA *just maintains her masklike smile.*]

VERA: ... Don't get home enough as it *is*! [*Fierce.*] I WANT YOU *HERE* WITH *ME*, YOU DO LIKE I *SAY*! — [*Then quiet.*] Think I'm kidding you? Oh, you think I'm *kidding* you, huh? — ?? [*Making a gesture of rejection.*] All right, go. Just go get out right now. I'll tend to Ma Rose myself since you wanna be that way — there's the door. Come with that attitude then — GIRL I WILL *BLESS* YOU OUT!! — Fly on back outta here from where you came — !

[ROSA *reaches into her pocket, pulls out a bottle of pills and swallows two of them in one dry gulp.*]

VERA: [*Instantly soft, coming to* ROSA*'s side.*] Baby, that stuff's to be had with *milk*, ain't it? That stuff's no penny candy —

[ROSA *is silent, her smile drops.* VERA *watches* ROSA *in a contrite silence.* VERA *moves over to* ROSA *and tentatively attemps to pat her shoulder.*]

VERA: Why don't you just curl up in the back seat and rest. I'll drive the first hour, then you take over —

[ROSA *just moves away in silence. She is well aware that she is making* VERA *"pay" for her tantrum.*]

VERA: — How 'bout it? Hum? [*Silence.*] I don't know why we got to always get into it. Let's get down on our knees and pray ... Let's

ROSA: Uncle said for us to get there as soon as possible.

[*As* ROSA *turns to move away,* VERA *grabs her on impulse.* ROSA *rears back startled, but* VERA *is not even aware of her grip or of* ROSA*'s reaction.*]

VERA: [*Smile of astonishment.*] [*Gently.*] I am not prepared for this. [*Pauses, pleading to* ROSA.] I am *not* prepared for this. [*Laughing to herself.*] Ain't that something? Old as I am. [*Turning to* ROSA.] I am not prepared ... !

ROSA: [*Awkward and gentle.*] It's gonna be all right ... you'll see. It's gonna be all right ...

VERA: See — she's my mother. See? She's *my* mother.

[*Fade out on* VERA, *the spot remains on* ROSA *as gospel music is heard upstairs, "Peace Be Still." The singing of the choir then blends with the voice of* MA ROSE *singing in the darkness as the lights rise on Scene 2.*]

SCENE 2

Lights up on ROSA *dressed in business suit, seen in the spotlight staring out.*

We now hear the raw, a capella voice of MA ROSE *coming from the darkness. Lights up on her, a woman in her early sixties, dressed in a formal church dress with a Sunday hat, she is finishing the ironing on a frilly little girl's silk dress and she playfully sways her hips from side to side, singing her version of Bessie Smith.*

MA ROSE: "Love oh love oh careless love — love oh love oh careless love ... /love oh love oh careless love oh see what careless love can do ... "

ROSA: Sing some more Nana ...

MA ROSE: Ha! Chile, back when I was a pretty little young thing, 'fore I settled down and got wedded, I was a "pistol" yes I was!!! ... "Oh see, C.C. Rider ... Oh see what you done done, Lordy Momma, see C.C. Rider see what you done done ... oh you made me love you now you up and gone ... !!" Chile, I just feel so *good* this morning! We gonna have ourselves a *great* day this day! Yes ma'am! A great day!!

ROSA: [*Joining* MA ROSE, *imitating her, it is clear that* ROSA *is transported back in time — she is clapping and laughing.*] Sing some more ... Nana! Sing some more ... !

MA ROSE: [*She holds ribbons in her hand and playfully crosses over to an imaginary girl, as if to begin plaiting them in the girl's hair.*] Come on you put on your dress —

ROSA: [*Suddenly she is a little girl, imitating* MA ROSE.] "Oh see, C.C. Rider ... oh see what you have done, Lordy Momma, see C.C. see what you have done ... oh you made me love you, now you up and gone ... !"

MA ROSE: Aw right Madam! Pick that up that *quick* huh!?

ROSA: [*Transforming back to adult reflective manner of the present* — MA ROSE *is in memory and does not acknowledge her remarks.*] ...Ha! [*Swaying her hips back and forth.*] ... You oughta see me imitate you to m'"sweetheart"! [*Pauses.*] *Former* sweetheart.

MA ROSE: [*Addressing the invisible child in memory.*] Mercy Lord — what grade you in now ... ?

ROSA: [*Holding up four fingers as a child.*] Fourth ... *teach* me.

MA ROSE: Chile, that old gut-bucket foolishness. Naw, you up for much better things. You the promise. You my future girl. Oh, if your daddy was alive and living — you say a prayer for your daddy every night? [ROSA *nods "yes."*] Good girl — that was a good man, thank you Lord ... best thing your Momma ever done — [*Calling out.*] VERA-ROSE!! VERA-ROSE! HEY VEE!

ROSA: [*The adult.*] ... What will I say when I come face to face with *you. You* ...

[VERA *suddenly appears from out of the shadows,* ROSA *jumps.*]

VERA: [*To* MA ROSE.] Uh-uh, she ain't wearing that outta here Momma, that's her best dress. Ro, go put on your plaid jumper — that's what Momma wants you to wear —

MA ROSE: [*Happily ignoring* VERA's *comment.*] And to *think* Lord done seen fit for m'lil Rose to be with me on today of all days! Ain't she gonna be fine?! Fine as wine —

VERA: [*To* ROSA. *Insistent but with effort to stay calm.*] Go get your other dress like I say ...

ROSA: [*The child again. Very obedient, nervous.*] Yes, ma'am.

MA ROSE: [*Calmly.*] Naw-naw, we got you in what you gonna wear ... turn 'round for Momma to see. [*She turns* ROSA *in a small circle.*] [*Turning to* VERA.] Ain't she gonna be something walking down Main Street? Ha! The cutest little thing you ever wanna see!?

[VERA *stares at her mother in frustrated silence.* MA ROSE *smiles back at her in the full assurance of power.* VERA *is holding her temper with great effort.*]

VERA: Momma, I don't braid her hair with them ribbons 'cause it won't *stay* ...

MA ROSE: Vera, bring the baby's "go-to-church hat" and hurry on up. They be gathering 'round the Courthouse by now ... Is your brother here yet??!!

[VERA *turns and disappears into the shadows.*]

MA ROSE: [*To* ROSA.] ...We making *history!*

ROSA: [*To* MA ROSE *as an adult.*] — How bad off are you? "...

mind not right ..." How bad off are you?

MA ROSE: [*To the invisible* ROSA.] Tell me something, precious ...

ROSA: [*As an adult anticipating what* MA ROSE *will say.*] "Who you named after, Baby ... ?"

MA ROSE: Who you named after, Baby?

ROSA: [*As a child.*] M'Momma. [*As an adult, she calls into the shadows.*] Mom? Momma?!

MA ROSE: Yeah, but *who* you *named* after?

ROSA: M'Ma Rose.

MA ROSE: [*Clapping with delight.*] Oh, I just *love* to hear you say that! [*Imitating* ROSA *as a little girl.*] "M'Ma Rose." Gimme some suga! [*She reaches out to kiss* ROSA.] Bless her heart — Bless her *sweet* heart — ! [*To* ROSA *as a child.*] C'here turn 'round, 'lemme put this on you. [*She takes off a locket from around her neck and fixes it on* ROSA.]

ROSA: [*Undoing the clasp and gazing at the picture.*] Pretty!

MA ROSE: Oh, you know it too! And pitch, pitch black with hair down her back like a Indian — could sit on her hair — half-blood Cherokee, matter-fact.

ROSA: [*As adult.*] Now *that* [*Referring to the locket.*] *That* I want passed down to *me* — [*Stopping herself in shock, her hands fly to her mouth.*] *Shit* — WHAT ARE YOU THINKING!! Got my eye on your *things* already! — Naw-naw, that's not *me*, I'm not like that — Rosa shame on you — !

[*Suddenly there is a man's voice from out of the shadows.* WAYMAN *appears beside* VERA. *We should have a sense of them standing in another room. He is dressed in a sober Sunday suit. He carries a set of car keys in his hands, which he jangles impatiently.*]

WAYMAN: [*To* VERA, *warm but firm.*] Shame on you. Now Vera, now you not ten years old — now if you can't go in there and just *tell* Momma, then shame on you —

VERA: [*She is fingering a medium-sized painted placard that reads:* "We Shall Overcome"] Have I *no* say-so? Brother, she talking 'bout she gonna take my Baby on out here to this thing here —

WAYMAN: And you come to town on vacation, supposed to be relaxing and just look at you. [*Pauses.*] See now, if it was *me*

I'd go on in there and tell her to her face — oh yes I would!!

VERA: She just gonna take my Baby right on out from under me —

WAYMAN: [*Jingling his car keys in his hand tensely.*] Naw, wait now, Rosa can't go! ... We don't know *what* to expect out there this afternoon! Okay, it ain't Mississippi, but then again who *knows* what they gonna do — if it was *my* kids I wouldn't stand for it Vee — no I wouldn't —!

VERA: *Oh* if only my husband was alive and living! *He'd* stand his ground! That's how come Momma never *took* to Eli, *he'd* put her in her *place*!

[VERA *reaches into her handbag and pulls out a wallet-sized photo which she holds before her, dabbing her eyes.*]

WAYMAN: [*Shaking head back and forth.*] Now, Sister — now, Sister — see and you gonna go get yourself all worked up now —

VERA: —Brother — [*She brushes the side of his head.*] got some lint on you right there — Brother — would you —

WAYMAN: Ah naw-naw now — it's up to *you* Sister — it's up to you — but if it was *me* I'd go on in there and tell Momma! And you got yourself a situation here now — 'cause now Momma done latched onto *your* child more than my kids, O.Z.'s kids, Dolores ... anybody in the family — and you just gonna hafta put your foot down and straighten it ...

[*Lights return to* MA ROSE *speaking to "little* ROSA*" as she holds the locket in her hands.*]

MA ROSE: Come outta slavery at near 'bout 16 years old — that lady there — that there's your Great-Grandma Ma Rose, *my* Momma, Big Momma "Ma." Passed on in '37 —

ROSA: [*As little girl.*] Can I wear some ah your perfume, Ma Rose?

MA ROSE: Lemme show you something. [*She takes the long, blue hair ribbons she has pressed on the ironing board. She lays each ribbon in long strips that drape from the length of* ROSA*'s shoulder.*] Now you wanna talk about some "whippings"? Ha. M'Momma come out of "bondage" tattooed with the lash! Lashes long as these here ... ha. I used to run my fingers along her scars when I was a li'l chile — [*She playfully rips the* *ribbons off* ROSA's *shoulder.*] ... Ha. Spooky, huh — ?! [*She begins dabbing perfume onto* ROSA's *neck and arms.*] [*Singing.*] " ... Well, I woke up this morning with my mind staying on Freedom ... " Chile, I'm so excited! See [*Pauses.*] here turn 'round ... good. [*She nuzzles* ROSA.] Ummmm! Smell so sweet! [*Pause.*] See, way I see it everybody's got this better half of theyselves, see? "In here" way down deep somewhere ... [*Pointing into her own chest.*] This better half of us that's got more sense and more guts than what we usually own up to in the everyday. Some of us got it way down deeper than others, but we all got it, see? And when you stand up for what you believe in? Then you have a reunion with yourself ... with your own soul's better half ...

[*Lights return to* WAYMAN *and* VERA *in another room.*]

WAYMAN: [*To* VERA.] Look it's just like this here march to the Courthouse — you standing up for what you believe in, ain't you?! — Well — You gotta do the same on the home front — 'cause-'cause-'cause Rosa she just a child and she can't help it, she just gotta be guided right. She gotta be spanked so she can *know* who to mind and who to look to. And it's up to *you.* You gotta put your foot down and say "No, Momma!" — Enough is enough!

[VERA, *spurred on by* WAYMAN, *rushes over to* MA ROSE *and* ROSA. VERA's *mouth is open, she is ready to confront* MA ROSE.]

MA ROSE: [*Stopping* VERA *in her tracks.*] Hold on, Sister, something's getting 'way from you here ...

[*She indicates for* VERA *to turn around so that her back zipper can be pulled up.* VERA *obeys dutifully and frustrated.*]

... And you just trimming down that backside nice and pretty ... turn around ... [VERA *obeys.*] Good! Go 'head!

[VERA *makes an attempt to speak up but* MA ROSE *interrupts her.*]

[*To* VERA.] I'm telling the Baby here — just the thought of folks standing up to be counted! PEOPLE DEMANDING RESPECT! [*She claps as if in church.*] It's when you come on home to your own soul girl — you seen me fall out in church? With the Holy Ghost? Can't help it, spirit takes over in ya and you find you just gotta do what you gotta do and devil take the rest —!

[VERA *makes an attempt to speak up but* MA ROSE *interrupts her.*]

[*To* ROSA.] Now, then, you just hold onto Nana's hand and walk slow with me in the line. We gonna be marching up to the Courthouse and then to the Square. See — we gonna show our support for the folks down South — yes, ma'am! They say they ain't riding they buses. Say they gonna hold out and walk *everywhere.* HA! Yes, ma'am! Seem like to me them folks down there is going through a reunion of the best part of they souls with they better selfs!

VERA: [*Sudden, rigid, hurt, to* ROSA.] What's this I smell on you?

ROSA: [*As a child, frightened.*] Nothing.

VERA: [*She makes a motion to hit* ROSA.] Now, haven't I told you 'bout lying to me?!

ROSA: [*Trembling.*] M'Rose's —

VERA: [*With great effort holding her anger.*] Momma, I don't ... I don't allow her to be wearing perfume at her age. [*She turns to* ROSA, *trying to be gentle.*] Didn't you *tell* your Grandma I don't 'llow you?

MA ROSE: [*Ever so pleasant.*] Oh it weren't *her.* I know what you don't 'llow. But after all she's in *my* house and with *me* — so what *you* don't 'llow don't have to mean that I *don't,* now *do* it?

[VERA *stares into* MA ROSE's *face, in frustration and fear, swallows deep, turns away and exits.*]

ROSA: [*Turning to* MA ROSE.] I don't feel like going.

MA ROSE: Eh? What's this?

ROSA: Don't feel good.

MA ROSE: [*She indicates* ROSA's *stomach.*] I bet it's that old "serpent's tooth" in the tummy — huh?

ROSA: [*As adult.*] Ha! *Yes,* I 'member now — *That's* what you called it — !

[MA ROSE *puts her arm gently around* ROSA's *neck and leads her across the stage into the pool of light where* VERA *and* WAYMAN *wait.*]

VERA: [*To* WAYMAN.] Brother, I don't know what comes over me, I get in there and seem like my strength is waning and 'fore I —

WAYMAN: [*To* VERA.] Your problem is you don't know how to *handle* Momma —

[*Suddenly he is surprised to find* MA ROSE *standing behind him.*]

MA ROSE: [*To* WAYMAN.] Son, where's your wife?

WAYMAN: [*Smiling broadly and timid.*] Waiting in the car, Momma, we waiting on you.

MA ROSE: [*Looking him over.*] Too hot to be sporting 'wool' ain't it? Seem like to me you'd wanna wear your cotton *summer* suit — [*Then to* VERA.] Vera-Rose, Rosa here tells me she don't feel that well —

VERA: [*With instant relish.*] Oh, she's got tummy-ache, I bet [*To* ROSA.], don't you?

ROSA: [*Pressing her fists into her stomach and speaking as an adult to herself.*] "Serpent's tooth" yes — oh, yes —

VERA: [*Satisfied.*] She gotta lay down. [*Taking* ROSA's *arm.*] Here, let's get this stuff off, y'all have to march without me, I'm staying with my Baby …

WAYMAN: Well, come on, Mom, let's go. You know they lining up —

MA ROSE: [*To* VERA.] Seems like she be getting these tummy aches too often, seems to me —

VERA: [*Friendly, at ease.*] Oh, Mom, I take her from one doctor to the next — they say lay off starch, lay off that, lay off this. [*Turning to* ROSA.] Let's get you to bed — [*Back to* MA ROSE.] What works is her getting right into bed — give Grandma back her necklace. Here Mom.

MA ROSE: [*Friendly.*] I'm thinking she should spend the year with me.

[VERA, WAYMAN *and* ROSA *all stop in their tracks.*]

MA ROSE: [*To* VERA.] You working after all. I can watch her diet up close. Soothe that tummy with my herbs and home grown stuff. She'll lose that trouble once she's spent some longer time down here in the counrty with her Nana.

VERA: [*Tense.*] This is *my* child, mother. She lives with *me*.

MA ROSE: [*To* VERA.] Why *sure* she lives with you — you're her Momma — and I thank Jesus you able to concern yourself with her —

VERA: Concern — *yes* I'm able to! *Course* it concerns me —

MA ROSE: Well, I'm glad to hear it. [*She simply stares at* VERA.]

VERA: [*Blustering under her mother's gaze.*] Well — ah — ah you don't have to look at me like *that*, Momma — !

WAYMAN: Vera, now don't get excited —

VERA: [*To* MA ROSE.] Well, don't — don't be looking at me — look, they say she's got nothing major wrong, you know that —

WAYMAN: [*To* VERA.] Sister, you are working yourself up now—!

VERA: [*To* MA ROSE.] I get her checked, tested — Momma you — you — you

WAYMAN: Vera, I'm trying to *tell* you something —

VERA: [*Frenzied.*] I'm *sure* she feels better already — don't you Baby?! [*To* ROSA.] Just something that comes and goes in passing — queasiness when she gets a little nervous — [*Speaking to* ROSA *the invisible child.*] You feeling better already, huh! Not even nothing to lie down over really. Tummy all gone, huh? Tummy all gone!

MA ROSE: Well then, now that she's feeling better and there's nothing to lie down over, *fine*, wonderful. Let's all go get in the car, come on sweetness — [*She takes* ROSA.]

[VERA *is silent, in frustration and defeat.*]

[*A pleasant afterthought.*] You know, they'll all be clamoring for me to sing a solo probably on the steps of the Courthouse, too, you know — nobody done said nothing, but just in case I done planned it —

WAYMAN: [*Shaking his head at his mother.*] If words could speak ... if words could speak ...

MA ROSE: [*Clapping her hands cheerfully and she puts on her white gloves.*] [*To* ROSA.] Clap your hands, Baby — I'm gonna do one of my favorite foot stompers, rouse the crowd ... that's right ... keep it going.

[ROSA *laughs and claps.*]

MA ROSE: Keep it going ... [*She begins her singing as the lights fade.*] I'm so glad/ trouble don't last always/I'm so glad/ trouble don't last always/singins/I'm so glad/trouble don't last always ... / Oh My Lord/ Oh My Lord/ What *shall* I do ... ?

SCENE 3

MA ROSE's *singing from the previous scene blends into the lights up on the living room of* WAYMAN's *house in the present as suggested by minimal set pieces and shadows.* VERA *and* ROSA *have just arrived, which should be suggested from the presence of their suitcases.* WAYMAN *and* ETHEL, *his wife, are present.* ETHEL *is serving coffee.* ROSA *is pacing, she and* VERA *still dressed in their clothes from Scene 1.*

WAYMAN: [*To* VERA *and* ROSA.] I mean her hair was all over! Sticking straight up off the top of her head!

VERA: Ump-upm-upm ... !

WAYMAN: All over her head! Just like a wild woman! Robe all hanging half off her ... HAIR ALL OVER HER HEAD ...

VERA: Surprised to find she ain't hurt none, carrying on like that —

ROSA: You say she didn't know *who* you were? She *didn't* know you?!

ETHEL: [*To* VERA.] Naw, she ain't hurt. Just backed up in the corner — eyes staring wild in her head like she gone wild or something!

WAYMAN: Well, I didn't know what we'd find ... creeping through the house like that. No sign of her. I'm steady calling: "MOM?! MOMMA"?!

ETHEL: Like I say, he just went by to check up on her. He drives up ... house if flooded with light! *Every* light on in the house — like it was on fire or something —

WAYMAN: First I couldn't find her —

ETHEL: And then he found her —

WAYMAN: Took one look at her —

ETHEL: And his heart like to stop —

WAYMAN: Here I'm steady walking through the house —

ETHEL: Every light on in every room, in every corner!

WAYMAN: One door then the next ... hallway no sign of her ... bedroom, no sign ... parlor nothing ... past the shiffrow ... no sign ... took one look and my heart like to stop!

ETHEL: He took one look and his heart like to stop!

VERA: Well, I guess it *did*!

ROSA: Gawd. And you say she didn't *recognize* you?! [*A beat.*] She didn't *recognize* you?!

ETHEL: Wayman said she was barefoot. She was barefoot, wasn't she, Way? [*Pause.*] I told him this morning, I said, get you on the phone! Get you on the phone *now*. Who are we to know what's gonna happen? HUH?! Who are we to know???

VERA: You right — you right — you right —

ETHEL: *Sure* I'm right!

ROSA: [*Pacing back and forth.*] Well. [*Pause.*] First off we gonna hafta try and help each other stay calm for the time being, [*Referring to* VERA.] Huh, Ma?

VERA: [*To* ROSA *regarding her pacing.*] Ro-daughter please have a seat, 'cause I just — just — ooooh m' nerves —

[ROSA *instantly sits. But in a few moments she is up again pacing around, her hands clasped as she is intently trying to figure out what to suggest, what to do.*]

ETHEL: [*To* VERA.] Not for us to know what will happen. But, it's up to us to ready ourselves. To prepare ourselves and that's *why* we called you. Now am I right? Tell me am I right?

VERA: No, you right. You right — you right —

ETHEL: Well, *sure* I'm right!

WAYMAN: She's been started talking out of her head —

ETHEL: Since the last time you been here on Mother's Day she been talking out of her head ...

WAYMAN: You right, you got that right.

ROSA: Hold it. What?! What's this, Momma? You never — I didn't know.

ETHEL: When your mother was here last. Vera, you 'member. Last Mother's Day of this year.

ROSA: Oh, I was planning to come but I had that conference in San Di-

ETHEL: Well, that's how come you didn't know it then, 'cause your Momma couldn't *find* you — and Vee, my kids the *same*, half the time I don't know where this "new breed" be at, 'cause they be jetting all over creation!

WAYMAN: [*To* ETHEL.] Naw-naw, don't be dragging up all that now — !

ETHEL: [*To* VERA *regarding her coffee*.] Vee, you take Sweet and Low? And that's *another* thing — several times I done caught Ma Rose using *salt* and thinking she's got *suga* — and last Mother's Day of this year, when we was all ready to sit down to supper, Vera, you was here … Ma Rose *jumps* up from the table and starts hollering "TAKE ME HOME. TAKE ME HOME. I WANNA GO HOME"!

VERA: That's right, 'cause —

ROSA: Oh, Mom — !

ETHEL: [*To* VERA.] 'Cause you the one went on and *took* her home …

WAYMAN: Ethel, let her tell it — !

ETHEL: Ma Rose was so riled up she didn't even wanna *wait* and let Vera finish her meal —

VERA: Well, you know Momma can be *real* "um" when she wanna be ,

ETHEL: Well, I been her daughter-in-law for 40 years, I *know* she can be!

VERA: Yeah, well, *I* got the backside to *prove* it.

ETHEL: And I ain't two minutes cleared the table, when here Vera come bringing Mom back *again* …

VERA: That's no tale. [*To* ROSA.] Here I am out here in the middle of the *freeway* —

ROSA: Yeah, and — ?

ETHEL: And Ma Rose started asking Vera about *dinner* now didn't she? She told Vera to "call on everybody to come sit down to table and say the grace," now didn't she Vee, didn't she!

WAYMAN: Ethel, will you let *her* tell it!

VERA: I say to Mother, I say, "Mother, we're out here on the freeway! We not at Wayman's house now! We on the way back to *your* house — "

ETHEL: But in her *head* she's still thinking she's back here at our house, ready to sit down to table with us —

ROSA: [*To* VERA.] Well, I *know* that threw you. [*A beat.*] Wish you had been able to find me.

WAYMAN: [*To* VERA.] Yessir. Didn't wanna worry you, 'less I absolutely had to.

VERA: Brother, you ain't done nothing but what you supposed to. Something happen here, we'd *all* feel responsible ...

ETHEL: If those, them weren't all scattered around the country we woulda called on *them*. But like I told Wayman, I said, "Wayman? Wayman," I said, "it's just you and Vera that's living near enough to this way. Now if you can reach her, you call on her, you call on her right away — "

VERA: You right, of *course* you call on me —

ETHEL: Well, *sure* I'm right!

ROSA: [*To* VERA.] Momma, and *you* call on me.

VERA: [*To* ROSA.] Well, what you think?

ROSA: [*Pacing.*] Of course, *you all* are the ones in charge. But if I can, uh, "suggest" ... well ... One: ... it is well, y'know true Ma Rose is kinda "partial" to *me* — hate to *say* it that way [*Quickly turning to* ETHEL *and* WAYMAN.] — I mean I'm sure she's "partial" to the other cousins, too — all I mean is she has always kinda singled *me* out — and all I'm saying is that — well, she — I mean with you all's *approval* — y'know — I think if I can just sit with her by myself and talk to her and see where she's —

ETHEL: Vera? After Ma Rose scaring us like that last night? I thought Wayman was gonna hafta carry *me* to the hospital!

WAYMAN: Robe half hanging off her. Hair every which way on her head. All wild and backed up in a corner ...

VERA: And you say she was *barefoot*?

ETHEL: Just *wild*. Looking right through you. Didn't know where she was. Wayman had to go up to her and call out several times. "MOM!" "MOM!" 'fore she even know him. [*Pause.*] He had to go up and call out to Mom *several* times 'fore she let him sit her down, 'fore she know *who* he was ... !

WAYMAN: Then on top of that she ...

ETHEL: *Made* him *get* out of the house!

VERA: *What*?!

ETHEL: So he got out! Like she said. What's he gonna do? Overpower her? Have her scratching and clawing at him?

WAYMAN: 'Course I ain't getting into all of that.

ETHEL: Vera, for the past week Momma ain't let *nobody* in that house. Not the doctor, pastor, *nobody*.

ROSA: [*Clapping her hands together with resolve.*] Okay then. Here's what we do. First, I'm obviously the one to talk to her. I can't see her turning *me* away ...

ETHEL: [*To* VERA.] And Vera-Rose, get ready for this — I drove over there night 'fore last and here was Ma Rose, standing out in her nightgown *in the snow.*

VERA: *WHAT*?!

ROSA: Well then, I'm obviously the one to get her to a doctor —

WAYMAN: [*To* VERA.] She's not lying — I just didn't call *then* 'cause I didn't wanna worry you.

ETHEL: [*Acting out* MA ROSE.] Vee, she was talking 'bout, "This house is my tomb! This house is my tomb! They's dead people in there, I gotta get away ... "

VERA: WAYMAN — WAYMAN — WAYMAN!

ETHEL: I almost had a conniption there and then.

ROSA: [*To* VERA.] Okay, Mom. Give me a minute to just — col-

lect my thoughts here — I'll take your car, Mom. I think it's
best I go there by myself at first to see —

ETHEL: I think we should pray.

VERA:
WAYMAN: } A-men.

[WAYMAN *and* VERA, *on instant reflex, join hands with* ETHEL *to
form a circle.* ROSA *stands apart, struggling not to show her impa-
tience and annoyance. Then after a beat of hesitation,* ROSA *joins
hands with* VERA. VERA, ETHEL *and* WAYMAN *all close their eyes
in a beat of silent prayer.* ROSA, *however, stares out, her eyes wide
and worried. She is only going through the motions for the sake of
pleasing them.*]

VERA: [*Turning to them all.*] And y'know? Momma's always been
so clear-minded ... I just can't — it's so hard for me to
imagine.

ROSA: Let's first just follow my plan. [*A beat.*] One thing I'll
show you, I *never* just plunge in blind if there's a problem.
My first rule of thumb is *always* first get a *plan* —

ETHEL: Niece, this ain't no "Seminar," this is *real* life, this is
family.

[*Pause. Silence. There is complete stillness.*]

ROSA: [*A tense half-smile.*] "Excuse" me?

ETHEL: This is your mother's mother and this is your uncles'
mother.

WAYMAN: [*Rushing to get his coat.*] Well, let's get on over there
then. See what she's up to now. I'll warm up m'car. Y'all
come on.

[*He exits.*]

ETHEL: [*Following right after* WAYMAN *and yanking on her coat as
she speaks.*] Vera, just slam the door. [*Calling after* WAYMAN.]
Wayman! Way! You put a hat on — last thing I want is for
you to get *flu* on top of everything else!

ROSA: [*Calling after* ETHEL.] Now *look* at ya — just *look* at ya!
Running out here and don't have a *bit* of idea of what you
gonna do, now *do* you!? And that's *exactly* what's gonna bring
trouble!

VERA: Rosa, you don't hafta preach at us now — you don't have
to —

ROSA: I AM *NOT* HAVING THIS TURN INTO NO
WHOLE LOTTA MESS — *THAT* I WILL *NOT* HAVE!!
[*She calls out into the shadows.*] UNCLE WAYMAN —
COME ON *BACK* IN HERE —

VERA: [*Warning* ROSA.] *Who* do you *think* you talking to??!!

ROSA: [*She turns to* VERA *and* ETHEL *with authority.*] — Now
there is no *immediate* danger. We gonna take a half hour right
now and we gonna *plan.* Matter-fact we better *counterplan.* I
just am not gonna leap into something I can't *handle.*

ETHEL: [*To* ROSA.] You just help us get into the house and that'll
be enough.

ROSA: *YOU* DON'T TELL *ME* WHAT TO DO!!!

VERA: [*With a grimace of warning to* ROSA.] ...Go slow, girl —
You better take it easy — you hear — ?!

ROSA: *LOOK.* I am *here* now. I'm the one to help you straighten
this out and I"m gonna *straighten* it all out. But let's get *one*
thing straight — I WILL *NOT* BE *TOLD* WHAT TO DO.

VERA: [*Suddenly fierce.*] YOU BETTER *DRAW BACK* UNDER
CONTROL!!

ROSA: [*Cowers on an instant, smiling, hands wide in placating apolo-
getic gesture.*] Kay — okay — kay — okay — kay — okay —
kay — okay — Momma —

VERA: [*There is an instant pause. Then* VERA *suddenly in the full
force of feeling offended, balls up her fists and shrieks.*] E-E-E-E-
E-E-E-U-U-U-U-U-U-U-U *WHO DO YOU THINK YOU
ARE*!!!

ROSA: [*Her hands fly to her face in terror and protection.*] Mommy
— Mommy — don't — okay — okay —

VERA: My nerves are frayed *already*!

ROSA: Yes, ma'am.

VERA: Don't you try me ...

[*There is the sound of* WAYMAN's *car horn, insistent.*]

VERA: [*Pointing a warning finger at* ROSA.] Don't you *try* me.

[The lights fade to a spotlight on VERA *and* ROSA. ROSA's *smile fades into frustrated but suppressed fear and rage. The car horn sound continues, then lights fade to darkness completely.*

The sound of the car horn continues and blends into the sound of a door buzzer, shrill and insistent. Lights come up on VERA, WAYMAN, ETHEL *and* ROSA, *all standing in a line at* MA ROSE's *front door.]*

SCENE 4

The buzzer continues to sound, as WAYMAN, ETHEL, VERA *and* ROSA *knock and knock. Finally they all pause and tense up as we see* MA ROSE *peer out from the shadows. She is seriously disheveled, leaning on her cane, her eyes appear slightly disoriented.*

WAYMAN: *[His hand raised in a placating gesture.]* Now Ma ... now Mother ... don't get riled up and excited now ... We all just come by to pay a call on you and see how you feeling this evening. How you feeling?

MA ROSE: *[Immediately wary upon seeing* VERA.]* Wha ... ? Vera-Rose? What you doing down *all* this way? How come—you—

VERA: *[Straining to remain casual and cheerful.]* Hullo, Momma! Oh, I'm just uh ... passing through ... town ...

WAYMAN: She passing through town, Momma — on her way to — she just passing uh through — on her way —

VERA: *Look!* Look who I brought! All the way from New York! Somebody that somebody else is *sure* gonna be sure glad to see! Lookit here, look... !

[VERA turns sideways to reveal ROSA *standing behind her.]*

ROSA: *[Stepping forward, her arms outstretched, her smile radiant.]* *[Singing.]* " ... love oh love/ oh precious love ... love oh love ... " Hey there! How ya doing m'darling! *Good* to see ya!!!

[ROSA steps forward and attempts to take MA ROSE *in her arms for a kiss but* MA ROSE *backs away in surprise and shock.]*

AH!!! It's *so* good to see my Nana!!! Oh — I have *missed* my sweetness, oh *yes* I have!!!

MA ROSE: This ain't —

VERA: *Yes* it is!!

WAYMAN: Ma, we gonna go inside now, okay?

[MA ROSE *throws up her hand warning them back.*]

MA ROSE: Naw!

VERA: [*Continuing to remain casual.*] Yes it is — yes it is —

ETHEL: Now Ma — Momma — how 'bout we all helping you to come on inside and take a seat —

VERA: Yes, ma'am! This is her! Your favorite "grand," your favorite, oh you'll wanna hear what she's been up to, Momma, will make you *so* proud —

MA ROSE: [*Backing off.*] Something ain't right. This don't feel right. [*Turning away.*] I'll be seeing ya.

WAYMAN: WAIT! WAIT! — Wait a minute, Ma — hold on !!!

ETHEL: Way, take it easy —

ROSA: Nana?

VERA: See, I told her she oughta come by and see you, I told her. You ain't seen her since when, Mom?

MA ROSE: [*Confused.*] I dunno — I —

ROSA: [*Turning to VERA.*] Mom, if you just — please — I think I can be the one to talk to Nana —

VERA: [*Ignoring ROSA.*] — Not since that awards banquet when she got that plaque — thought it was *time* to bring her by for a visit — so good to see you, Momma —

MA ROSE: [*Flinging up her arm to stop VERA in her tracks.*] NO! You hold it right there! Just hold it!

ROSA: [*Softly so as not to frighten MA ROSE.*] Even *me*, Nana? Me too? You don't mean me, do you? Not *me*?

MA ROSE: [*Suddenly perking up, a spark of her former vigorous days.*] Naw-naw — you come on in here, gal, see your Ma Rose!! Bless her heart!! Ain't laid eyes on you since I don't know *when*, my goodness — [*Shooing away the others.*] — Rest a y'all clear on back home!

ROSA: [*Turning to VERA.*] Mom, I'll call you at Uncle Way's house, we'll get this all straightened out —

VERA: You just hold it!! [*Blocking* ROSA.] You *don't* know what you doing!! This is *my* Ma —

WAYMAN: [*Suddenly erupting with frustration.*] Now *look*! Enough of this now! 'NOUGH OF THIS NONSENSE!

ETHEL: You tell 'em, honey —

WAYMAN: We coming in there and we coming in there *now* and that's all there is *to* it —

MA ROSE: [*Rearing up with all her strength.*] BOY, WHO YOU THINK YOU TALKING TO, HUH! WHERE YOU THINK YOU GOING WITHOUT MY PERMISSION! HUH! YOU BETTER BACK OFF 'FORE I TAKE A STRAP TO YOU! AND YOU *KNOW* I'M THE ONE TO DO IT, TOO — I'LL KNOW YOU TO KINGDOM COME!!

[ROSA *starts to move inside with* MA ROSE.]

VERA: [*Stopping* ROSA.] Where you think *you* going without my permission!

[ROSA *freezes*.]

VERA: Now I mean it, I will raise a hand to you girl, 'cause I sure *will* raise a hand to you!!

[*There is a suspended pause, then —*]

MA ROSE: [*Suddenly jolly.*] Well, everybody, I had a good time. Thanks for coming. It was nice, real nice. Good to see all of you. Enjoyed myself thoroughly. Next family reunion we'll do it up even more. Rosa, you staying with me, rest of y'all get home safe and take care —

[MA ROSE *forcibly takes* ROSA's *arm, pats her cheek and starts to lead her inside.*]

MA ROSE: [*To* ROSA.] This here's my *namesake*, my name —

VERA: [*Stunned.*] I am your namesake too — I fit in there some-where, too, don't I? Well, don't I?

ROSA: [*Turning to* VERA.] There is no reason to get your feelings hurt —

VERA: [*Plaintive to* MA ROSE.] *I am* your namesake, too!

WAYMAN: And me too, me too! Here I done given her all my life! Given, given, given, [*To* ETHEL.] and you see how she treats me, don't you?! All I spend taking care of her, seeing after her!!

ROSA: There is no need to get agitated —

VERA: WELL, I *AM* AGITATED, GOT TO BE AGITATED, HOW ELSE I'M GONNA BE *BUT* AGITATED!

WAYMAN: [*Throwing up his hands.*] All right, I'm done with it! She wanna act like she ain't got *six* living sons and *four* living daughters and —

ETHEL: — and all them grands and great-grands —

VERA: And great-great grands —

MA ROSE: Ain't nobody denying y'all, I gave life to you! I did! *I* gave life to you!

VERA: Momma, Wayman didn't mean that. We know you love your family. This is family, sure you love us, don't you? 'Course you do— [*She suddenly takes* MA ROSE*'s arm.*]

MA ROSE: [*Caught off guard by* VERA, *confused, alarmed.*] Wait — I — I —

VERA: Momma, you said for me and Rosa to come on in and for Way to wait —

MA ROSE: [*Confused.*] I said that? I — ?

ROSA: [*To* VERA.] Ma, don't do that to her —

[VERA *gives* ROSA *a warning look,* ROSA *cowers and backs off.*]

ROSA: All right, fine, fine — let's just please not fight —

[VERA *leads* MA ROSE *firmly by the arm into a new spot of light which designates the inside of Ma Rose's house. As lights come up in the house we see old newspapers and rags flung about.*]

VERA: Now, Mother, you just lean on the cane and lean on me.

MA ROSE: [*Confused.*] I said that? But wait — wait — I said that?

VERA: That's right. Okay, here we go. Let's sit you down. You rest now. You rest.

[VERA *walks* MA ROSE *over and sits her down.*]

WAYMAN: [*Calling out as they leave him and* ETHEL *standing out-*

side.] A man just oughta get the respect he's got coming!!

ETHEL: AMEN! From his sister as well as his mother!

[*Lights fade on* ETHEL *and* WAYMAN *as they back away.*]

MA ROSE: [*Confused, to* VERA.] Girl, I'm all right — I don't want — I'm all right —

VERA: You *sit.* Just sit. You stay put. I'm here now. I'm in charge. I'm gonna see what's what, you just stay put.

MA ROSE: [*Turning to* ROSA *in shock.*] They got in — they got in —

VERA: [*Shaking her head back and forth.*] Ah, Mother, Mother, Mother! And just *look* at your hair — and your skin — and — and you just ain't been taking good care of yourself at all —

[ROSA *gazes both at* MA ROSE *and at the surroundings, speechless and in shock at the disarray.*]

VERA: Rosa — sit here with Grandma till I see what's what ... [*Suddenly.*] Smell smoke ... ?!

[VERA *runs out toward the kitchen.*]

ROSA: [*Lovingly.*] Oh —
Lemme squeeze — so so
good to hug you!! How
you doing? Hum? How
are you!?

MA ROSE: Oh — girl, I'll do
— I'm all right — lemme lay
eyes on m' namesake — bless
her heart — how you doing,
Babbee?!

[VERA *enters wearing a potholder mitt and holding up a horribly burnt and melted cooking pot.*]

VERA: Momma, this was burning up on the stove. Flames leaping high up!

MA ROSE: I did not.

VERA: Evidence don't lie! Here it is big as life! High — high up —

[MA ROSE *drops her head embarassed.*]

VERA: And you claim you gonna stay here by yourself. *How?* How you gonna stay here by yourself?

MA ROSE: Put that back! Who told you you could mess in my kitchen! Clear out! Clear out!

[VERA *turns and exits back to kitchen shaking her head.*]

[ROSA *puts her arm around* MA ROSE.]

[*To* ROSA.] See, girl, I'm *fine* — they don't know it — ya mother and them but I — don't need no taking care of — them trouping in and out and spying —

[*There is the sound of clanging and clattering dishes, pots and pans and silverware, from off-stage as they are being sorted by* VERA *off unseen in the kitchen.*]

[*Pointing toward the sounds coming from kitchen.*] Demons in my house!

[*She rises slowly and with great effort on her cane.* ROSA *rushes to her but she waves* ROSA *off. She seems to peek out of a window.*]

Demons outside there! They ain't drove off! They parked out there, I see 'em! Out there planning and scheming! Leave me be! Just leave me!!!

[ROSA *reaches* MA ROSE *and holds her.*]

[*Suddenly laughing at her own tantrum.*] Yessir! Your old Nana *still* got the salt left in her — you watch me — [*Whispering to* ROSA.] Always watch it when people come *claiming* they wanna do *for* ya — when it's for *they* own sake and not for what *you* want —

ROSA: Coming to help means we just love you *more* — care so much about you —

MA ROSE: M' namesake — oh — turn 'round lemme look at ya!

ROSE: What if we — if *I* — could find someone to come live — wait not so fast — hear me out, Nana —

MA ROSE: Don't need no taking care of — no — no! I'm fine — carrying on just fine — folks leave me 'lone — I do fine.

ROSA: You *deserve* some help! Doesn't have to mean that you can't take care of yourself — Together you and me can find somebody in town here — somebody who can make sure you're — who can —

[VERA *comes from the shadows, alarmed that* MA ROSE *is standing.*]

VERA: Mom, I thought I told you to sit down and stay down —

MA ROSE: [*She slowly approaches* VERA, *her cane raised, but strained with the effort.*] [*She quietly speaks to* ROSA *as she approaches* VERA.] She know better than to try me ...

[VERA *stands still and frightened as* MA ROSE *approaches. In slow steps* MA ROSE *is finally face to face with* VERA, *their foreheads almost touching.* VERA *is shaking visibly.*]

MA ROSE: [*Referring to* VERA *as she speaks to* ROSA.] ... She *know* to bow her head and tremble when she face me — she been raised on the "overseer head-whipping" that *my* momma taught me — *Ask her*! — she *know* not to mess with me!!!

ROSA: [*Gently holding* MA ROSE.] Nana, no — Nana, — don't be like this — Don't now — Nana, please ...

[*Several beats of silence. Then suddenly* MA ROSE *weakens and must lower her raised cane in order to keep herself from falling, her body collapses and* ROSA *quickly helps her to stand.*]

ROSA: [ROSA *then leading* MA ROSE *to her chair.*] There now — there now — there — there

MA ROSE: They on the prowl! They on the prowl!

[ROSA *silently raises her hand behind* MA ROSE's *back, trying to plead with* VERA *to leave off and return to the kitchen.* VERA *returns* ROSA's *silent gesture, urgently motioning for her to follow her into the shadows — all is done behind* MA ROSE's *back.*]

VERA: [*In a pleasant voice that is forced.*] Mother, now, there ain't *no* sense in you getting all excited when we just come to help — Ro? Come get some tea for your Granma.

ROSA: [*To* MA ROSE.] I'll talk to Momma — sh-h-h-h-h now — you rest and let me —

[ROSA *moves off with* VERA, *anxious to speak with her.*]

MA ROSE: [*Gesturing to* VERA *with her warning cane.*] A shut eye ain't always sleep! A shut eye ain't always sleep! [*Calling out after them.*] Get your butts out from nosing 'round! Y'all ain't getting me out! Y'all ain't!

[*Lights up on* VERA *and* ROSA *in another room of the house. They're both whispering furtively and desperately.*]

VERA: [*Whispering conspiratorially to* ROSA.] *See* how she looks!

[ROSA *nods anxiously.*]

Gawd, Rosa — lookit — whole ice box filled with rotted I don't-know-what! Mom could *poison* herself with this here! And back in the bathroom? There's weeks-old stale water just filled to the rim in the tub! Uncle Wayman has got to get in here and help me — !

MA ROSE: [*Calling out.*] Y'all ain't getting me out!! I am *not* a child! A Child of God, but not no child!

[VERA *startles and holds to* ROSA *at the sound of* MA ROSE'*s voice.*]

VERA: [*Holding tight to* ROSA *and speaking in hushed, furtive tones.*] Sh-h-h-h-h! Keep your voice down! [*Placing her palm on* ROSA'*s cheek.*] See how clammy?

ROSA: Mommy, listen now, look — you're a grown woman, don't be scared — just speak up — as her daughter it's got to come from *you* — you see, she's weak, she can't hurt you — tell her that her mind is slipping and that she needs help —

VERA: Me? You the "favorite" — you do it — I — I — ain't *never* been able to get nowhere with Momma.	ROSA: Okay, then. [*Firm.*] We gonna do this *my* way — right? Agreed?
Sh-h-h-h-h-! Keep your voice down — *you* the one. Not *me*.	Okay then — I can do it. Don't worry none, just *let* me. I can do it —

[ROSA *stares at* VERA *a brief moment, then turns and returns to* MA ROSE.]

[ROSA *enters from the shadows with a cup of hot tea on a tray which she offers to* MA ROSE *as she then proceeds to smooth out* MA ROSE'*s hair and to rebutton her ragged sweater.*]

MA ROSE: I remember when you were just l'il bitty "l'il Rose" — I remember — I haven't forgot anything — they told you I forget stuff —

ROSA: They told me this, that — long as I see for *myself* that's all

I want.

MA ROSE: I forget a few things — *everybody* forget a few things — but I don't never burn up nothing on no stove —

[MA ROSE *catches* ROSA's *eyes — they smile at her fib and finally laugh together out loud.*]

MA ROSE: Chile, it ain't all that dumbfounding as you trying to make out. [*Pause.*] Getting nearer the grave is all. Nothing to fret over. Just waiting and ready for the harvester and the harvest and that's all —

ROSA: No — no — no! Don't even *think* anything like that — no.

MA ROSE: [*Insistent and annoyed.*] You *hear* me! Got many more waiting for me on the other side than I got here. That's what I got. And I'm ready any time. Don't *want* no taking care of. Don't want to be *put* nowhere. Don't want nothing long and drawn out. Don't want to leave my house! Now you just make 'em leave me be. *Please.* That's all I want!

[VERA *suddenly appears from the shadows. Relieved,* ROSA *runs to her.*]

VERA: [*Her attention gentle and tense is focused on* MA ROSE.] Mom … ? … *Look.* You gonna have to help me. You gotta help me take matters in hand. See er — Mom — your thoughts are starting to slip. You sense of making sense is starting to er —

[MA ROSE *merely stares* VERA *down.*]

MA ROSE: [*Quiet.*] What cha doing Vera-Rose? Tramping through your *Mother's* house? Fiddling in your *Mother's* stuff? This your *Mother* talking to you!!

VERA: [VERA *withers, backing away.*] [*To* ROSA.] *That's* what I get for listening to *you*, thank you very much.

[VERA *returns to the shadows.*]

ROSA: [*Gently.*] Nana — look, we can see you having trouble getting 'round and doing for yourself, and keeping your house up, feeding yourself, we can *see* that —

MA ROSE: [*Referring to* VERA.] Child thinks she know *everything*! Nobody can't tell her nothing! Well sir, I raised her — yes, Lord, I pay the coin for that — she's my doing — [*She whis-*

pers to ROSA *quietly*.] Hump — see that's how I be passing these last days — dredging up the days I done passed on the river side, dredging on history — [*Laughing*.]

ROSA: Please, please, there's no "last days" yet for a *long time* — don't want you *thinking* this way —

MA ROSE: — Now *my* momma? We used to think she had a branding iron for a backbone, she was so rough — now I stand in my vineyard — now that m' harvest is come I got to look over my crop — [*Thoughtful again*.] It's a wonder how *clear-sighted* waiting on your grave makes ya!

ROSA: [*Stunned for a beat*.] If you could just — show Mother you know she hurts — if you two could just *show* each other —

MA ROSE: And what about *you* showing your Momma *you* — the "for real" you? [*Silence*.]

ROSA: [*Smiling*.] [*Silence. Then*.] Look — let me find somebody to come here and help you.

MA ROSE: Naw, ain't gonna have "them" thinking I can't fend for *myself*.

ROSA: *You* was somebody else's maid all your life! — It's time we set you up with somebody to do *your* bidding — somebody to see and look after and — you deserve somebody just to stop in now and then — just to —

MA ROSE: [*Stopping* ROSA *with her voice*.] Listen here, m' namesake — m' namesake — you don't got no peaceful face on you. When you last caught a glimpse of your "real" face —

ROSA: [*Laughs*.] Well, I guess you caught me with my "jet-lag" circles under my eyes for *one* thing —

[*She crosses over to another spot and lifts up a small bottle from the floor in a corner*.]

Nana, these the pills Uncle tells me you're not taking?

[*Suddenly* MA ROSE *lifts an earthen pottery jar with a sealed-on lid from underneath the scattered pile of objects on the floor. She shakes it. It is obviously full of pennies*.]

ROSA: [*Turning to the sound in recognition and shock*.] GAWD! I	MA ROSE: HA! "Make a wish" —' member? 'member?

DON'T BELIEVE! HA! *WHERE* DID YOU — ??

Childhood stuff — oh, sweetness, you could of thrown all this out — !

I appreciate but — no sense in having junk cluttering things up.

Ha — I found it — 'member 'fore you took off to college or what was it — you keep on coming and going so till I hardly recollected — but you was leaving for somewhere, member and member me sealing in all the "wishes" — Oh, I got it *all* — I 'member

MA ROSE: You still climbing up higher and higher in the wide world — still winning prizes?

ROSA: Ha! *Every* opportunity! I won't let you down!

MA ROSE: [*She shakes the jar with the sound of pennies.*] And just as shapely as she *wanna* be — turn 'round! Haha! So how you *doing*! How you be!?

ROSA: Like my hair?

MA ROSE: —Still think of you as kinky headed.

ROSA: Ha — My 'fro was in my other life and former days.

MA ROSE: So how you doing? How you be? [*She gives the jar a shake.*]

ROSA: [*Twirling before* MA ROSE.] Well, take a look for yourself and *see* !! Tell you what — I'll stay for the weekend and see how you get along —

MA ROSE: How you doing?! *Answer* me.

ROSA: Ha! Lemme tell you — see in New York City when you get an office with windows in either side of the wall and you have a corner view and you can look out see the city below you, that's your sign ... that's your solid signal — Nana, I got windows on *both* sides of my wall four ways 'round — my office is so big — couch I can sink into.

MA ROSE: —That's *what* you doing, but *how* you doing? How you?

ROSA: [*Suddenly realizing.*] Ah! Forgetting something — *What* is wrong with me! [ROSA *goes to her briefcase, takes out a wrapped gift and places it in* MA ROSE's *hands.* MA ROSE *opens it. It is a long piece of very expensive lace.*]

MA ROSE: Things. You know I *know* you, see. I know when I look in that face and *see* you and when I *don't* see you.

ROSA: *What is it?*! What am I doing wrong — What? What?!

MA ROSE: Answer me — *How* are you? You got friends?

ROSA: Oh — Ah!! Here we go — now you not gonna try and tell me I need to have "Mister" wrapped 'round my name as my badge for proving I'm happy or not happy?

MA ROSE: *Do* you have people 'round you who care 'bout you—?

ROSA: When I have time to see them, I have friends — okay?! Satisfied?

[*There is the sudden sound of clanging, falling objects offstage.*]

VERA: [*Offstage.*] LORD HA'MERCY MOMMA *WHAT* IS THIS HERE!! —

[VERA *appears from the shadows. She is maintaining a false effort at smiling calmly.*]

VERA: Er — now er don't get excited now Momma, it's all under control — er good, Ro, you keep her company — I er —

[VERA *disappears back into the shadows urgently.*]

ROSA: [*To* MA ROSE.] How you like your present? It's handmade — 'member my postcard from Florence, I wrote you —?

MA ROSE: [*Stopping* ROSA *with her voice.*] And you way up there now, huh?

ROSA: [*Playful.*] Lotta windows in my office.

MA ROSE: And you can see outta all of 'em when you want to.

ROSA: It's the mark of making it, Nana.

MA ROSE: Got any mirrors in there? Windows you see out of — mirrors for seeing into?

ROSA: [ROSA *laughs.*] I hear you! I hear you!

[*She is frustrated and uncomfortable and in order to get away she takes up the tea and saucer* MA ROSE *has finished and moves to take if off into the kitchen.*]

[*There is a loud crash of boxes, furniture, the sounds of spilling. The crash offstage startles* ROSA *dropping the cup that was resting in the saucer.*]

VERA: [*Heard offstage.*] AND WHAT IN THE WORLD IS ALL THIS IN HERE, MOM — THAT'S OKAY — YOU SIT AND LEAVE IT UP TO ME — THAT'S OKAY —

[*Suddenly a louder banging sound.*]

VERA: [*Having hit herself on something.*] OWW! [*A beat, she calls out.*] I'M OKAY, Y'ALL, Y'ALL JUST — RO, JUST KEEP MOM COMPANY —

ROSA: [*Turning on MA ROSE.*] D'you know what's *wonderful* about my life?! *Winning* is wonderful! D'you *understand*!? No, I don't think you do! There's a thrill when you win — when you plan to win and make your move and then find that you have *won* — and figuring how to win *more* — winning my place in that wide and rough world out there — fighting my way in and *winning* and winning 'cause I *deserve* to!!

MA ROSE: I can see you go through day after day after day of feeling like you ain't been inside your own flesh — I can see that.

ROSA: I have my bad days just like everybody else! Just bad days like everybody else!! And you just make up your mind you're gonna go *forward* no matter what — that's all! And you go *forward*!

MA ROSE: I can see there be times when you be wishing you could hear your own deep down inside voice 'stead all that "empty" you be — be "mouthing" ... and fronting

ROSA: [*Silence. She is stunned.*] "Empty" —

MA ROSE: *Many* days when you feel like you ain't been doing *nothing* but mouthing "empty" — it's all traced out on your face.

ROSA: Fine — I've had to accept that there are certain rules that have to be played by, followed. Okay, there is a way you have to "be" — Took some — getting used to — but I've made my — peace with it — Don't worry 'bout me, okay? [*Pause.*] You can *see* all that, huh? [*Pauses.*] "Inside voice" — my "inside voice" is my *personal* life.

MA ROSE: Do you *have* one?

ROSA: Funny-funny-funny   MA ROSE: *Do you?*

ROSA: I have set certain goals for myself and I have *accomplished* that — can't you — see that — just see that!!

MA ROSE: All I see is that you right away mouth up whatever you think anybody wants to *hear* — that whatever win you the world's pat on the head, then that's what you bow to — all I can see is that that crust of that false-face is scratching you and scratching you —

ROSA: I've adjusted and made my peace — I'm *all right* — you get used to how you have to "be" — how you have to conduct yourself — you — you —

MA ROSE: [*She shakes the jar of pennies.*] "Make a wish ... "

"Do" I remember!? "Do" I!??

'Member that day when we marched?

MA ROSE: [*She pulls out packet of letters she has saved from* ROSA, *sent throughout the years, all wrapped up in faded ribbon.*]

And all them *other* marches and travels and stops along the way you done wrote me ... What was it then you wanted? What was it you told me then you was wanting to be ... ? Something other than this Demon false-face, I recollect —

[ROSA *takes the packet of letters from* MA ROSE's *hand, amazed at the sight of them.*]

ROSA: *These*!? People *change* — obviously — what I *was*? What I *was*? *Why* should I be what I "was"? Be proud as I *am* — all you have to do is be *proud* of me!

MA ROSE: [*She takes one from its packet and recites as if from memory.*] "*I* was part of that one *small* thing — *I* was part of that ... "

ROSA: [*She reaches for the letter and begins to read it out loud for herself — the lights fade to a spot that illuminates her face as she reads.*] " ... of that one *small* thing — we got the public library here to *finally* send out a bookmobile over to the Jefferson Projects for the children — Day one — so many kids turned up *and* parents — our first reaction was to panic — but people started bringing out card tables and crates, radios and before we knew it we ended up with a neighborhood block party — just that one simple step — Oh, I feel — I feel — Nana — hon' — I feel so *alive!* —"

[*The lights return to the present.*]

[*She is stunned, a startled awareness now crosses her face.*] "I feel so alive" ... — not a morning I don't wake up feeling my "realness" drifting off further and further — not a morning — I just want to wake up one day and not feel such a cold scare flooding through me —

MA ROSE: That there Demon with a false face is a tough Demon.

ROSA: "I feel so *alive.*"

MA ROSE: [*Suddenly she is seeing a vision before her.*] And there go that false-face Demon being bred in you! There you go l'il Rose — running from them whippings — running from that strap — and two-facing — pleading and begging and wetting yourself — and lying and screaming anything you think will save you —

ROSA: Don't bring all that — up — no — I don't feel like — That stuff, I've put behind me — don't, please don't.

[*There is the sound of clanging and falling objects offstage.*]

VERA: [*Offstage.*] MOTHER, YOU JUST GOT ALL THIS STUFF EVERY WHICH WAY — I JUST DON'T KNOW — I JUST DON'T — !

MA ROSE: [*To* ROSA.] When you gonna cast off the veil off your spirit and face her face to face and face your demon face? — The child of my third generation and life got you all backed up in the corner — What's chasing you so? *What* you turning into? You my namesake and ever since you come out the womb with your eyes blinking full ah blood and womb water I done *known* ya. Yessir. I *know* ya —

[ROSA's *hands fly up to her face and she weeps.* MA ROSE *slowly, on her cane, walks up to her and embraces her. The sound of* VERA *rummaging through boxes and objects falling, increases in pitch — there is the sound of glass breaking.*] [*A pause,* VERA *appears on-*

stage.]

VERA: [*She remains in the entrance, awkward.*] Mother — [*She is too bewildered and overcome to continue, just shakes her head and exits.*]

[*Suddenly* MA ROSE *jabs her cane out into the air in rage, brandishing her arms in the air.*]

MA ROSE: GET-GET — GET OUT! GET OUTTA MY STUFF! GET OUTTA MY HOUSE! GET OUT! GET OUT!

ROSA: [*Struggling to calm her.*] NANA, SIT ... PLEASE ... SIT.

MA ROSE: THIS IS MY HOUSE AND MY STUFF AND I'LL TAKE LEAVE OF THIS WORLD ANY WAY I WANT!

ROSA: [*Trying softly to quiet* MA ROSE *and to lead her to sit.*] Yes, ma'am, yes — yes — sh-h-h-h-h-h —

MA ROSE: [*Resisting* ROSA's *pull.*] Yessir! *Any* way I want!

[*Just as* ROSA *almost soothes* MA ROSE, *leading her to sit, she and* MA ROSE *both slip on the cane in almost reaching the seat. They both fall flat out on the floor.* ROSA *leaps up.* MA ROSE *is on her back and struggling to lift herself up.*]

ROSA: NANA ROSA!

MA ROSE: You get back! You leave me 'lone and lemme ... Hear?! *Leave* me.

[VERA's *voice is heard offstage as she rummages through boxes.*]

VERA: OH, GOD, MOMMA — YOU COULD KILL YOUR-SELF IN HERE — !

MA ROSE: [*At the sound of* VERA's *voice she suddenly clutches* ROSA.] Look, don't let 'em take me. You my nameskae now. Don't let 'em take me ...

ROSA: If she gets in here and *sees* you ... !

MA ROSE: [*As* ROSA *struggles to help her up.*] Sh-h-h-h-h — just stay quiet and help me — nobody need know but us — just you and me —

[VERA *suddenly appears in the shadows, carrying a huge pile of very soiled clothing.*]

VERA: Rosa? [*Immediately screeching at the sight of* MA ROSE.]

MOMMA!!! OH, MY GAWD, LORD, WHY DIDN'T YOU *CALL* ME!!! WHY DIDN'T Y'ALL CALL ME — OH, MY *GAWD*, MOMMA OH MY GAWD — !!

[VERA *runs to the edge of the stage, calling out into the shadows.*]

VERA: WAYMAN!! ETHEL!! GET IN HERE QUICK!! MOMMA'S DONE TAKEN A FALL!!!

[VERA *rushes back and kneels down to* MA ROSE.]

MA ROSE: Baby, I'll be all right, please — please —

VERA: Sh-h-h-h-h-h HUSH! REST!! DON'T MOVE!! [*To* ROSA.] DON'T MOVE HER!! [*Her harsh tone giving way to softness.*] Momma, momma, momma, you won't listen to let us try and help —

MA ROSE: [*In anguish and fear.*] Please, I don't wanna go, please — children, please this is your mother asking, pleading with you, please —

[WAYMAN *and* ETHEL *rush in with cries of shock and concern. They push* ROSA *away as they close in on* MA ROSE. ROSA *begins to slowly move to the front of the stage, standing in a single spotlight, apart from the rest of the family. The others surround* MA ROSE.]

VERA: [*To* ETHEL.] Call the hospital and get her coat. [*To* WAYMAN.] Don't move her, brother, get a blanket ...

MA ROSE: No. I don't wanna go! I don't wanna go!

WAYMAN: Momma, we ain't taking you nowhere. We just gonna let the hospital make sure you ain't hurt none. We bringing you right back home.

[ROSA *just stares out, hardly able to bear it.*]

MA ROSE: [*Pleading.*] Right back home?

VERA: We won't take you no place you don't wanna go.

MA ROSE: I'm coming right home?

VERA: Yes, ma'am.

WAYMAN: Yes, ma'am — yes.

MA ROSE: Vera, thaw out that cut-up veal I got in the icebox — when we get back everybody stay to supper —

VERA: Yes, ma'am, now Mommy, you could be hurt on the inside, now calm down —

WAYMAN: Rest now, you done fought the good fight.

ETHEL: Thank God we was here when this happened!

MA ROSE: Now I'm coming right back home?

ROSA: [*Standing apart fromthe others, a spotlight on her face as she whispers to herself in anguish.*] You coming *right back home* —

MA ROSE: Y'all bringing me right back, right? Lemme see your eyes — lemme see your faces —

ROSA: [*Standing apart from the others, a spotlight on her face as she whispers to herself in anguish.*] We bringing you right back home, Nana —

VERA: Yes, yes, yes, Momma, yes, yes, yes —

MA ROSE: Lemme see your eyes — lemme see your faces —

[*A slow fadeout on the family grouping, one last spot on* ROSA.]

END OF ACT ONE

ACT TWO

SCENE 1

Spotlight up on ROSA. *She sits on the edge of a bed, dressed in a white, silk kimono. Lights come up on a separate area of the stage and we are back in the past in* ROSA's *mind. There is the sound of gulls and other birdcalls, and the languid lapping of waves.*

MA ROSE *appears, dressed in a casual house dress and barefoot. She is a younger woman again. She is clapping and laughing.*

MA ROSE: [*Motioning to* VERA.] Come on, Vee —! Let's wade on in — let's *try it* — !

VERA: [*Laughing and removing her shoes,* VERA *enters. She mimes approaching the shoreline of a large body of water.*] Momma, you are something else! Ha! *Look* at you! Lord — and she don't even have a *swimming* suit! Out here stripping — lookit Miss Sexy — [*Laughing.*] Momma, you are a *mess.*

MA ROSE: I wanna wade on in —

VERA: But it looks *deep* — Why, I don't even know if Negroes are *permitted* over on this side — You are *something* Momma — !

MA ROSE: [*Warmly holding* VERA's *cheek.*] You *trust* me. Just hold onto me.

VERA: [*She gestures to* ROSA.] 'Lil Ro? Come on! Let's see if Momma can hold you —

MA ROSE: [*Also gesturing to* ROSA.] Come on, Baby — Just hold onto Momma and hold on to me —

ROSA: [*Staring out with a tentative but very hopeful smile on her face.*] That's right! *Hold* me — hold me tight — *hold* on to me.

[*Lights down on the memory.* VERA *silently appears at* ROSA's *side,* ROSA *startles.*]

VERA: [*Quizzical to* ROSA.] Huh?

[ROSA *lets out a forced laugh and shakes her head, "nothing."* ROSA *has walked to the front of the stage and appears to be gazing out of a window. There is the sound of a fierce wind blowing outdoors. Both women gaze out.*]

VERA: Ha' mercy and if *we* hadn't showed up today — Momma could be right now standing out there in the storm — out of her head and snow piling up around her!

[ROSA *and* VERA *cross over to a simple low platform center stage — which suggests a bed surrounded by darkness and void.*]

VERA: Look what I turned up! My "Mz. Sassy"! My Mz. Sassy! Ha. [*Pauses.*] [*She holds up the doll.*] Used to give her spankings and whippings and more spankings and ohhh ha!! Lord lookit this — lookit what I done come up with!

ROSA: Used to give her "whippings" did you?

VERA: Ha. Oh, yes-s-s-s ... used to hide up here underneath the bed here ... see ... after one of *my* whippings? [*Holding up the doll.*] And I'd crawl up under here and — [*She stops abruptly.*] Oh, I don't remember. [*She fingers* ROSA's *kimono.*] Silk. Pure silk.

ROSA: It's a kimono, Mom.

VERA: Yeah, but your bosom half-shows when you raise up your arms, so what's the sense of it? That's what y'all sophisticated ladies wear in New York?

ROSA: Am I just chilled? Is that what — 'Cause I can't stop shaking — I just oou — I just — I just.	VERA: Now-now — never mind now — Come on here you take one half — I'll take one half.

[VERA *indicates the blanket and* ROSA *crawls in beside her.*]

VERA: [*Laughing.*] Ooou, girl, don't you be touching me with them icicle-toes! — Don't touch me! You stay on your side now — go on!

ROSA: [*Laughing.*] Hey, but you snatching all the cover, Ma — See there, now you tell me "come on in" then you bunch it all up to *your* side —

VERA: You gonna hafta get out anyway soon 'cause I'm gonna be sleep. You gonna hafta get on back out in the cold ...

ROSA: [*Opening the Bible.*] Okay, Mz. Vera-Rose ... What verse you wanna go to sleep to?

VERA: Ah, ain't you sweet. Read me something from the Psalms, please, Ro.

ROSA: "Psalms" [*A beat.*] Love the feel of that going through my throat ... "Psalms" ... [*A beat.*] Can't stop shaking, Mom.

VERA: [*She spreads her hands over the quilt.*] Hey, Ro, I recognize this! This here's a piece of Great Grandma's head rags here, so you know this must be near a century old ... and here's a piece of m' Daddy's long john ... Just think, your Ma Rose brought 10 living babies into birth laying up underneath this here — There be many lives bound up with a ole piece of tatter!

ROSA: [*She smooths her hands over the quilt.*] *Your* Daddy —

VERA: *Your* Grandad — wish you'd know him.

ROSA: What about *my* Daddy, Ma —

VERA: Now, that's *one* thing 'bout Ma Rose, boy!! Boy, did she stand up for me!

ROSA: She seems to have liked Daddy.

VERA: 'Cause his people, them Negroes was the worst bunch of "pure-blood" thinking so and so's you ever wanna meet — *his* Momma come claiming I was "too yella tainted" for her precious boy — ! Boy, you shoulda seen Ma Rose light into that woman! And in full view of the wedding guests, too — [*She pauses.*]

ROSA: Tell me — was he — ? Tell me something 'bout him —

VERA: [*Looking* ROSA *over.*] Pure *silk* you say? Oh, if Eli coulda lived to see *you* — Just to think — me a 15-month bride laying 'cross that coffin with my dress soaked in breast milk and trying to figure rhyme or reason for this world and what in the world did God intend for me to do —

[ROSA *suddenly places each hand on top of* VERA's *for a beat.*]

ROSA: But what was he *like* ?

[*A beat.* VERA *is clearly in too much pain to open the subject.*]

VERA: [*Speaking to herself in a revelry.*] Ha — had me at least *something* she couldn't snatch from me — something for me to have to myself at last — till Jesus decided *he* needed him —

ROSA: [*She leans into* VERA *eagerly.*] "She"? Ma Rose? "Snatch from you" — who — who snatch from you — who?

VERA: —Hush, that ain't nothing — Christ say "Let the dead bury the dead."

ROSA: [*Eagerly piecing things together.*] You mean Ma Rose. *Tell* me, woman-to-woman, tell me.

VERA: [*Abruptly reaching for the Bible.*] We gonna find us some Peace of Mind in this here and then get to bed and call it a night and get rest, that's what — [*Finding a passage.*] Here, now — lemme hear that "pleasing" voice — sound it out —

ROSA: [*She stares at* VERA *in frustration, pauses, then reads in a dull voice.*] [*Reading.*] "I cried unto God with my voice and he gave ear unto me ... "

VERA: Gotta tell ya — sound like you come to them words like a stranger passing through some unfamiliar place.

ROSA: It's time you got to *know* me — wanna be up front with you — first thing is, I guess you know by now I'm not too religious ...

VERA: Ain't tell me nothing I don't know. Just wish there was a way for folks to get educated and not stray from how they was raised and here the Lord has been the comforter of your folk down ...

ROSA: ...This *doesn't* mean you and me can't still be good, close friends —

VERA: ... through the generations and — and that alone gotta mean *something* — I may not be — be so sophisticated in the eyes of the world, but that is a stone fact ...

ROSA: Tell you what I'm ... er ... looking forward to — [*A beat.*] You and me being good buddies. Working together. Planning together. You and me settling Nana back here in her home, Mama. This whole thing bringing us together, Ma, me and you —

VERA: [*Indicating the Bible.*] Read it over once more, Ro — sound it out like when you used to stand 'fore the Sunday School. —

ROSA: I still see her on that stretcher ... wheeled away —

VERA: Ro, now — Ro, nothing's gonna happen to your Nana. Now, you saw her, didn't you see her cleaned up, decent, safe and sound?

ROSA: Right, you right — hey and the fact of no broken bones — when the man said, "Just rest and she can come back home," ooh Momma! —

[*Referring to herself and clapping with relief.*]

You talk about somebody wanting to sing and shout!

VERA: [*Smiling gratefully.*] On this very night at last — safe and sound at last, at last thank you Almighty God.

ROSA: [*Leaping up out of the bed exiting into the shadows as her voice trails off.*] ... Now I have tomorrow's plan all worked out — [*She re-enters with her briefcase, and a phone directory.*]

VERA: [*Indicating the brief case.*] Girl, that thing trails after you like afterbirth — and I *wish* you'd cut the cord —!

ROSA: [*Smiling at* VERA *as she removes various pamphlets from her briefcase, showing them to* VERA *as she talks.*] ... Had a brief talk with the hospital social worker — I dunno, where do they *find* these people?! Couldn't answer *half* my questions to my satisfaction — so now after we check in on Nana in the morning — let's head out to Meridian County Social Welfare and get this homecare business straightened out —

VERA: [*She reads from Bible.*] " ... Save me oh God for the waters are come in unto my soul ... "

ROSA: [ROSA *takes a hair brush from behind the bed and begins brushing* VERA'*s hair.*] Momma, we need a — a pact with this situation, me and you — see, Uncle Way — Oh, he's a very good son to Ma Rose, held her together in this town, thirty years, nobody's denying him his due — but still, it's not like the woman understanding that *you* bring to this as the one daughter present.

VERA: [VERA *nods vigorously.*] I hear you —

ROSA: Right. And I can help you. The point is to get Ma Rose back home — I'm not above scheming if we have to — anything to get her to realize and accept that she can't live here alone —

VERA: [*Suddenly* VERA *grabs the brush in* ROSA'*s hand and holds it. It is full of strands of hair.*] Ro, it's coming out — out, Ro.

ROSA: Naw, that's just —

VERA: [*She clutches* ROSA'*s hand.*] Getting so I'm looking like a old —

ROSA: [*Reassuring* VERA *gently.*] No. No. No.

VERA: [*Suddenly seeing* ROSA'*s hands.*] Girl, lookit them long and pretty fingernails!! [*Her voice drifting off to sleep.*] Guess you go to saunas and stuff like that, huh? [*Pause.*] Girl, am I beat. [*Pause.*] I guess the smalltown homeboys 'round here and down at the plant — that kinda man — don't hold much interest for you —

ROSA: Well, hey — ! You got something there — Now why don't I while I'm here, just go on down there and hang out and see who available and hand out m' business cards and —

[*She stops at* VERA'*s expression.*]

Just kiddin' — ha — don't look at me like that — Come on. [*Pause.*] Nothing *wrong* with the men 'round here but when you advance in life you get expectations, Momma, that just comes with the territory ... I'm working on it ... working on it — I just broke up with a very nice man.

VERA: Then *why* "broke up with"?

ROSA: *Why* is it *you* never remarried?

VERA: *Me*?!

ROSA: All that time? It would have nice to have had some "rusty-butt" gentleman ...

VERA: [*Smiling.*] Watch you mouth —

ROSA: ... to' hold me on his lap — somebody to catch you snuggling up to —

VERA: Talk sense — had m' little girl to raise — no time to be selfish 'bout myself.

ROSA: I was no excuse for you to have to give up sex.

VERA: [*Astonished at* ROSA.]   Will you hush — what's got into you!

ROSA: Mother — speak to me like you and any one of your women friends do! If we're going to be *real* friends — look — you see me and you think, "Oh, there's my V.P. daughter, there's my Rosa." — Fine, wonderful — let me *really* tell you — [*A pause.*] "Success" don't just turn up to ring your doorbell — know what I mean? Success don't just all a-sudden decide to pay you a courtesy call, y'know what I'm saying? And I'm on the front lines each and every day — Mommy, then that fright can come on me without warning — I start thinking I don't "deserve" this position and I can't hold it — but still I stand for my people, I stand for the family — everybody's got a stake in where I'm at — But still I'm thinking, "God, don't let them find me out ... " It's a trip to keep down this — this fear that *in spite* of my credentials, I could be this imposter, this total failure, this "jive" ...

VERA: You just keep them newspaper clippings coming on back home — : and whatever notice you get — wherever you speak and things, or whatever — no matter how small — I wanna know —

ROSA: Wheeled away — [*She blinks and shakes her head as if trying to cast out an image.*] — When you wanna get a headstart on out to the Social Welfare in the morning, Ma? —

VERA: [*Indicating the Bible.*] Here's one I wanna hear you on — and call it on out to the air — like when you lead the youth choir —

ROSA: Momma, whatever's in your head is not *me* — [*A beat.*] Momma — Momma — Momma — you 'member all that time it took Nana to help me get over being scared of the dark? Well, it never took. I travel with my night light at all times — [*Laughs.*] still scared I might wake up in the middle of the night to the total dark, Momma.

VERA: Nonsense, you doing just fine — just fine. Why, this what's meant to *be*, Rosa — we just going through the trial of being part of the line of generations — what we seeing with Ma Rose is just the cycle of life and we gotta bear up — we — er

ROSA: Ma, you're gripping my hand — you're hurting me, Momma —

VERA: Oh, pardon me — pardon me — er — I

ROSA: [*Moving to wipe* VERA'*s tears.*] Here, lemme —

VERA: Quit. I'm okay — I'm fine — I'm just cold — durn old drafty house —

ROSA: *Now* she is curled up in her bed up at Crestwood ... now she's warm and she can sleep ...

VERA: Yeah! Yeah! Tell me more ... tell me more ... *You* picture Ma Rose and tell me ... you talk it so well ...

ROSA: She's all curled up in the hospital bed ... it's all warm ... she's been given the right dose of her medicine ... Here, get down in the covers, good ... She resting calmly and safely....

[ROSA *bends down to try to kiss and hug* VERA.]

VERA: [VERA *moves her head away, uncomfortably.*] Now-now we don't hafta get all mushy and carried away, now ... that's okay.

[ROSA *stops still, a flash of rage across her face.*]

VERA: [*Looking up at* ROSA.] What?

ROSA: [*Smiling falsely.*] Nothing.

VERA: ... Keep talking ... talk to me ... talk to me ...

ROSA: Uh-Hum ... she's sleeping peaceful ... nurses come in and check on her and make sure she's safe ... Tomorrow we'll get there ... we'll bring her flowers, bring a present ... tell her about coming home this weekend, she'll be *so* happy ...

VERA: Keep talking ... keep talking ... keep talking ...

[*Lights slowly fade.*]

SCENE 2

We hear a gospel choir singing "Near the Cross." As the lights fade slowly on the previous scene, we see VERA *rise from the platform which has been her bed, remove her bathrobe, so that she now stands in a plain street dress. She now sits on the platform which is now a chair in the waiting room of the hospital.* ROSA *also removes her bathrobe and stands in a plain skirt and blouse.* WAYMAN *and* ETHEL *enter from the shadows and stand alongside of* VERA.

VERA: Um-um-um-um-um ... [*She is laughing, smiling and laughing, frantically fanning herself and laughing.*]

ROSA: Just lemme hold her, Auntie, just lemme hold her ...

WAYMAN: I'm going back in there. I'm going on back *in* there ...!

ETHEL: Wayman — now Way —

WAYMAN: Naw-naw, I'm a-going back *in* there ...

VERA: [*She is laughing and laughing, softly laughing.*] Well — well sir — *well* — *so be it* — ! Ha! So be it —

[*She is biting all around the edge of the styrofoam cup that she holds in her hand.*]

[*To* ETHEL *as she refers to the cup she is holding.*] Ever see anybody t'love's to bite into this stuff? Stills m' nerves.

ETHEL: Sh-h-h-h-h now, Vee, now Vee.

ROSA: Auntie, lemme hold her — [*Holding* VERA.] Okay, now, rock with me now, rock with me ...

VERA: Spit in my face — spit in my face — SPIT IN MY FACE — didn't she? *Didn't* she? You saw it. You a witness to it. Okay! Okay! Well! Well sir — ha ha — I'll live through it! Ha! So be it —

ROSA: I can't *believe* Nana would *do* something like that — *terrible* thing for her to do — !

ETHEL: Oughta be *shamed* of herself! Vee — want water? Lemme get the nurse t' get you some coffee ...

VERA: See, I don't pay no 'ttention to her, Rosa, I just don't even let it phase me, see, but it's a back-breaking load to tow, I ain't gonna lie to ya.

WAYMAN: I'm going right on back in there — She can't get away with treating you like that — !

ROSA: She'll ask your pardon once she realizes, you wait and see if she don't. She'll come around, she'll realize what she's done once we get her back home — terrible thing to do!

VERA: Ro — Ro, she just never took to me, Ro [*Shaking her head back and forth and smiling.*], that's all there is to say — never did — that's all. No big "lamentation" about it — I *don't* pity myself none — you gotta drink from the cup you been given, bitter or sweet — that's just the way life is, Ro — that's just the way life *is*.

ROSA: Mom, she's so scared right now she don't know what she's doing — we'll bring her home this weekend and Mom? I'm gonna *make* her apologize to you — She's just so *scared* right now — I'm not *excusing* her but you know, a strange place to spend the night, then with the doctors telling her she can go home, but yet she's not being *taken* home —

ETHEL: [*Indicating* VERA's *necklace.*] Vee, you done broke your cross — !

VERA: Lemme just hold it in my hand. [*She makes a tight fist.*]

WAYMAN: Time for me to go on back in there — Ethel — Vera — Here I'm a grandfather myself and can't even — ain't never even stood m' ground with her —

ROSA: She'll make it up to you, you watch, I'll get her to come around.

WAYMAN: Vee, I'm gonna go back in there ...

VERA: She gonna "shun" me! You heard her ... calling me "serpent"! Calling me "serpent"!

WAYMAN: Now-now Sister, now Sister.

VERA: Well, Lord, I have lived to have to come to this fork in the trail! Oh, yes! Rosa, "everything comes past your gate sooner or later, if you *stand* there long enough." —

ROSA: She is gonna be *so* ashamed of herself when this all works out.

VERA: Well, I'm like some cast-off devil to her — she won't even *curse* me — ! Oooo! Take these flowers outta my face, hate that scent, they 'bout to choke me! See, Ro — she gives you a different face on the coin. You blessed, yes-yes-yes, I count you so blessed, if the truth be known. Yes.

WAYMAN: Time I face her out and go on in there and give her a piece of m' mind. I'll have her come 'round Sister ... lemme go on back in there *now* — Rosa, you stay with your Momma, this here's between me and Ma. Vera, we don't haveta take this kinda attitude from Momma. Ailing or not ailing, she don't treat us like this — oh, no!

[WAYMAN *crosses over into the light where* MA ROSE *is.* MA ROSE *is dressed in hospital gown and is seated in a wheelchair.*]

[*For several beats he stands back from her some distance as though he cannot quite bring himself to fully enter the room proper. He is stock still staring at her.*]

ROSA: See, Momma, *this* is why I try to start out every day with careful *planning* — 'cause things can get carried away and out of control and 'fore you know it —

VERA: Ever since I brought you in this world, she has lit up just to hear your name — and I do count you blessed — What y'all two find so much to talk about all the time, huh? How'd you get her to sing to you?

[*After a moment,* WAYMAN *starts to point his finger at* MA ROSE *and is about to speak. But some inner force paralyzes him and his pointing finger freezes abruptly in mid-air, held there by the force of his mother's eyes. A beat.* WAYMAN *crumples against* MA ROSE'*s knees.*]

[*Blackout.*]

SCENE 3

TIME: *later that same night. Lights up on* MA ROSE*'S house.*

ROSA *is seated beside a small radio that sits on top of a second small end table. The radio is one of the early portables, circa 1950's.* ROSA *turns the dials, the low hum of static is heard as* VERA *switches the dials back and forth.*VERA *is seated opposite* ROSA *rocking and trying to calm herself. The phone rings and* WAYMAN *grabs it.*

WAYMAN: [*Speaking into the phone.*] NOW - now look here, now! I been dialing "7-5-3-3-9-6-7" for twenty-five years, so don't tell me I "got the wrong" *nothing* ...! Now, look here, Miss, now I'm real upset, now, got me a family emergency in my family, and I need to speak to my brother ... that's "2-1-3" ... right , ... "2-1-3" ...

[WAYMAN *hangs up the phone, crosses over and begins to help* VERA *with the radio dial.*]

VERA: Lord help m' nerves. Lord help m'nerves ... Lord help me.

[ETHEL *enters wearing rubber gloves and carring a quart-sized plastic bottle in her hand which she holds up, displaying to* VERA *and* ROSA.]

ETHEL: Now, see here, Vera? See here, see?

VERA: Um?

ETHEL: [*Holding up the bottle in her hand.*] Now, this here ain't your usual store-bought stuff, see ...

ETHEL: This ain't store-bought stuff, this is mail-order stuff — been bringing Ma Rose some and all my neighbors down my street some and *I* use it ... this stuff gets off ole dirt and grime just great — just *great* ... [*She exits.*]	VERA: Um-hum Yeah — is that right? Um-hum Yeah? Ummmm ...

[*A gospel song suddenly blasts up loud on the radio.*]

ROSA: —Here we go, Mom — here's your favorite ... [*She claps to the music and sings along.*] "We've come this far by faith/ leaning on the Lord .../ trusting in His Holy Word/ He's *never* failed me yet ..." Tell you what, family — the "spirit of forgiveness" has gotta move *through* us —

[ROSA *turns back to* VERA, *and joins her clapping to the music on the radio.*]

... Uh-oh, Momma! Here's where your choir starts that ole foot stomping, like they do ... Uncle, here's where Momma's choir brings the roof down, don't they, Mom?! ...

VERA: Ha — oh yes they do! Yes indeed they do!

[ROSA *begins stomping in time to the music,* VERA *claps along.*]

ROSA: You know, Family — Uncle, Mom — what we need is to hire a home care worker here to stay with Nana. We *know* we got to do that ... [*She continues to clap in rythm to the music.*] ... We need to get somebody to watch her safety here in the house ... live with her and make sure she takes her medication ...

[*She claps to the music.*]

WAYMAN: Don't we wish — don't we wish.

VERA: Brother, all we can do is to know in our heart we doing the best we *can* do, that's all we can do.

ETHEL: [*Entering with a cheesecloth and a pot in one hand.*] Say, Vera, check this out ... see that ... lookit that spot ... lookit that spot coming off there so easy ...! And this here is even cheaper than what you find out there on the market, see — Oh, I'm just getting off all that ole crud and whatnot, come on back here, Vera, — come take a look — I want you to see. [*She exits.*]

[*The gospel song: "Peace Be Still" comes over the radio.*]

ROSA: [*Moving to stop* VERA *from leaving.*] Uh-oh! Uh-oh! [*Indicating song on the radio.*] Know who's good on *this* one?! Uncle O. Z.!

VERA: Yes, he is! Sure 'nuff, oh yes he is!

ROSA: 'Member how he'll *raise* his hand "on high" like this here ... [*She demonstrates.*] 'Member how he had the crowd "Amening" and shouting up to heaven, 'member? 'Member that day we was all together — marching down to the square ...?

[*She begins to sing along with song.*]

"... Master, the tempest is rising/ the wind and the billows are tossing high/ in this deepest hour so many, many are frightened ..."

WAYMAN: [*To* ROSA, *clapping along.*] Sing the song, girl! Keep going — keep going!

ROSA: [*Clapping and timing her words to the rhythm of the music.*] Oh, when we *marched!* When we marched! Finest day of my childhood — when we marched down the Square!

WAYMAN: Who can forget it?! Who *can* forget it!

ROSA: [*Clapping and timing her words to the rhythm of the music.*] Okay, well — we *have* been through a hellish day today — [*Referring to* VERA.] Poor Momma — but I see I gotta ask you and Uncle to come on back to what y'all brought *me* up with — with this here [*Indicating the gospel singing.*] —The "spirit of forgiveness" —

VERA: [*Clapping to the rhythm of the music.*] Daughter, lemme just calm m'nerves till we talk to O. Z. and Clarisse 'n' them.

ROSA: Sure - sure — I understand — Ma Rose done dealt you a *blow*, Momma ... and no excuse for it — but what you bring me up to believe in, Momma? ... Sing the song with me, Uncle ... Come on, Momma , you join in!!

WAYMAN: [*To* ROSA.] *You* sing! Lemme hear you sing ... *Amen*, sing the song! Amen! ...

ETHEL: [*She re-enters carrying in her hand the shiny grille from a refrigerator shelf.*] Y'all just raising up the Lord in here something fierce! Lookit here, Vera! Sprayed on my "magic" mail-order stuff and just could *blow* the grime off! [*She exits.*]

ROSA: [*Singing and clapping to the music.*] ... "Peace be still/ peace be still/ peace be still .../" [*Clapping out the rhythm as she speaks.*] Now, that's what y'all taught me the Scripture was all about — willingness to forgive and let go.

WAYMAN: Well, sir ... after all, she *is* our mother. 'Course she didn't mean it —

ROSA: 'Course not! Now, I want us working together — I plan on setting up a Family Fund for Nana's care —

[*To* VERA, *indicating the radio.*] Uh-oh, Mom! Here comes your favorite! Come on, sing with me! Sing with me! Don't be bashful, sing!

[VERA *shyly joins in.*]

ROSA: "... Precious Lord ... take my hand ... I am weak ... help me stand ..."

[*She stands in place rocking back and forth to the rhythm as she speaks.*]

See ... all right— okay, so I'm out in the "big, wide world" but don't think I forget *where* I come from and what I was *taught* and what I got to be *proud* of!

WAYMAN: [*To* ROSA.] Well, speak on, Niece! *Speak!*

ROSA: Hey, I've taken the *best* of what I was brought up with and I've made something of it! I'm *so glad* I came back this weekend. Why? 'Cause "family" is just what my spirit needs — just what's gonna renew my strength to "keep on keeping on" out there in what Ma Rose would call "the wilderness" — that's what's gonna revive me — the "spirit of forgiveness" —

VERA: Amen.

ROSA: [*Swaying along to the music.*] I *know in my heart* that y'all are willing and able to go to Ma Rose and *forgive* — 'cause you're big-hearted people and you're *able* to forgive —

WAYMAN: [*Referring to* ROSA.] She's got us there, Vee — ha! Ha' mercy, she's something else!

ROSA: [*She continues clapping and refers to* VERA.] Momma, sing up like you do when you think nobody can hear you ... come on!

VERA: [*Smiling shyly.*] Girl, quit!

ROSA: [*Swaying in time to the music.*] Okay, now look. I'm gonna use my private secretary to call up each and every one of my cousins, all those 35-40 grands, great-grands, and whatnot that Nana got. I'm gonna just collect us a yearly Family Fund to support Nana's care.

WAYMAN: Well, 'course now, that *is* something to think over ... [*Phone rings. They startle.* WAYMAN *runs to it, answers,* ROSA *turns the radio down.*] [*Hearing his brother's voice on the line.*] WELL, SIR *FINALLY!* HEY, BROTHER!! —

[*He holds the receiver, his face deflates, he turns to the others.*]

— We got cut — [*He stands holding the receiver and speaks out to* ROSA.] —Go on, li'l Rose, I hear ya —

ROSA: I'm telling you this is in the bag! We can provide for home care for Nana — 'cause, okay — Medicare ain't but a "drop" — but I hereby put myself in charge of all my cousins paying up small installments — on a regular basis, look — with my new salary, I'm willing to assume the major cost — oh, yes — we gonna *work* this thing, here!

WAYMAN: Well, on the one hand, it *don't* sound impossible.

VERA: Well, we can't be hasty, now — There's so many unanswered things — see what I mean? — This, that, and the other to think of.

ROSA: Shoo! I'll be on the phone to you and Momma week to week. Keeping in touch with what's happening here with the home nurse.

VERA: [*To* ROSA.] You gonna have *time* for all that?

ROSA: *Time?* Mom, now you 'member how you'd tell me how well you recall *your* Grandmomma talking 'bout what it was like being born a slave, right? Am I right? [*Pause.*] Well, welcome to the *wide* journey, Momma! From your Grandmomma's lifetime to mine! [*Pauses.*] You *watch* me make time!

WAYMAN: The Bible do say, "Be ye not afraid, only *believe.*" *Something* might could work.

ETHEL: [*Entering and overhearing.*] Bible say, "Thy will be done."

WAYMAN: A-men, and all we got to do is give it on over, and I trust that, I *know* we can trust that.

ROSA: That's right, Uncle! Talk it, Uncle! That's right, talk! Ha, talk!

VERA: Well, no, I *am* willing to stand on hope.

ROSA: Sure, you are! Without that, what do we have? And the "Spirit of Forgiveness'" yes?!

ETHEL: [*To* VERA.] Vee, now I got Momma's Fridgidaire all fresh and looking like she'd *wanna* have it!

WAYMAN: Long as I know to my satisfaction that I been a good son to Momma, and if that's all that's given me to know —

then so be it, that's all I wanna know then —

ROSA: That's it! She raised you, now it's *your* turn to give back — [*Pause, she looks at all of them then,*] Here, everybody, let's join hands —

[*They all join hands in a circle, all except* ROSA, *close their eyes in a silent prayer. She meanwhile glances over the others with the satisfied smile of a saleswoman who has finally convinced her "customers" to purchase her product.*] [*Phone rings,* WAYMAN *is right there to pick it up.*]

WAYMAN: HEY, BROTHER! HOW YOU?! OH, KEEPING WELL ENOUGH — KEEPING WELL ENOUGH — HUH?? CAN'T HEAR YA TO GOOD — HUH?? —

VERA: Wayman, if you're willing to then I'm willing to —

WAYMAN: [*His hand over receiver.*] Oh, I'm willing to!

ROSA: Well, then!!!

WAYMAN: —[*He holds the receiver and turns to them.*] Hold it, y'all — they *still* messing with me — now they talking 'bout "hold the line" — now, soon as we hook and I give the news — Li'l Rose, you get on with the "Family Fund" —

[ROSA *hugs* WAYMAN, *attempts to hug* VERA *awkwardly but they don't quite make it, then she moves to hug* ETHEL .]

ROSA: You know you always been one of my favorite aunts?

ETHEL: Aw, naw! Stop!

ROSA: [*To* VERA *and* ETHEL.] ... I think it's 'cause you all had boys, 'cause I 'member it used to tickle you so when you'd catch me trying on your high heels and jewelry ... [ETHEL *and* VERA *laugh.*]

WAYMAN: [*On the phone.*] OH, IT'S COLD HERE, *SNOWING* ... OH, YEAH! YEAH ... OH, WE ALL KEEPING WELL ENOUGH, EVERYBODY'S DOING FINE. JUST FINE. YEAH, I CAN HEAR YA BETTER, NOW — okay, Operator, we'll hold — [*Turning to the others.*] *Blast!* And *then* they wanna come talking 'bout "reach out and touch someone!" [*There is a tense silence.*]

WAYMAN: [*Suddenly booming forth on the phone.*] WELL-ALL-RIGHT, NOW! *FINALLY!* Oh, keeping well enough, keeping well enough ... *you?* That's good, that's good, and how's Clarisse doing? That's good. Oh, it's *cold* here, *snowing* ... yeah ... nope, from Momma's house, yeah, from Momma's ... [*He listens.*] Well sir ... I don't have such good news ... [*Suddenly.*] AW-NAW-NAW!! NOT *THAT*, NAW! Momma's just fine, well, she ain't *fine,* but she ain't "the other," don't let me fright you now, no! [*Turning to* VERA.] He thought we was calling to say ,"you know."

VERA: [*Taking the phone from* WAYMAN.] NAW, NAW, BROTHER, WE DON'T MEAN *THAT!* HEY ... Vera, it's Vera ... naw, we don't mean "that" but we had to put Momma in a "home" for a while ...

ROSA: *Just* for one more day ... we'll have her home, tommorrow evening ... [*Talking into the phone.*] HEY, UNCLE "O," HOW YA DOING?

WAYMAN: [*Into the phone.*] See, we gonna have this Family Fund set up and ... well, what it is, is a hospital with a rest home kinda attached to it, uh-huh ... run by the county ... thing is ... er ... er ... [*Turning to* VERA .] You get on, Vera ...

VERA: [*Into phone.*] Brother, Wayman called me day 'fore yesterday, Wayman called me, I mean — I mean, Wayman called me *yesterday,* and, er ... no, day 'fore yesterday, no, oh *when* was it! I'm just getting *confused,* I'm upset so!

ROSA: Momma, you rest — I'll tell him my plan —

VERA: Yeah, Rosa's here too, Rosa's here too, yeah, "our exec" ... Wayman called me 'cause Momma wasn't acting right, um-hum ... yeah, Brother, she was, er ... yeah! [*Turning to the others.*] He knows! [*Turning back to the phone and listening.*] See! See! See there!

ETHEL: 'Cause he knows how Momma was acting when they visited here last, and when he calls long distance, *sure* he knows!

WAYMAN: [*Talking into the phone with* VERA.] Uh-uh! Well, you 'member when you was here this summer for the family reunion, you know how Momma was ... !

VERA: [*Into the phone.*] Oh, yeah, talking out of her head, yeah ... You got it! You got it! [*Turning to the others.*] He knows! See, he knows!

ROSA: Family Fund, Uncle … Family fund …

VERA: Rosa, now your Uncle's talking, he's doing the talking, now …

WAYMAN: Burning up stuff, yep — talking "dead people in the house" … [*Turning to the others.*] He knows the *whole* thing …

VERA: [*Grabbing the phone.*] See, then, top it all off, day 'fore yesterday, she fell!

ROSA: She *slipped*, Mother — she just slipped …

VERA: [*Into the phone.*] On her side, uh-huh — now what was we to think, behind all that… !

[*Talking into the phone receiver while it is still held in* VERA's *hand.*]

ROSA: … But she's gonna be all right the doctors say, she didn't break nothing — Now, I got this plan to talk over with ya — see, for Nana's care? When we get her back home tommorow —

WAYMAN: [*Into the phone.*] Yes, it *has* come down to that — it *has* come down to that —

[*Talking into the phone receiver while it is still held in* WAYMAN'S *hand.*]

VERA: Oh, Brother - Brother - Brother — when I come in and saw Momma had fallen like that, oh, I like to just die — I like to just die!!

ETHEL: [*Suddenly breaking in and talking into the phone receiver while it is still held in* VERA's *hand.*] BROTHER O. Z. ?! HOWDIE-DO — ETHEL, IT'S ETHEL — OH, BROTHER — BROTHER, THANK GOD YOU DIDN'T SEE WHAT WE SAW — OH, WE ALL JUST LIKE TO *DIE!* AND ON TOP OF *THAT*, MOMMA *SPIT* IN VERA'S FACE THIS MORNING, BROTHER! NOW YOU *KNOW* THAT AIN'T THE WOMAN WE KNOW!!

[*Suddenly* ETHEL *has, in her frantic energy, tangled* WAYMAN, VERA, *and* ROSA *up in the phone cord. They are all locked into a tight bunch and in confusion and frustration scramble to break free.*]

EVERYONE: OH *LORD* SOMEBODY SOMEBODY HOLD

STILL — *HOLD STILL!* — GET - GET - NAW - THIS
WAY — NAW NAW TURN BACK TURN BACK ...
TURN IT LOOSE —

WAYMAN: [*Into the phone.*] HOLD ON, BROTHER, HOLD
ON —

ROSA: Wait a minute, everybody, hold it — *hold it* — calm down
— keep calm — Momma, you walk this way — Uncle, you
move *this* way — now, let me slide between you — right —
now, Auntie, turn 'round and come out here — okay — there
— *there!*

[ROSA *untangles them from the cord.*]

WAYMAN: [*Into the phone.*] Yep — I *know* it's a shock! In Vera's
face, Brother, yes she did!

ROSA: But tell him how scared she was, tell him —

WAYMAN: So behind all that, we done had to put her in the
hospital ... 'till we can see what's what ... I'm with you *SURE*
— *SURE* ...! Oh, well, we ain't gonna decide nothing till we
see what's what with the hospital ... Oh, yeah, she gonna be
in there for a while ...

ROSA: *She's coming out tomorrow.*

VERA: Rosa, he can't hear good if you talking, too. Please let
him try to talk ...

WAYMAN: [*On phone.*] Yeah ... why, of course, this is the best
thing for her — of course — yeah! ... They watch 'em, see,
and that's what we want! Oh, they watch 'em pretty good,
see, oh yes!! Oh, some of 'em strapped to the bed if they get
too rambunctious, oh yep — teach 'em a lesson, that's right!!
She's in a nice room — yeah — yeah, yeah ... un-huh, naw,
this house ain't all that liveable—

ROSA: LIVEABLE! *LIVEABLE!*

WAYMAN: Little Rose, now,	VERA: [*To* ROSA.] *WILL*
I can't hear...	KEEP STILL!? AND WAIT
	YOUR TURN?!

ROSA: Well, *when* — when *is* my turn!!!???

VERA: [*Into the phone.*] Yeah, what's that, Clarisse? Uh-huh ...
Which drawer is that — which is that — [*She turns to*

ETHEL.] Ethel, would you go in there in Momma's bedroom and — and [*Into phone.*] Which drawer? Third drawer down ... [*Turns to* ETHEL.] third drawer down ... [*Back to phone.*] ... yeah — yeah.

ETHEL: [ETHEL *has gone out, then returns with a folded pile of cloth in her hand.*] They got these here pretty crocheted sheets — tatted lace ...

ROSA: This is not happening ... this is *not* happening ...!

VERA: [*Into the phone.*] Crocheted, yeah, we found 'em ... okay ... okay ... well, we gonna keep y'all posted ... oh, yeah ... we'll be on to you ... you take care, now ... yeah, long as we know we got you all's support and you all's approval ... yeah ...

[*To* ETHEL *as she hands the phone to* WAYMAN.]

O. Z. say he'll go by what *we* do since we the ones here and we the ones seeing the situation for what it is ... and Clarisse say you know all them fine linens and flatware and glassware and quilts, all that oughta be packed up right now, right away — you know, things Momma wouldn't want ruined, you know, she would want passed down through the generations —

ROSA: NO — NO!! HOLD IT — THIS IS *STILL* HER PRIVATE   HOUSE — WE'RE   NOT   TAKING ANYTHING OUT OF THIS PLACE 'LESS SHE TELLS US ...!

VERA: [*Pause. She starts to rock back and forth in a slow building fury.*] *Are* you telling me my Mother wouldn't want us to care for her things and to *preserve* what she has saved to pass down to us?!

WAYMAN: [*On phone.*] Okay — you'll hear — yep — YOU RIGHT — SHE DON'T KNOW WHAT'S GOOD FOR HER OWN WELFARE — YOU GOT THAT —okay — okee-do-kee — God-bless, love you — bye, bye.

[*He hangs up the phone.*] [*He turns to others.*] Clarisse say them hand-crocheted sheets she had when she was eighteen, Momma made 'em for her trousseau, said you can have 'em, Rosa, you can have 'em.

ROSA: NO. NO STUFF GOES OUT OF THIS PLACE 'LESS SHE TELLS US —

VERA: [*To* WAYMAN, *rocking back and forth in a rage.*] Brother, you better talk to her — 'cause I'm 'bout to - to - to ...

WAYMAN: Little Rose, now, m' brother's just suggesting that we pack up a few of Momma's good things just away like she would want — just to help save stuff ... even coming back, that's what Momma would want ... Momma might be here and people be breaking in and carrying on you don't know what ... and now Momma's sick, she don't know no better 'bout storing this stuff up ...

VERA: [*Nodding vigorously with* WAYMAN.] *Tell* her. Will you *tell* her!

ROSA: YOU'RE NOT *LISTENING TO ME* — YOU'RE NOT LISTENING TO ME — NOT LISTENING TO ME — NOT LISTENING TO ME!!

[*They all turn to her with warning signals of rage in their faces. She pauses stock still and panting. Silence.* ROSA *turns to* VERA's *scowling face.*]

ROSA: [*Suddenly she holds her side and stomach.*] It's ... it's — er — it's kicking up on me, that's what, sorry. 'Scuse me. It's kicking up — kicking up on me.

[VERA *turns to* ROSA, *reaches for her,* ROSA *backs away.*]

VERA: [*Staring at* ROSA.] Well, you shoulda told me sooner. You shoulda told me.

ETHEL: That stomach's acting up on you, huh? You should eat more regular, Rosa.

VERA: Daughter, you better go on in and have a lie down.

ROSA: Yes, uh — excuse me, everybody — excuse me.

[*The spot fades down on* WAYMAN *and* ETHEL, *remaining on* VERA *and* ROSA *who stare at each other, neither one moving.*]

SCENE 4

In the darkness we hear the loud, raw, jolting sound of canned laughter from a TV sitcom. Lights up on MA ROSE *in a wheelchair.* ROSA *is standing behind and beside her. They are encircled by a pool of light surrounded by shadows and darkness.*

MA ROSE: [*Shouting because of the TV sound.*] WHEN YOU COMING FOR ME?

ROSA: MAKE IT UP TO THEM, *LISTEN* TO ME —

[*She steps into the shadows briefly and mimes turning down the volume of an imaginary TV set.*]

— Tell them you're "sorry" — They keep thinking they got to fight you in order to "help" you, the minute you rear up, they gonna rear back, *believe* me —

MA ROSE: I ain't got to beg! I ain't got to plead! Y'all *promised* me —

[*The canned laughter comes up very loud again.*]

ROSA: *PLEASE,* NANA — PLEASE —

[ROSA *steps into the shadows briefly and mimes turning down the volume.*]

MA ROSE: Y'all just get me *home.* Home is where I'm to wait out for the Angel. *My* home — where I come to as a young bride, raised up them that was born to me, saw my husband cross over, and where now I'm to *wait* for him to come fetch me —

ROSA: [*She pushes the wheelchair to face* MA ROSE *directly.*] Look. In my business, we learn when to cut our losses, when to compromise and work out a deal, if we want to get what we *want* ...

[*The loud volume of sitcom laughter comes up full.*]

ROSA: [*Shouting to some unseen person in the shadows.*] *HEY!* — TURN IT - KEEP IT *DOWN,* PLEASE —

[*The volume lowers only slightly.*]

ROSA: Tell them you're sorry. Make it up. Tell them what they want to hear — if you don't feel it, then pretend it —

[ROSA *steps into the shadows briefly and mimes turning down the volume.*]

MA ROSE: — Nunno — *NO* — Can't be lifted up to glory with a false face on my face — *no* — how they gonna *know* me —?!

ROSA: Look now — compromise is how we operate where I come from, Nana. If you got to stretch the truth a little to get what you want, then —

MA ROSE: [*She grabs* ROSA'*s hand fiercely.*] Nunno — Don't you *ever* lemme see you mistake the *dry* river bed for the creek — Roots don't take to dry silt-land — YOU *HEAR* ME —?!

[ROSA *is stunned for a few beats and pauses trying to grasp what* MA ROSE *has said.*]

[*Just as suddenly* MA ROSE *releases her hold, turns and looks at* ROSA *as though she is a total stranger.*]

Hey — you, there — Miss — Miss Lady — Need you to do something for me — You go tell m' Grandbaby Rosa — Little Rose — you go tell her come see me — She the one know who I am — Please?

ROSA: [*Frightened by* MA ROSE'*s sudden transformation.*] Nana??!!

MA ROSE: [*Cautiously looking around her, then to* ROSA *as if she were a stranger.*] Sh-h-h-h-h — Please. Miss Lady, please — Go find m' namesake and bring her to me — Miss — Miss — I done been left off here in this shadow place —

[*She looks around, frightened.*]

Who these folks?! Please Miss — please — how the Kingdom-come Spirits gonna know where to find me if I'm hid away in this place —!

ROSA: This *is* Rosa — this *is* me —

[*There is an indistinct cry or moan heard nearby.*]

MA ROSE: [*Responding to the sound and suddenly realizing who* ROSA *is.*] Li'l Rose! Done watched *so many* all down through the years take they leave — now, here *I* stand, me. *My turn.* Posted at the "lookout" and that wide open bright, bright beam of "shining" is seeking me — closer — closer — [*She holds on to* ROSA.] Baby, this here a hellish place to have to be — baby, *please*, please — when you coming *for* me? —

[ROSA *shakes her head back and forth at a loss as to what to say or do. Suddenly the volume of the television sitcom laughter increases in pitch.*]

ROSA: [*Yelling out to an unseen person in the shadow.*] YOU TURN THAT *DOWN*! [*Calling out to get someone to hear her.*] CAN SOMEBODY *STOP* THAT LADY, *PLEASE* —!

[ROSA *turns back to* MA ROSE.]

You will *not* stay here — I will not let this happen — you *will not*—!

MA ROSE: [*She takes off the locket from her neck, handing it to* ROSA.] Come outta slavery at near 'bout sixteen — that lady there. That there's your Great-Grandma Ma Rose. My Momma. Big Momma Ma. Take it. —You the onliest one I want to have touch it.

ROSA: No — there is *still* someway to — to right this and straighten this out with *everybody* — not just me —!

MA ROSE: BUT *HOW* IS MY MOMMA GONNA KNOW WHERE TO *FIND* ME?! Please, now — please — I'm being looked for, sought after from over yonder — I gotta get back to my waiting place — Tell me tomorrow for *sure* you'll be coming for me. Promise? Promise me. Promise me — promise me —*please* —!! Tell me tomorrow you coming for me —

ROSA: [*She wants to promise* MA ROSE *but is clearly paralyzed and frightened.*]

[*The lights fade to black.*]

SCENE 5

Lights up on MA ROSE*'s house that same evening.* WAYMAN, ETHEL *and* VERA *are surrounded by boxes.*

ETHEL: Now, Dolores said that she wants the settee ...

VERA: All these photos, now this gonna be a project ...

ETHEL: Well, divide up the weddings, the graduations, the baptisms, the army and service, and the holiday ones, and each immediate family can be sent the ones pertaining to them.

VERA: Good idea ... right.

WAYMAN: Well, now, 'member to even up the ones of Ma Rose so each and everybody got a good one of Momma.

ETHEL: Oh, everybody'll have a good one of Ma Rose, that's important.

VERA: 'Specially the ones from back in the "teens" and "twenties" and the little girl ones, let's not have no fussing and fuming over the antique pictures of Momma.

WAYMAN: Oh, no! Now, this all can be done with fairness and good faith, after all, this is *family*.

VERA: *This* is family, all right — she can't rely on us to come through with what we promised her, but this is "family."

ETHEL: Tell you one thing, Vera, I'm gonna be up there next week and give her a bath! She gonna give me some stuff, but I'm just gonna tell her that Vera's gonna be up there next week! Ha! Then she'll straighten up!!

[ROSA *enters and stands in the background watching them*.]

ETHEL: And the nurse and them try and give Mom a bath and she up there giving 'em what for about it!! Then she up there talking 'bout she's not gonna take a bath and she's not gonna do this and not gonna do that ...! Well, then, I just say, 'kay then we just not gonna take you nowhere, then ...

[*She pauses and pulls a crystal wine glass out of a box*.]

Vera, you gonna want any 'these antique wine glasses Momma got here? ... You gonna want this, uh-uh — now here's this, uh, coffee table — hand-carved coffee table, Granddaddy made this here with his own hands, you gonna want that ... ?

WAYMAN: [*To* ETHEL:] Honey, I'd like to send that to O. Z. Like to think of it going off to California, that way they can sit 'round it and it'll bring 'em in mind of Momma ...

VERA: [*Seeing* ROSA *for the first time*.] Rosa, I want you to have some of these antique wine glasses Momma got here, hear? ... No need in your cousins having all of 'em.

[ROSA *is silent*.]

Momma got a ole time butter-churner you can have, take back to your big fancy office — put some potted plant in it, make yourself a "conversation piece" ...

[ROSA *is silent*.]

Rosa, you gonna want this old set of books, I *know* that ...

WAYMAN: Oh, some of them go back to the nineteenth century, some of 'em got that ole leather binding.

VERA: [*Indicating* ROSA.] Ha. Well, we know "our Exec" — gonna want to have 'em ...

ETHEL: Here's one on "Female Complaints of a Delicate Nature." ...

VERA: Ha! Rosa, here, take a look —

[ROSA *is silent. She just stares at* VERA.]

VERA: [*Low and trying to control her fury.*] Do you hear — HEAR ME SPEAKING TO YOU!!?? ... Well, *SPEAK*!! ... Are you gonna *WANT* this or aren't you??!! Well, just forget it then, okay!! OKAY!!

ETHEL: Well, what's — what's with — with ...

VERA: [*Attempting to laugh it off.*] Ah, don't pay no 'ttention ... she just acting STUPID ... don't pay no 'ttention to her, don't pay her *no* mind ... 'cause- 'cause- 'cause it just makes me SO DISGUSTED, uh- uh- uh ... she wanna act out and carry on, and act a-fool, ... I DON'T CARE *WHAT'S* WRONG WITH HER!! So there!! We'll just give it to your cousin Mae, just give it to your cousin Mae!

[*Struggling to control her fury.*]

You gonna act up on *ME*!? Naw- naw- 'cause- 'cause I ain't gonna have it ... *I ain't gonna have it*!! ... GONNA ACT *RIDICULOUS ON ME*? NOW just what do you expect us to *do* with Ma Rose!!?? What do you *expect* us to do!!

ROSA: We stood there making all kinds of *promises* to Ma Rose and you — you ask me what I *expect*?

VERA: [*Struggling to remain patient.*] Ah, that ain't nothing, I mean — I mean there things you just gotta bring yourself to do in spite of a person — 'cause you know it's for they own good — now, you got sense enough to know *that*! Momma's gonna have to get used to it — and that's *real* — that's good common sense.

ETHEL: Right, you gonna haveta grow up, Rosa, now, and face facts and we don't like it, but sometimes this is how you gotta deal ...

WAYMAN: And Momma herself — Momma herself, I swear to God, I do believe Momma *herself*, if she was in her right mind, would understand the circumstances, and — and understand.

VERA: Right! Understand she's being taken good care of and that it's all in the best and what *must* be and that's all there is *to* it!! Now, what about these hook rugs. Think you might want one of them shipped out to you, don't worry, I can get it out to you if you want ...

ROSA: My Gawd.

[ROSA *just stares at* VERA.]

VERA: [*It is all she can do to try and control her temper one last time.*] Look, you gonna act like that then, just get outta here then, okay ...?! JUST GET OUTTA HERE AND GO ON HOME — you gonna act like that then I don't even want to be bothered now — now- now — just go on — just- just- just — get on outta here and go on back home!!

WAYMAN: Now- now, Vera, now Vera, don't upset yourself now ...

VERA: GO ON!! YOU GONNA ACT LIKE THAT — THEN JUST GET ON OUTTA HERE AND RIGHT ON BACK TO WHEREVER YOU WANNA COME FROM 'CAUSE I don't wanna be bothered with you 'cause I don't even wanna her from ya with that kinda attitude!! Just *sick and tired* of it and I just- just don't even wanna *HEAR FROM YA*!!

[ROSA *is silent.*]

I will turn you out — I will turn you out of my sight.

[ROSA *is silent.*]

Don't make me have to turn you 'way from here now.

[ROSA *is silent.*]

ETHEL: Oh, *sure-* sure ... [*Pointing to* ROSA *sceptically.*] *She* gonna take care of Ma Rose, see, she and the rest of my kids ...

WAYMAN: Rosa, now that's enough, now. That's *enough*. Sister, what of the family Bible?

VERA: Brother, as the oldest *you* should have the old Bible.

WAYMAN: [*To* ROSA.] This here's got dates back into slavery. Births on up to the here and now, gravesites of the old ones listed ... all thems that tied in "Holy matrimony" since your Great-great was living and breathing, all — all listed in this here ...

[ROSA *just gazes back at them in silence.*]

VERA: [*Suddenly the weight of* ROSA'*s presence is too much for her.*]
NO YOU AIN'T none of mine with that kinda attitude. You
think just 'cause- 'cause- 'cause you got all this education and
whatnot and things and PH and Ds and whatnot behind your
name that you can just forget your upbringing and what's decent and how to treat people ...

[ROSA *is silent.*]

ETHEL: [*To* ROSA.] Now, okay, you tell me how many times you
done called your Ma Rose, phoned her, over the past year,
tell me that! Now, Vera, you ain't said nothing, but I suspect
your daughter here's just like my Justin —

ROSA: This is *her* house. We can't just — just dispose of her
house!

ETHEL: [*To* ROSA.] See your cousins come calling us 'bout they
new swimming pool — but did they think to call up Ma
Rose? Oh sure, they ask about her, but y'know that's like asking if the rain done come, y'know what I'm saying, Vera —
sure — sure y'all keep checking on Momma, for what? A
month or two, let's say three, maybe, then soon as schedules
"don't permit," then what? Naw-naw, ain't like back in the
"old time," ain't like back with the "old ways" ...

VERA: Ethel, you take this — some of this flatware here for your
daughter-in law.

ETHEL: [*To* ROSA.] Y'all wanna talk about what y'all will do but
when it come to the doing, what you gonna do is you jaunt
off to St. Thomas and — and every where else 'cross the
planet y'all go to. The family's so far-flung so till I don't
know what.

WAYMAN: Can't hardly get people on the phone when you want
'em.

ETHEL: Amen!

ROSA: Look, I admit it — you're right. Everything you say —

ETHEL: And Wayman, it'll be me and you and Vera left with the
"keeping" and the "doing," ain't that so, Vera?

VERA: I ain't even got nothing to say to *her*. I've had it with her. I've *had* it.

ROSA: [*To* ETHEL.] I guess you'd say I got a lot of "gall" to ask you to let her come live with you ...

ETHEL: Yes, I would say — yes, indeed — and I see you don't dare ask your Ma — 'cause you *know* what Ma Rose might put *her* through —

VERA: Ethel, I apologize for her rudeness ...

ROSA: Look, if I *could* ...

ETHEL: Yes, if only you could! But I don't see you willing to have Ma Rose intrude on *your* lifestyle, now *are* you?

ROSA: True. All true. [*Pauses then takes them all in.*] *Still*, you're marked with a *lie* — *still* you *know* you bold-faced *lied* to her!

WAYMAN: [*Turning to* ROSA.] Baby — now... li'l Rose, I'm gonna ask you now to stop it, okay? I'm asking you to stop.

[VERA *leaps up, storms off, returns with* ROSA's *briefcase, tosses it to* ROSA, *it splatters on the floor.*]

ROSA: *GIVE* ME A FATHER TO REMEMBER!! I AM SICK AND TIRED OF ONLY HAVING YOU — JUST *YOU* — I DON'T *WANT* YOU —!

[VERA *is stunned and stops stock still.* VERA *suddenly breaks from* WAYMAN, *runs up to* ROSA, *her arms extended,* ROSA *flinches, yells out in terror and cowers as if to ward off a blow,* VERA *turns away just as suddenly and runs offstage.* ROSA *trembles so violently that she nearly falls over.*]

WAYMAN: [*To* ETHEL.] Honey, go see to her.

[ETHEL *goes running off for* VERA.] [*To* ROSA.]

Blast you! Don't know when to quit, do you! Yes, we all hoped and everything for Momma but this — this is what the Almighty intended —

[VERA *comes back from out of the shadows, frantically searching in her purse which she clutches distraughtly. She finds a pair of gloves which, because of her sobs and trembling, fall to the floor. She manically reaches down, retrieves one of the gloves, and places it on her right hand. She holds the gloved hand high in the air for them all to see. There is a beat of silence, the others stand poised, bewildered as to what* VERA's *next move will be. She holds her gloved hand high, then in a sudden gesture, yanks it off, rips it apart in a single tear, holds it up in the air, she crumples it in her hand, flings it off toward* ROSA.]

VERA: [*To* ROSA.] I CAST YOU OUT! *OUT!* I SHUN YOU — NONE OF ME AND MINE — I SHUN YOU!!

[*Lights fade down to a spot on* ROSA.]

SCENE 6

ROSA: [*Shouting back at* VERA — *there is no time lapse from the previous scene.*] *I* SHUN *YOU!* I SHUN YOU —! I - I - I — I SHUN YOU — I - I - I

[*She suddenly calls out.*] Momma? [*Pauses.*] Ma Rose?

[*She is surrounded in darkness.*]

[*She calls out into the air.*]

Yeah, Ma Rose, there be demons!!!

[*She indicates herself, her own mind and body.*]

There be demons down in here!! *HEAR!!??* There be demons day and night and every step I take and everywhere I look — YES, I BLEED — BLEED *BLOODY* — I AIN'T NO WOOD THING, *NO!!!* —

OH YEAH - YEAH, I BEEN TRYING NOT TO GET STEEPED IN BLOOD, — YEAH *YEAH* THERE BE DEMONS DOWN IN HERE, OH YES — OH YES —!!

[*Suddenly we hear* MA ROSE's *voice from the shadows.*]

MA ROSE: … It's when you come on home to your own soul, girl … it's when you have a reunion with *yourself.* With your own soul's better-half …

ROSA: WHAT WILL I DO IF THEY CAST ME OUT — yes, I got the fierce "fright" demon on — YES — OH YES — WHAT WILL I DO IF — IF I FAIL *YOU* — WHAT WILL I DO IF I FAIL MYSELF — WHAT WILL I DO IF I — FACE THE DEMON FACE, WHAT WILL I *DO!*

HOW WILL I LIVE — yes, I got a second coat of flesh on me made of fear and fright and trembling — OH YES — OH YES I DO — AND HOW WILL I LIVE AND — WHAT WILL MY LIFE *BE* — WHAT WILL I DO??!! WHICH OF MY FACES IS MY *REAL* FACE —!

[*There is suddenly the soft a capella voice of a single singer singing, "On the Banks of the Jordan."* ROSA *exits the stage, lights change,* ETHEL *and* WAYMAN *enter, both dressed in black and clear the stage of the few pieces of furniture and props as the music softly plays. There is an interval of two minutes.* VERA *appears from the shadows dressed in black with a black veil.* ROSA *appears from the darkness, wearing a black coat. She and* VERA *stand facing each other, both very awkward.*]

VERA: It's good to — you looking well —

ROSA: How you been?

VERA: You?

ROSA: — in her sleep?

VERA: [*Nods yes.*] Hated for it to have to come to *this* for me to finally call you —

ROSA: It's not been easy not to see you …

VERA: Never did find that locket.

ROSA: *I* got it — I've had it —she gave —

VERA: You? She —? [VERA *is about to burst in questions, she stops and just nods.*] [*A beat.*] Been missing you. — Not knowing how you been — not —

ROSA: I know you have been, Momma — [*Shaking her head back and forth sadly.*] Yes — yes, Momma — me and you — *me* and *you* —

VERA: Ro — it all jus' tore me up so and scared me so and — and I — I did what I *had* to do — You think I don't reflect on it all? Well, I do.

ROSA: I *know* you do.

VERA: Two years is too long. I've *missed* you.

ROSA: In her sleep.

VERA: She's done "made it 'cross the wide water," Ro. [*She pauses. Then tentatively.*] We gonna march two by two from the church to the ... cemetery ... the whole fifty or so in the clan ... the whole entire family. [*Pauses.*] I 'preciate it if you ... join me.

[ROSA *pauses and just stares at* VERA, *then she nods slowly, agreeing to do so. Slowly she and* VERA *begin to put on their funeral gloves.*]

[*The shadow of* MA ROSE *appears upstage. She is dressed in the same Sunday church suit from the day of the march in Act One. She is once more in* ROSA's *memory.*]

MA ROSE: [*To* ROSA.] Now, then, you just hold on to Nana's hand and walk slow with me ... It's when you have a reunion with yourself ... with your own soul's better half ... [*She begins her singing as the lights fade.*] I'm so glad/ trouble don't last always/ I'm so glad/ trouble don't last always/ singing/ I'm so glad/ trouble don't last always .../ Oh My Lord/ Oh My Lord/ What *shall* I do ...?

[*A spotlight remains on* ROSA.]

ROSA: [*Whispering out into the air as she hears* MA ROSE's *voice in memory.*] Ma Rose? I'm beholding to you. Yes. I'm beholding to you ...

[*Fade out. End of play.*]

THE END

ETTA
JENKS

by

Marlane G. Meyer

The ape, alone in his bamboo cage, smells
The python, and cries, but no one hears him call.
The grave moves forward from its ambush,
Curling slowly, with sideways motion,
Passing under bushes and through leaf tunnels,

Leaving dogs and sheep murdered where it slept.
Some shining thing inside us, that has
Served us well, shakes its bamboo bars.
It may be gone before we wake.

— *Robert Bly, "Defeated"*

CHARACTERS

Etta Jenks, a woman in her early thirties
Clyde, a man in his mid-thirties
Burt, a man in his late twenties, deaf
Sherman, Burt's twin brother, blind
Ben, a man in his forties
Dolly, a woman in her forties
Dwight, a man in his late twenties
James, a man in his late twenties
Spencer, a man in his early fifties (actor may double as Clyde)
Sheri, a woman in her mid-thirties
Kitty, a woman in her early twenties
Alec, a man in his early twenties (actor may double as Dwight)
Max, a man in his late thirties (actor may double as Burt and Sherman)
Shelly, a young girl, eighteen (actress may double as Kitty)

(This cast can be doubled down to nine actors.)

PRODUCTION NOTE
With the exception of Etta, Burt and Sherman, the characters should all be possessed of a certain animal quality, subtly suggested through makeup or gesture, the effect to be not cartoonish but queer. The landscape should suggest a kind of contained isolation that might be found in an empty aquarium at an abandoned sea park.

SCENE 1

Darkness. A train whistle blows in the distance. The engine becomes audible. A covered light hangs down center stage. It comes up to reveal ETTA *standing on a small platform. She wears a long coat and carries a large suitcase. She seems to be leaning into the sound of the train, waiting, as the train approaches. The lights flicker and turn flashing as the sound of the train roars by.* ETTA *disappears in a blackout. The train sound recedes in the distance.*

The lights come up on a bare stage. We hear the sound of a busy train terminal; a voice announcing arrivals and departures, people milling, voices calling to each other. ETTA *is center. She pulls a map from her purse. A young man enters with a load of luggage. A baggage handler,* BURT, *he glances at her briefly before unloading the luggage. A man approaches. His name is* CLYDE.

CLYDE: How you doin'…

[*She moves away.*]

Excuse me.

[*She moves away.*]

Miss? Excuse me … but … Miss? I can see you're from out of town …

ETTA: Please don't.

[*She moves away.*]

CLYDE: I see you have what looks like a map?

ETTA: No.

CLYDE: Well, it sure looks like a map.

[ETTA *approaches* BURT.]

ETTA: Could you help me?

CLYDE: I could help you.

ETTA: Please leave me alone.

BURT: I have to see your lips when you talk.

[CLYDE *steps between* BURT *and* ETTA.]

CLYDE: I'm insanely good with a map — like the Army was havin' a hard time trainin' their guys to read a map? And they heard how good I was and they snapped me out of civilian life

— bad knee, I had a metal plate in my head — they did not care 'cause I'm so good with a map, they flang me smack to the middle of Nam...

ETTA: [*To* BURT.] I fell asleep and I don't know where I am.

CLYDE: Angel City.

BURT: Los Angeles.

ETTA: [*To* BURT.] I am looking for someplace to stay, someplace cheap.

CLYDE: I know just the place. Let me help you with your bag.

[*They struggle with the bag.*]

BURT: Like a motel.

ETTA: I'd like it to be cheap.

CLYDE: You can stay with me for nothin' ...

BURT: You got any money?

ETTA: Not a lot.

CLYDE: I got a lot of money and I can show YOU how to get a lot of money ...

BURT: Say again ... ?

CLYDE: Meeting successful businessmen ...

ETTA: I have some money.

CLYDE: Eating at expensive restaurants ...

BURT: I have a brother might be able to rent you a place. You'd have to be out during the day.

ETTA: Out where?

CLYDE: Out on your ass.

BURT: Wherever it is people go when they're not home.

ETTA: Oh.

CLYDE: Oh. See? You don't even know where you're gonna be.

BURT: It's a sleeping room, jus' someplace t'sleep.

CLYDE: That means no visitors and suppose I want to visit?

ETTA: [*To* BURT.] Well, I'll probably be workin' in the movies.

BURT: [*Thinking.*] That's day work.

CLYDE: [*He stares at* BURT, *then at* ETTA.] Oh, shit ...

ETTA: I can start anytime so there shouldn't be a problem ...

BURT: [*Nods.*] Okay ...

CLYDE: I see it now. I see the attraction.

ETTA: I imagine I'd be gone quite a bit ...

CLYDE: Contract negotiations, celebrity luncheons.

BURT: My brother, Sherman, it's his house. He's a veteran and he's blind but he can hear if you stay in the room.

CLYDE: Hey, wait a minute ... you don't even know this guy or his blind brother.

ETTA: Yeah, and I don't know you ...

CLYDE: We could fix that.

ETTA: What's your job?

CLYDE: My job?

ETTA: [*She looks him over.*] What do you do ... get girls as they're comin' off the train?

CLYDE: Get? I don't have to get! They come!

ETTA: Why is that?

CLYDE: Why do you think?

ETTA: They're stupid.

BURT: You wanna call?

ETTA: Yes, let's call.

[*She takes his arm and moves down and away from* CLYDE.]

CLYDE: Oh, yes, let's call ...

BURT: I could take you there after work. I'm off in about thirteen minutes.

ETTA: That would be good. [*Looks back at* CLYDE.] That would be real good.

[*They move downstage, freeze, he looks at them, turns away.*]

CLYDE: What's my job ... shit, where do these bitches come from?

[*Lights fade on* CLYDE.]

SCENE 2

BURT *watches TV.* ETTA *wears a slip. She sets her hair with hot rollers. Beat.*

ETTA: I think my throat is closing up. Those French fries were so dry, I think they're caught ... like a lump in my throat.

[*She nudges* BURT.]

I think those fries got caught in my throat.

BURT: Drink water.

ETTA: I wish I had a coke. I saw this science experiment once, where they put this tooth in coke, and over a period of a few weeks or days ... or maybe it was just one day, it completely fell apart. Just disappeared.

I guess that could happen with a whole set of teeth if we were to sit around with a mouth full of Coca Cola day and night. I wonder how it would work, the teeth comin' out, would you swallow and then what, would they come back in ... somehow?

God, I'm stupid. What am I supposed to do? I thought by now I'd at least have some kinda extra work, somethin' ...

I met this girl, Sheri, at the lunch counter? I thought she was pretty weird but she came out to be nice and she said that one way to break into movies is to have a videotape of yourself made.

Performing a scene with someone or maybe doin' a monologue. But the problem is, it costs. I wonder how I could get five hundred dollars?

I had four hundred, but that's just about gone. I wonder if I could find somebody with one of those video cameras you use at home?

[*She nudges* BURT, *he looks at her.*]

ETTA: Do you know anybody with a ... home movie camera?

BURT: I know people with video equipment.

ETTA: You do? Video! Yeah, that's what I need!

BURT: It's very expensive equipment. I don't think they'd let you just use it, just like that.

ETTA: I need an audition tape. [*Beat.*] This is great. I'll brush up on my monologue or maybe get somebody to do a scene with me. When do you think you could ...

[*She nudges him, he turns.*]

When do you think we could use the stuff?

BURT: What stuff?

ETTA: The videotape stuff.

BURT: I gotta ask.

ETTA: Do it.

BURT: I don't know.

ETTA: What do you mean?

BURT: This guy is not a very nice guy.

ETTA: Yeah?

BURT: He's a creep.

ETTA: What do you mean, a creep?

BURT: [*Beat.*] I don't really know.

ETTA: [*She touches him.*] You lie to me 'cause you think it's for my best good but all it does is make me not want to trust you. Don't lie to me, Burt. It makes me mad.

BURT: He's like, not a human being exactly.

ETTA: Go ask him.

BURT: He makes movies of women.

ETTA: Can you ask him now?

BURT: He's weird, Etta.

ETTA: I'll ask him.

BURT: [*He looks away. Beat.*] I'll ask him.

[*She kicks him, he looks up.*]

ETTA: Now.

[*He stands.*]

And while you're out ... get me a Coke. Please. Okay? [*Beat.*]

Okay?!

[BURT *moves upstage to* BEN. *The lights fade on* ETTA.]

SCENE 3

BEN *is seated up left. He looks like a man mutating into a wolf.* DOLLY *is standing down and right of him. She faces out with a drink.* BURT *enters.*

BEN: [*Beat.*] Dolly, could you make our guest a drink?

DOLLY: [*Exaggerated.*] You want a drink?

BURT: Well, if you're gonna have one...

DOLLY: I've got one.

BEN: Get his drink! [DOLLY *exits.*] What else?

BURT: Her name is Etta. She's got long arms and a big head.

BEN: [*Nods.*] A big-headed girl.

BURT: A natural blond.

BEN: Personality, or no.

BURT: [*Beat.*] It's very difficult for me to say, because I can't hear. I can read her words, but since I can't hear how she says them, it's hard to say what she's like. You can tell a lot by how people sound, beyond what they tell you. If someone were to ask me, what's the worst part of losing my hearing, I'd have to tell them that it's not being able to hear if someone is sincere. Like with you for instance? I have never heard your voice and it's hard for me to know what kind of man you are.

BEN: I'm an asshole.

BURT: I guessed that.

BEN: I'm not ashamed, I'm not proud, but I don't try and put it on like I'm anything but an asshole.

BURT: I'd have to say ... she could be anything.

BEN: Anything at all.

BURT: She spends hours making up. Even when there's no place to go. She likes to look her best.

BEN: [*He stares in the direction of* DOLLY.] Vain. They are all vain, and then when they get old and they look like shit, they get pissed off! [*Beat.*] So ... she would like to be an actress?

BURT: She would like to be.

BEN: Is she any good?

BURT: I don't know. I do notice one thing. When she's talking, and she's excited, her face doesn't move. In my opinion, I'm not sure...that would make a very good actress. A wooden face.

BEN: Is she an easy lay?

BURT: Yes.

BEN: Details.

BURT: She came on to me the first night.

BEN: SHE came on to YOU?

BURT: She likes to have sex.

BEN: With a lot of white around the eyes?

BURT: Not at all.

BEN: She sounds like she has definite star quality.

BURT: [*Pause.*] How's Millie?

BEN: Millie ... seems to have dropped out of sight.

BURT: Millie had star quality.

BEN: But she was unreliable.

BURT: She had a good sense of humor.

BEN: She was an addict.

BURT: After.

BEN: [*Cocks his head, shakes it.*] I don't know. I hate drugs myself. I don't even drink.

[DOLLY *enters with two drinks.*]

My wife is a drunk.

DOLLY: I didn't drink at all when you first met me.

BEN: So what? What's that supposed to mean? That I made you a boozebag?

DOLLY: Maybe.

BEN: That's shit! You just need a way to sit still. 'Cause if you stopped drinking you'd probably have to get up and live! And the pressure's too much! It's too damn much! Life scares the living shit out of you, and you're trying to blame me!

BURT: [*Facing away.*] I wish she wouldn't get involved with you, Ben ...

BURT: [*To* DOLLY.] Oh, Christ! You piss me off!!!

[*Lights fade.*]

SCENE 4

[*Four women sit on a wooden bench.* ETTA *is among them. A voice speaks to them from the dark.*]

VOICE: Hi. I'm the director, Thomas Schultz, and this is my A.D., Valerie. She'll be handling most of our problems and she'll be answering any questions you might have about your part. Today we're casting for the role of the maid. It's a non-speaking, non-paying part. You'll plan to be here every night for rehearsal and provide your own costume. It would help if one of you were really a maid?

All right. Who's first?

[SHERI *rises and moves downstage.*]

SHERI: Hi, Mr. Schultz, my name is Sheri Shineer and I'd like to do a monologue from the musical "Hair."

VOICE: That won't be necessary, because you won't be talking. The deal is, and I want to be as honest as I can with you up front, your type is not the type I had in mind.

SHERI: What type did you have in mind?

VOICE: I don't know, but you're not it.

SHERI: I am not my body.

VOICE: Maybe if you could all step up to the front of the stage and ... yes.

[SHERI *watches the remaining women move forward and exits.*]

VOICE: That's right. [*Beat.*] Okay, you ... second from the left, what's your name?

ETTA: Uh ... Lana?

VOICE: Don't you know?

ETTA: I'm changing it.

VOICE: Okay, the rest of you can go. Thanks so much.

[*The other women exit.*]

Have you ever worked in the theater before, Lana?

ETTA: Oh, yes, I have, yes, I worked as an usherette for two and a half years at the Rialto ...

VOICE: Wait a minute ...

ETTA: Uh, Mr. Schlitz? Did I understand you to say that nobody was gettin' paid here?

VOICE: Yes. We work for free. I mean, most of us work for free, and some of us work for a token salary ... Valerie?

ETTA: Well ... [*Chuckles.*] How can that be?

VOICE: Lana, this is equity waiver theater. I told you at the beginning the part was non-paying.

ETTA: It took a minute to sink in.

VOICE: Yes, well ...

ETTA: I guess I could do it for the practice?

VOICE: Make up your mind.

ETTA: I haven't really worked in two months.

VOICE: That's not my problem.

ETTA: I used to work at the Thrifty Lunch Counter but I burned my hand and they had to let me go and I was hopin' to begin to pursue my professional career now that I was between jobs.

VOICE: Do you want the part or not?

ETTA: No money at all?

VOICE: And you have to provide your own costume.

VOICE: Are you getting paid?

VOICE: [*Calling.*] Valerie?

ETTA: I really think I should have some money.

VOICE: The people producing this show can't afford to pay everyone. I'm not making that much myself.

ETTA: Like how much do you make?

VOICE: [*Beat.*] I make ten dollars every night the show is up.

ETTA: Ten dollars? How do you live on ten dollars? You know in a movie you get paid no matter if you're just standin' around in the background ... ?

VOICE: Lana ...

ETTA: It's evil not to pay people for work they do. That's the time of their life.

VOICE: That's their choice.

ETTA: This can't be right. Man. I hate theatre.

[*Lights fade out around her.* ETTA *remains lit, she turns, lights come up on* SHERMAN *and* SHERI.]

SCENE 5

SHERMAN *is cleaning his M-16 at a kitchen table and listening to the ball game.* SHERI *and* ETTA *enter and sit.*

ETTA: Sherman

SHERMAN: Home so early AGAIN, Etta?

ETTA: I don't know what to do. I could take a job typing. I'm a pretty bad typist.

SHERMAN: You'd improve.

SHERI: I hate office work.

ETTA: It makes me feel like I'm in a box.

SHERI: That's real.

ETTA: What would you do, Sherman?

SHERMAN: It doesn't matter. You and I have nothing in common. What do you want to do?

ETTA: Be a movie star.

SHERMAN: What's that?

ETTA: You know, like ... be an actress.

SHERMAN: And what's that?

ETTA: Sherman ... ?

SHERMAN: Like, what does SHE think it is?

ETTA: It's like ... people are giving me money ... 'cause of who I am.

SHERMAN: And who's that?

ETTA: [*Beat.*] I don't know.

SHERMAN: Maybe that's why you're not making much money.

ETTA: I'm not making anything.

SHERMAN: Maybe that's why. This is what stops most people — not knowing who they are or where they fit in the marketplace.

ETTA: Where do you think I fit?

SHERMAN: Well, let me just say this. I imagine that you are pretty, even when you lie or steal my cigarettes or when you stay for days on end in a room I specifically told you for was for sleeping only!

[SHERI *and* ETTA *giggle silently.*]

SHERMAN: I still IMAGINE you're a good-looking girl.

SHERI: She takes a good picture ...

ETTA: You think so?

SHERI: Oh yeah, definitely.

SHERMAN: But that's not all, see what I'm saying?

SHERI: No.

SHERMAN: People can imagine what they want about her. Tabula Rasa.

SHERI: People can project what they want ...

SHERMAN: She's like an archetype.

ETTA: Is that good?

SHERI: I think so. [*Nods.*]

SHERMAN: [*Emphatic.*] No.

SHERI: Like Monroe? [*Beat.*] Oh, yeah.

SHERMAN: Icons who ascend to a level of worship and perish. It's a cliche.

SHERI: Maybe you shouldn't be in the movies.

ETTA: It's my only dream, Sheri.

SHERMAN: You've had no interest?

ETTA: Burt has a friend. I don't know, though, I don't know about that. I'm supposed to go talk to him. But, I don't know.

SHERI: He said she could make three hundred dollars a day.

SHERMAN: Burt's friend.

ETTA: Ben.

SHERMAN: Primordial ooze.

SHERI: He makes movies.

SHERMAN: Pornography.

SHERI: It's a service industry, Sherman.

ETTA: I could use three hundred dollars a day.

SHERMAN: Pornography in its focus on the genital experience creates an ultimately carnal mind that is necessarily death oriented since the body is always in a progessive state of decay. The earth begins to crawl up inside you ...

SHERI: Ugh.

ETTA: We're dying anyway, who cares?

SHERMAN: The day you wake up with a mouth full of dirt, you'll care.

SHERI: I don't think it's like that.

SHERMAN: You start thinking you're a body, you're not a body.

ETTA: Then why did I get a tattoo?

SHERMAN: It's macho.

SHERI: I got one when I first moved here, a snake on my shoulder blade. I hate it.

SHERMAN: It made you feel like you had some control over your
life.

ETTA: I think I should have had something by now, don't you? I
mean, maybe this guy Ben is a break and I don't know it. I
mean, how WOULD I know it? I have never had a break. I
don't even know what a break looks like, do you?

SHERMAN: You can't know.

ETTA: Well, see there?

SHERI: I just do what's up next, and it seems to work out.

ETTA: And you know, it could be these films are artistic.

SHERI: Yeah, Sherman.

SHERMAN: The difference between erotic art and Ben's business
is the difference between gourmet dining and eating fifty
pounds of raw sewage in one sitting.

[ETTA *sneaks a cigarette.*]

ETTA: What do you think of the name Lana, Sherman.

[*He catches her hand, takes the cigarette back.*]

SHERMAN: It sounds like a fat girl trying to be thin.

[SHERI *lifts her skirt, flashes him.*]

SHERI: I bet he's not really blind.

[SHERMAN *slowly points his gun at her,* ETTA *laughs, blackout.*]

SCENE 6

BEN *and* SPENCER *sit downstage. Lights flicker across their bodies.
They are watching a movie.*

SPENCER: [*Pause, disgusted.*] I hate dogs.

BEN: [*Absorbed.*] How can you hate a dog? Dogs have some of
the best qualities of men.

SPENCER: How old is the girl in the doghouse?

BEN: Old enough ...

SPENCER: How old?

BEN: These children are ancient sexual beings. They teach me.

SPENCER: God ...

BEN: Don't God me, Spencer, I built the pyramids. Don't use that superior tone with me, I'm you.

SPENCER: [*Beat.*] Remember decolletage, Benjamin?

BEN: What's that supposed to mean?

SPENCER: A flash of thigh, a bare shoulder. Evening gowns, Grace Kelly, a single strand of pearls. Teeth. A slight overbite?

BEN: [*Sighs.*] God, Spencer, you are so romantic.

[ETTA *knocks and enters.*]

SPENCER: [*To* ETTA.] Welcome to the glue factory.

[SPENCER *exits,* BEN *looks at* ETTA.]

BEN: [*Beat.*] I've heard very good things about you — high praise from my friend Burt. He thinks you have talent. And after meeting you, I have to admit, I'm impressed.

ETTA: Thank you.

BEN: I met Burt when I started out in this business, but not many peole make it the way I have. Most lose their stuff — like Burt — he couldn't handle the pressure.

ETTA: What pressure?

BEN: I personally don't know. Just, when people get out of the business they say it's 'cause of the pressure.

ETTA: Burt thinks this is a mistake.

BEN: Burt thinks. Yes. Burt is a big star.

ETTA: He says it's the quickest way to ruin your chances.

BEN: I have footage on Burt. He's a lame dog.

ETTA: He never said anything about that.

BEN: Burt is a loser. I think you know that already. Am I wrong? Okay. Good. Now, let's talk about you. I know you want to make a short video, is that right?

ETTA: I want to make a tape of myself doing a monologue or a scene so I can send it to casting directors or producers ...

BEN: Okay. Back up. Has Burt told you I'm a producer?

ETTA: Not exactly.

BEN: I am. I make movies.

ETTA: Yeah, but ... what kind?

BEN: Okay, let's not fool around. You know that.

ETTA: Yeah, I guess I do.

BEN: It's a business, Etta. That's all it is. Business. And I want to tell you one more thing here, Etta. Maybe you know this, maybe you don't, but many of our finest stars made their debut in a skin flick. Okay? That's number one.

ETTA: Like who?

BEN: I beg your pardon?

ETTA: Like what stars made their debut in a skin flick?

BEN: The world of cinema is like a secret society, Etta. I myelf would be happy to tell you the names of the other members, but these stars, these very rich and influential people, consider discretion to be the first responsibility of art. When and if you decide that this business opportunity is one that suits your needs, and if we find that you suit ours, within a very short time these names will be as familiar as your own. And believe me, Etta, you will be surprised and flattered to be among these elite. Now, where was I — number two?

ETTA: Number two.

BEN: Number two, you could make a shitload of dough doin' one film or maybe two films and use that money to start your acting career. Use that to finance your audition tape instead of coming in here and expecting me to bankroll your ass for no reason whatsoever. Did you stop to ask yourself that, Etta? Why should I do this tape for you?

ETTA: I thought maybe as a favor.

BEN: I hate doing favors, Etta, and you know why? Because in the long run you will resent me. That's right, you should always pay your way, Etta, and I'm speaking to you as a friend would. Owe nobody!

ETTA: How much money could I make?

BEN: How much could you make. [*Nods.*] I see. Cut to the chase. Okay. Let's just say this. It depends.

ETTA: On what?

BEN: Well ... we'd naturally have to talk about that. We'd have to see.

ETTA: See what? See what I look like without my clothes?

BEN: That's not the only consideration.

ETTA: I look fine.

BEN: Show me.

ETTA: [*Beat.*] Just like that?

BEN: Exactly.

[ETTA *removes her blouse, cross fade to* KITTY. KITTY *is facing upstage. She is nude from the waist up.*]

SCENE 7

Lights come up on SHERI *and* KITTY. SHERI *is dipping a big sponge in a bucket of makeup and wiping Kitty's back.*

SHERI: Like my dad was dying of cirrhosis, okay? Depressed, I mean, very. And he locked himself in his room with the windows closed and the gas going full blast and like that gas eats the oxygen in your body, so that when the cops opened the door he exploded.

VOICE: [*Off.*] Lana?!

KITTY: That's sad.

SHERI: It was a mess more than a feeling, Kitty, he was desperate. But like I started thinking about his body idea. Suppose you're not desperate, I mean, there should be a way to scramble your protoplasm and ... vamoose, you know? I mean, it would be like building a car without doors, you see what I'm saying?

[ETTA *enters wearing robe and wig. She drops the wig on the floor.*]

KITTY: No.

VOICE: [*Off.*] You have five minutes, Lana!

SHERI: I was just telling Kitty about disappearing the body.

ETTA: My hands smell like feet.

SHERI: I read about this yogi in India.

ETTA: [*She starts to sit down, grimaces.*] God, does anyone else have this infection ...?

KITTY: It's a fungus, everybody has it.

SHERI: This yogi had mastered dematerialization to such a degree that he could vanish at will.

ETTA: Sheri, will you shut up?

[*They trade;* KITTY *wipes down* SHERI.]

SHERI: So like that information is in race memory, Kitty.

KITTY: What information?

SHERI: Dematerializing ... That means it's available to anyone, through the subconscious.

KITTY: I don't get it.

SHERI: 'Cause we are one mind.

KITTY: What's the point of being able to disappear, anyway?

SHERI: You're walking down the street and a man comes out of nowhere waving a gun ... He feels like he's dead inside, misery loves company, he sees you. What happens?

KITTY: Get shot.

SHERI: Dematerialize, Kitty

KITTY: I never heard of that happening.

SHERI: I'm just saying we should have that option.

ETTA: You know, I used to really enjoy sex? Now every time I make love, even if it's somebody I like, I get this terrible urge that seems to come out of nowhere and it's all I can do to keep from gouging his eyes out or slitting his throat ...

KITTY: Or hitting him over the head with a crystal ashtray you had to work two days to pay for.

ETTA: [*Curious.*] Yeah, yeah ... what is that?

KITTY: [*Pause, thoughtfully.*] It's like some kind of rage.

SHERI: I'm not angry.

KITTY: Me either.

ETTA: I don't think I'm angry.

VOICE: [*Off.*] Lana?! Where's Lana?

ETTA: Shit ...

VOICE: LANA!!?

[*Standing slowly as she speaks.*]

ETTA: I AM NOT WEARING THAT STINKING COSTUME, YOU STUPID SON OF A BITCH. WHERE'S BEN!!!!

[ETTA *exits, they watch her.*]

KITTY: [*Beat.*] She hasn't been in the business very long to complain about a dirty rig.

[*Cross fade to* BURT.]

SCENE 8

BURT *sits alone watching TV. A suitcase is near his feet. Clothes are being flung into it from the shadows.* ETTA *enters a moment later. She's packing.*

BURT: He's married.

ETTA: Grow up.

BURT: What happened to just doing one film?

ETTA: What about it?

BURT: I thought that was the idea.

ETTA: What's your idea, Burt?

BURT: I don't know.

ETTA: If you don't have any ideas, you can't play.

BURT: What are you mad at me for?

ETTA: You can't be me and make my decisions.

BURT: I don't know what you're talking about.

ETTA: It's degrading.

BURT: What does that mean?

ETTA: You can't be anything to me, you can't be me, you can't do anything for me, what is it you want?

BURT: I don't want you to go.

ETTA: If I keep working like this, I'll make more money than my lawyer.

BURT: Well, is that the point? Money?

ETTA: Yes.

BURT: I think the point is not to screw your life up.

ETTA: Are you in love with me?

BURT: I used to think I was.

ETTA: Okay, so what do you want to have happen?

BURT: Get married?

ETTA: Oh, get married.

BURT: Yes.

ETTA: And what? Have a kid, have a child?

BURT: I like kids, I mean … yeah, kids would be fine by me.

ETTA: Right, kids … and what else? A house?!

BURT: Yes, yes!

ETTA: Jesus!

BURT: What?

ETTA: I don't want that, that's not what I want. House, kids, husband, prison, *National Inquirer*, sour milk, cheese every day, it makes me feel sick!

BURT: Marriage is a woman's destiny.

ETTA: What?

BURT: Nothing.

ETTA: If something is your destiny, it shouldn't make you feel like puking your guts out!!

BURT: What about our sex? What about that?

ETTA: I hate sex.

BURT: Our sex is a comingling of spirits. It's the kind of sex married people have, Etta.

ETTA: I can have sex with anything and make it look like I enjoy
it. I'm a pro.

BURT: You're just being mean now. You're just trying to make
me feel bad for complaining. All right. You don't want to be
with me. Okay. But you know it's not a good idea to do
things for money. Money is never good motivation. It turns
you hard.

ETTA: I don't do it for the money.

BURT: Are you on something?

ETTA: No!

BURT: 'Cause my brother hates drugs. He'd shit if he thought
you were on something ...

ETTA: Did you hear what I said?

BURT: You don't do it for the money. [*Beat.*] You don't?

ETTA: No.

BURT: What for then?

ETTA: I'm good at it.

BURT: Etta. That's disgusting.

ETTA: What's disgusting.

BURT: Don't you think I know what you're talking about?

ETTA: No, I don't think you do.

BURT: I've seen those movies, Etta.

ETTA: What am I talking about?

BURT: Screwing.

ETTA: What I'm talking about, Burt, is business.

BURT: Bullshit.

ETTA: Have it your way.

BURT: What about it do you like?

ETTA: I want to thank you for all the help you've given me,
Burt, I really appreciate it.

BURT: What do you think — you can just brush me off, just kiss
me off, just like that?! You think you need an excuse to be a
whore? You don't need an excuse. Money, no money, good,
no good, I don't know what you're talking about any more. I

can't see into your face, how you're talking to me ... it doesn't respect anything, Etta. I could be something to you. I could. But you won't have it.

[*He sits down, rubs his ears. Pause. She takes a box out of her valise.*]

[*She nudges him with a box.*]

ETTA: It's a gift. [*Beat.*] It's a white silk shirt.

BURT: Where am I supposed to wear this, the Academy Awards?

ETTA: Goodbye, Burt.

[*She takes the TV, crosses away.*]

BURT: WHY CAN'T YOU JUST TELL ME WHAT IT DOES FOR YOU??!

ETTA: [*Stops, beat.*] It makes me feel like I'm really here.

BURT: But what about me.

[*He turns away.*]

[*She exits.*]

When you leave, where will I be? Who's going to see me? Sherman can't see me. My job can't see me. Somebody needs to see me for me to be okay. I can't say I'm gonna be okay if I don't have that, Etta!

[*Lights fade out on* BURT.]

SCENE 9

Cancun. A beach in Mexico. Beach sounds are heard. A light comes up on BEN. *He is lying on a reclining lounge chair in Speedos and sunglasses.* ETTA *sits beside him sipping a drink. She wears a caftan. She watches him a long beat.*

ETTA: You have so many moles, Ben. Aren't you worried about getting skin cancer?

BEN: I can't stop thinking about it.

ETTA: You should wear sunscreen.

BEN: I'm trying to remember the color of the room I grew up in.

I think it was ... blue.

My bed was under a window. I would leave the shade up. Moonlight made the walls of my room look white. Sometimes I would wake up and there he would be, sitting on the edge of my bed, staring at me. I would ask him what was the matter, but he'd just sit and stare and not say a word. He was a drunk.

ETTA: Who?

BEN: My father.

ETTA: [Beat.] My dad and my mom's dad were the same person.

BEN: [Sits up, turns, beat.] Are you shittin' me?

ETTA: No ...

BEN: That's freakish. [Still staring.] Aren't you supposed to be dead?

ETTA: No.

BEN: It's a good thing you're not going to have a baby.

ETTA: Yeah.

BEN: It'd be a turnip.

[He lies back down. Pause.]

ETTA: He used to wrap himself up in a blanket and chase me around the house. One day my mom saw that and started screaming at him. And right after that we moved. We didn't see him again for a long time and then one day he showed up. We were watching the moonshot and he came to the screen door and looked in. I remembered him as this great big red-faced man, but it looked like he'd been shrinking. She unlocked the door and he came in and the three of us sat there without speaking, watching this guy walk on the moon, till finally ... he just got up and left, just ... slipped away, careful not to let the door bang shut, almost like he'd never been there at all. I looked at my mom and she wouldn't look at me. I told her she should go out and say goodbye, but she wouldn't answer. She was always quiet, but she hardly ever spoke after that. [Beat.] I don't like Mexico, Ben, it's too hot. I want to go home.

BEN: Go.

ETTA: What about you?

BEN: I made some bad deals. Spencer wants to pay me back. Screw him.

ETTA: You're not going back.

BEN: Correctamente bien.

ETTA: What about me?

BEN: Screw you.

[*He laughs a short convulsive laugh. She watches him.* ETTA *remains lit as the lights fade on* BEN *and the beach.*]

SCENE 10

A dance hall. Music comes up, Red Roses for a Blue Lady. *A couple dance in a spotlight. The woman looks at her watch, puts her hand out, the man gives her some tickets, they exit.* ETTA *and* SHERI *dance on after them.*

ETTA: So he said, you have such a cruel smile, right? So then I knew. I tie him up with his own necktie, step on his hand and call him dog. Dog. He gives me plane fare home and his Spanish Language edition of *Spanker's Monthly* and he's very clean. Japanese.

SHERI: I would love to have a stranger ask for my autograph.

ETTA: He wasn't seeing me, he was seeing Lana, in a leather bikini.

SHERI: It got you home. I have friends who've never come back from Mexico.

ETTA: Anything can happen there, it's so poor.

SHERI: Have you ever noticed how many miracles occur in third world countries? I think that poverty inspires a greater belief in the supernatural.

ETTA: Speaking of supernatural, look at this guy coming in.

SHERI: Psycho.

ETTA: His name is DWIGHT.

SHERI: DWIGHT, like Norman? Strictly from the Bates Motel.

ETTA: He seems like he's got a lot of money.

SHERI: He's a good looking white guy. He could date anybody. I
mean. Except for his eyes ... he's handsome.

ETTA: He has a funny arm.

SHERI: Look at his shoes, patent leather evening pumps,
two-hundred and sixty dollars. He's wearing an
eight-hundred-dollar suit. You have to ask yourself, what's
this guy doing paying you twenty-five cents a minute to
dance?

ETTA: He talks.

SHERI: To talk then.

ETTA: He seems like he's lonely.

SHERI: They're always lonely. It's because all their friends are
dead. Oh, here comes my dreamboat. He's looking for me.
He's waving.

[*She waves.*]

Ola Carlos! [*Quietly.*] You fat pig. See you later ...

[SHERI *moves off,* DWIGHT *enters.*]

DWIGHT: Hello there, Lana.

ETTA: Hi, Dwight.

DWIGHT: Business is slow tonight.

ETTA: Yeah

DWIGHT: You're looking especially pretty this evening.

ETTA: This is the same dress I always wear.

DWIGHT: [*Beat, he sighs.*] I would like it if you wouldn't use that
tone of voice when you accept a compliment. As if I was
insulting your intelligence.

ETTA: Well?

DWIGHT: If I think you look nice I say so. That's all.

ETTA: You want to dance?

DWIGHT: Not really.

ETTA: I have to take your tickets even if we just talk.

DWIGHT: I came over to ask you if you'd like to go out with me. Since it's a slow night, maybe they'll let you off. We could go someplace.

ETTA: Like where?

DWIGHT: Ladies choice.

ETTA: The health department closed the coffee shop, if that's what you're talking about.

DWIGHT: No. I was thinking we could have dinner someplace, a nice place, then maybe ...

ETTA: We could stop off at your house.

DWIGHT: My mother's away for a few days. I'd like to show you our collection of porcelain figurines. There's one that looks just like you.

ETTA: [*Beat. She looks away.*] I don't think so.

DWIGHT: Why not?

[JAMES *appears upstage. He lights a cigarette before making his way over.*]

ETTA: I don't date the customers.

DWIGHT: I thought by now we were friends.

ETTA: The manager is watching us. You'll have to give me some tickets.

JAMES: [*To* ETTA.] Hi, ugly.

ETTA: What are you doin' here, James?

JAMES: Spencer's been lookin' for you.

ETTA: So what?

JAMES: So he wants to see you.

ETTA: What for?

JAMES: How should I know. [*To* DWIGHT.] What are you lookin' at?

DWIGHT: Nothing.

JAMES: What are you tryin' to date my sister here?

DWIGHT: We were talking about having some dinner, yes.

JAMES: Oh, some dinner? I see, dinner. Are you eating these days, Etta?

ETTA: Get lost.

JAMES: [*To* DWIGHT.] I think she wants you to get lost.

ETTA: Not him ...

JAMES: This is a strange place to find a girlfriend, pal. You plug one of these and your dick falls off ...

ETTA: I'm calling the manager.

JAMES: [*Grimacing.*] What's wrong with your arm?!

ETTA: You're an asshole ...

DWIGHT: I had a muscle disease as a child.

JAMES: So now you're gimpified, is that right?

ETTA: Get the fuck out of here!

JAMES: Must have been something I said. Shit, I'm such a jerk.

[SHERI *enters as* JAMES *exits.*]

JAMES: Hi, Sheri ... how you doin'? What time you off?

SHERI: Two.

JAMES: Maybe I'll let you read my cards?

SHERI: I can't wait.

JAMES: We'll see you tomorrow, Etta.

[*He exits,* SHERI *exits opposite.*]

ETTA: [*Thinking, she shakes her head.*] Great!

[DWIGHT *takes her arm, squeezes, she pulls away, he holds on, they freeze.*]

DWIGHT: What about if I pay you?

[*Blackout.*]

SCENE 11

The lights come up on SPENCER *as he watches* JAMES *light a cigarette.*

SPENCER: [*Beat.*] GONE! Just like that, just like that! Shit.

JAMES: If you're so sensitive, maybe you should get out of the business.

SPENCER: You make me sick. You know that? You sicken me!

[*A knock on the door. Both men watch the door. The knock comes again.*]

Try and keep your mouth shut.

JAMES: Come in.

[SPENCER *glares at* JAMES. ETTA *enters. A bandage covers her left eye, her right cheek is bruised, her arm is in a sling.*]

SPENCER: Good to see you, Etta. [*Beat.*] You're looking well.

ETTA: I feel good.

SPENCER: Did you fall down a manhole?

JAMES: She's been bangin' freaks two at a time and she's getting what she deserves, isn't that right?

SPENCER: Shut up.

ETTA: Spencer. If the question is Ben, I have no idea where he is. He left me in Cancun with five hundred pesos and I haven't seen him since.

SPENCER: Ben is too slimy not to leave a trail, Etta. Ben is handled.

[JAMES *begins to laugh.*]

James doesn't know why he's laughing. Do you?

JAMES: I think something's funny

SPENCER: And he can't shut up, can you?

JAMES: Why should I?

SPENCER: [*Beat. He turns back to* ETTA.] What are you doing for work these days, Etta?

ETTA: I work at a dance place.

SPENCER: Like Arthur Murray?

[JAMES *laughs*, ETTA *laughs a beat later*.]

ETTA: Like taxi dancers.

JAMES: Like hookers dancing with scumballs …

ETTA: James is a regular.

JAMES: Eat shit.

SPENCER: So you're making a living wage?

ETTA: I do all right. I work part time and I go to school.

[JAMES *laughs*.]

I'm taking a class in court reporting ….

[JAMES *laughs harder*]

[*To* JAMES.] Screw you!

SPENCER: Etta, I have a little business proposition for you. Do you know what a talent scout is?

ETTA: Yes.

SPENCER: It's self-evident.

ETTA: It's somebody that scouts talent.

JAMES: Brilliant

SPENCER: You come into contact with a lot of young women. They are needy … they need things … money, a job, a place, but mostly they need money.

ETTA: Oh, brother …

SPENCER: Maybe movies wouldn't be an option, but you present it in such a way as to persuade …

ETTA: For Ben's business?

JAMES: No, for MGM.

SPENCER: It's not Ben's business any more. It's mine and I'm asking you to come in as talent coordinator.

ETTA: What's that?

JAMES: It's a hawk, idiot head.

SPENCER: You've made movies.

ETTA: That's right.

SPENCER: I want to make better movies.

ETTA: You want a class movie with class action.

SPENCER: I knew she was smart.

JAMES: Shit.

ETTA: Good looking women with no problems, no junkies, no freaks, and they want to make a pornographic movie that has the potential of coming back at them years from now when they want to marry a minister or run for Supreme Court.

SPENCER: This is business, Etta.

ETTA: I don't want to hustle anybody.

SPENCER: You don't have to. The dollar sign is the bottom line. Better pay, better working conditions equal better product. It's a whole different operation.

JAMES: You are making a big mistake here, Spencer.

SPENCER: Shut up!

JAMES: [*To* ETTA.] Stupid.

ETTA: Why don't you go home and eat a cockroach.

JAMES: I don't do that any more!

SPENCER: James had this job, isn't that right, James? But James cannot keep track of the women. They vanish, sometimes the day of shooting, sometimes in the middle of a film, or one or two movies later. You never know what becomes of them, they just disappear!

JAMES: Screw you.

SPENCER: Screw you!

[JAMES *moves away*.]

So. I am prepared to pay you three a week and fifty for every warm body you scare up. There's the deal.

ETTA: Is that what James was making?

JAMES: No way, bitch ... [*To* SPENCER.] Can you feature this?

ETTA: You want me to do a better job than James and you want to pay me less.

SPENCER: I'll pay you four a week and a hundred for every girl that completes an assignment.

JAMES: You're pissing me off, Spencer.

SPENCER: Why don't you get lost for a while.

[JAMES *and* SPENCER *exchange looks*, JAMES *looks at* ETTA.]

JAMES: Yeah, okay.

[*Laughing, he exits.*]

SPENCER: James is walking out to his car right now imagining that you and I are having it off. [*Sighs.*] James is a victim of this business. When he's not dreaming of latex miniskirts he's sitting in a quarter booth. Images of comfort and security.

[SPENCER *pulls three hundred dollars from his wallet.*]

One week's salary.

[*She starts to take the money, stops, moves away.*]

ETTA: [*Beat.*] I don't think so, Spencer.

[*She gathers her things to leave.*]

SPENCER: It's really not about thinking, Etta, it's about instinct, survival of the fittest, adaptation to environmental demands. Many women don't like business, they find it dull, or too competitive, or their priorities shift and they lose interest, but I don't think you're that kind of woman.

ETTA: What kind?

SPENCER: You ever been married?

ETTA: Once. Look, Spencer, the deal is, I'm gonna take acting class and get my SAG card. I mean, that's why I came out here and with court reporting, I mean, it pays real well, and you can work around auditions, so ...

SPENCER: You know, Etta, not everyone is Grace Kelly.

ETTA: Nobody is, Spencer, she's dead.

SPENCER: What I'm trying to tell you is, you're no actress, I think we both know that.

ETTA: Well, I'm better than I was.

SPENCER: But you're not good enough to overcome having done skin flicks.

ETTA: Overcome.

SPENCER: Yes.

ETTA: [*Beat.*] Ben said a lot of stars did movies to finance their careers.

SPENCER: He lied.

ETTA: Ben said that since they all did it, it was acceptable, and that nobody thought anything about it.

SPENCER: What world do you live in, Etta? What? Do you think legitimate actors and actresses risk their credibility to make porno? For what? For money? You meet actors waiting tables, tending bar; they could make better money here — why don't they?

ETTA: [*Beat.*] 'Cause it ruins your chances?

SPENCER: 'Cause people are hypocrites, Etta. If you and another actress are up for the part of the Virgin Mary and both of you are equally awful, who do you think they're going to give it to? You? With your spread shots from here to Timbuktu? It's a high profile industry — somebody is bound to recognize you, especially with your circulation. You're a star.

ETTA: [*Pause.*] It's my only dream, Spencer.

SPENCER: Dreams are a lot like movies. They function to keep you from seeing how shitty life is. But once you know that, you're free of those stupid expectations that drive people crazy.

ETTA: I feel like somebody slipped the bones out of my body. I don't know what I'm supposed to want if I don't want that, I mean, if I can't have that, what am I supposed to want?

SPENCER: Money is a good place to start. You have a little feeling for it, otherwise you would never have made your first reel, am I wrong?

ETTA: No.

SPENCER: Think about buying a fur coat and a closet to put it in ... think about a car the color of your eyes built in the country your ancestors came from. Think about getting into that car and driving home to visit those people who checked their ambition years ago. You're still gonna be in the movies,

Etta.

ETTA: My friend Sherman says that the way to get what you want is to keep a picture of it in your heart. That any image you can hold onto, you can make it happen in your life.

SPENCER: [*Beat.*] You go to the movies?

ETTA: I haven't been going much lately.

SPENCER: When you imagine yourself up there on the wide screen, with the big stars, what do you see?

ETTA: When?

SPENCER: In your head, in your heart, in your imagination, think. People are sitting in the dark, eating popcorn, watching you. What do they see?

[ETTA *takes a long beat to see what she actually thinks.*]

ETTA: Lana. They see Lana. Her body makeup streaked with sweat 'cause she's running a temperature from an infection she can't seem to get rid of. She's smiling at a man she hates, and giving herself to him, 'cause it's what he wants. It's what everybody in the audience wants.

SPENCER: And what does she want?

ETTA: [*Beat.*] Bigger tits.

SPENCER: And what do you want?

[*Pause. She looks at him, holds out her hand.*]

ETTA: A raise.

[*Beat. Blackout.*]

SCENE 12

Music, lights up, dance hall. SHERI *is standing downstage looking out,* JAMES *enters. He lights a cigarette before crossing to where she is.*

SHERI: Do you have to smoke so much? Christ ... !

JAMES: How you doin', Sheri?

[*She turns away.*]

What are you mad about — the other night? I had to work.

SHERI: Yeah ...

JAMES: So it's all the same, right? We both made money, except you came here.

SHERI: I came here, what's that supposed to mean?

JAMES: Just that you came here and picked up a few bucks, right?

SHERI: Yeah.

JAMES: I bet you can barely get high on what you make here.

SHERI: I'm not getting high like I used to. I'm changed.

JAMES: All I'm saying is you could do better.

SHERI: [*Beat.*] So, what are you doin' later on?

JAMES: I have some people I gotta see.

SHERI: Business again?

JAMES: For people like us, business is ninety percent of our lives.

SHERI: You and I are not the same kind of people, James.

JAMES: Well, anyway, my business involves one other person.

SHERI: I'm not loaning you any money.

JAMES: Sheri, you are so paranoid.

SHERI: I am not a savings and loan.

JAMES: And here it is, I used to get you high ...

SHERI: Please ... that shit you SOLD me?

JAMES: I just thought you might want to make some easy money, that's all.

SHERI: Nothing you do is easy James, that's you.

JAMES: That's me, what's that supposed to mean?

SHERI: How much?

JAMES: Ten big ones.

SHERI: What's a big one to you, James, a buck?

JAMES: A hundred is a big one, and ten big ones is a thousand dollars.

SHERI: Who do I have to kill?

JAMES: God, you know, you really have a good sense of humor?

SHERI: Eat me.

JAMES: Seriously.

SHERI: What's the deal?

JAMES: It's a movie.

SHERI: Why are they paying so much?

JAMES: Part of it's travel money.

SHERI: Where do I have to go, Mars?

JAMES: [*Laughs.*] Uranus.

SHERI: Where do I have to go?!

JAMES: Mexico.

SHERI: Mexico? [*Uncertain.*] No. [*Firm.*] No, forget it.

JAMES: Forget a thousand dollars?

SHERI: Don't you think I know what kind of movie they make in Mexico?

JAMES: What kind?

SHERI: You know.

JAMES: No, I'm stupid. You're smart. You tell me.

SHERI: [*Beat.*] You have to do it with a donkey.

JAMES: [*Bursts out laughing.*] Donkey?! [*Laughs again.*] I'm so sure! [*Calms.*] You don't have to do it with a donkey. No.

SHERI: So then what do I have to do.

JAMES: Although, it's not a bad idea.

SHERI: James ... !

JAMES: Lay there and cooperate.

SHERI: A thousand dollars.

JAMES: And I can get you high.

SHERI: Straight sex.

JAMES: And I'm driving your ass down there. We have a party in the car, I got some smack, some blow, I got a bottle of Chivas and some whites if we need them.

SHERI: A thousand dollars.

JAMES: You wear some rubber is all.

SHERI: That's not straight sex!

JAMES: [*Surprised.*] It's not?

SHERI: No!

JAMES: [*Beat.*] Okay, screw it, I'll catch you later.

SHERI: Hey! [*Beat.*] Are you going to be there or what?

JAMES: Yes, I am.

SHERI: 'Cause like I wouldn't mind a trip to Mexico, but like I don't want to get stranded, you know?

JAMES: [*Smiles.*] What do you think, I'm gonna leave your ass in Mexico? I'm so sure.

[*Freeze, blackout.*]

SCENE 13

Lights up. KITTY *and* ETTA *are seated in the office.* ETTA *is well dressed, upscale, business.*

ETTA: So tell me, Kitty, how's Moe?

KITTY: Moe's good, yeah, he's real good. He's been clean like, what three weeks?

ETTA: Three weeks.

KITTY: Pretty clean. Chipping on the weekends is all. Recreational. [*Beat.*] So what do you think, Etta?

ETTA: Let me see.

[*She stands.*]

KITTY: I wouldn't want anything to happen to the baby.

ETTA: It's not a baby yet.

KITTY: Moe wanted me to get rid of it.

ETTA: Moe is not as stupid as he looks.

KITTY: I'm two months.

ETTA: You look four.

KITTY: I can't remember.

ETTA: Okay, Kitty, look. I have a good doctor in Century City, a thousand dollars.

KITTY: A thousand dollars.

ETTA: You could make that in two days, plus five hundred extra 'cause you're pregnant.

KITTY: Five hundred extra.

ETTA: And you still have time to get rid of your problem.

KITTY: It's not a problem.

ETTA: It's going to be.

KITTY: You don't like kids.

ETTA: Don't pretend to know anything. What are you, twelve years old? You know something, you don't know shit.

KITTY: I know you don't like kids.

ETTA: I have a kid. She lives with people she calls mom and dad and when she gets sick she goes to a doctor and when she needs discipline she will understand why she's being punished. The element of random violence will not be present in her life.

KITTY: I want to keep my baby.

ETTA: And teach it what? How to be you? How to be Moe?

KITTY: What's wrong with Moe?

ETTA: Kitty, I'm sure you've noticed how a baby can scream? Did you know they're supposed to be allowed to do that? It's good for them? Because they're pissed off. They're pissed off about being in the world, and so they scream.

KITTY: [*Pause.*] One time I saw Moe rip a faucet out of a wall when he couldn't get it to stop dripping. He hates noise.

[KITTY *gets a cigarette out of her bag.* ETTA *lights it for her.*]

ETTA: Sheri used to work for Moe.

KITTY: Sheri did?

ETTA: She popped, he had her back on the street in two weeks.

KITTY: Moe said I didn't have to work any more.

ETTA: That's what he told Sheri.

KITTY: I didn't know Sheri had a kid.

ETTA: She doesn't. He's a memory.

KITTY: [*Beat.*] I don't believe you.

ETTA: [*Holds the phone out.*] Call Sheri, ask her.

[JAMES *enters. He's nervous, smoking. He sits down, stares away from the women.*]

KITTY: No.

ETTA: It's a simple solution to a complex problem, Kitty. Think about it and let me know today.

KITTY: I'm gonna see Moe and see what he says. 'Cause like, he seems happy about the baby and everything and I could see a baby making a big difference in our lives, a good difference, you know? We'd have a reason to get straight? For the sake of the baby? I'll call you, Etta, okay? I'll call you. Bye Bug.

JAMES: Bitch.

[KITTY *exits.* JAMES *lights a cigarette with one in the ashtray.* ETTA *makes a phone call.*]

JAMES: Isn't it fucked how sometimes you want things to work out a certain way but they never do, they just keep ... you know, screwing up, and I wonder, like do you think that's genetic?

ETTA: Shut up.

JAMES: Like with me and Dixie. We were gonna get married and like have a house, this and that.

ETTA: But you had to kill your parents.

JAMES: Just my mother. [*Beat.*] She made me kill her.

ETTA: [*She hangs up.*] Have you seen Sheri?

JAMES: WHAT DO I LOOK LIKE, PUBLIC INFORMATION? HOW SHOULD I KNOW WHERE SHE IS??

ETTA: Stop yelling.

JAMES: My parole officer says that every time a person commits a crime it's because they're reaching for a better life. What do you think? Do you think that's evolution expressing itself?

ETTA: Why don't you take a bath once in a while?

JAMES: You got any money, Etta?

ETTA: This is a loan ... Do you know what a loan is?

[*She digs in her purse, hands him twenty.*]

JAMES: What am I supposed to do with twenty dollars? I can't even get laid for twenty dollars. I mean I could, not that I ever pay for it ... I mean, I like to pay for it 'cause ... you know ... you can do what you want ... but not for twenty dollars. Etta, I need at least fifty.

ETTA: I'm not giving you fifty dollars to get laid.

[JAMES *lights a third cigarette with two going.*]

JAMES: How about you and me go someplace for a drink?

ETTA: No.

JAMES: You think you're too good to go out with me?

ETTA: Yes.

JAMES: Don't you think I know that? I'm offering to buy you a drink, I'd like to buy you dinner but I'm short. I mean, I'm not short, I'm average height for a man with my build, but I look that way 'cause I work out.

ETTA: What are you on?

JAMES: Speed.

ETTA: You're talking like a jerk.

JAMES: Etta, I take it every day. It helps me think.

[*She pulls more money from her purse and hands it to him.*]

ETTA: Here. Now get lost.

[*He looks at it. Beat.*]

JAMES: I don't want to go home right now. I don't really feel like being by myself and I don't feel like being with strangers and you and Spencer are the only friends I have. You don't have to loan me any money, here ...

[*He lays the money on the desk, he takes a chair, straddles it.*]

You don't even have to go out in public with me. I'll just sit here a while, I won't talk. If I could just stay here for a while I think I could be okay. If I could just get my breath and cool out I won't even talk and you can just do your work. Okay? Okay?

[*Pause.* ETTA *watches him.* JAMES *lays his arms across the back of the chair and puts his head on his arms. Freeze.*]

[ETTA *moves around her desk,* SPENCER *enters, they watch him.*]

SCENE 14

JAMES: [*Explodes.*] YOU ARE NOT MY BOSS!!

ETTA: I've been waiting a long time for this talk, James.

JAMES: Sheri could have been gone for months without a soul in the world being any the wiser except for YOU now have to be the big EYE.

ETTA: I love this. It's my fault, right?

JAMES: Yes! Because women don't belong in business.

ETTA: Did you know she was expected for dinner?

JAMES: How would I?

ETTA: Sunday night?

JAMES: Oh, Christ, Spencer ... !

ETTA: Her mother called me.

JAMES: So what?!

ETTA: She said Sheri left town with you.

JAMES: She's lying.

ETTA: She also said she called the police and they might be showing up pretty soon ...

SPENCER: What happened, James?

JAMES: How should I know ... ?

SPENCER: James?!

JAMES: I DON'T KNOW!

ETTA: [*Kinder.*] You know something, James.

JAMES: [*Beat.*] I heard ... don't ask me where, that somebody thinks she might have gone to Mexico to do a movie.

ETTA: Mexico.

SPENCER: Oh, shit.

ETTA: What in the hell did you take her down there for?!

JAMES: I don't know!

ETTA: [*Rage.*] GODDAMN YOU! I KNEW HER!

JAMES: [*Cowed.*] So you knew her? Big deal. Know somebody, it makes a difference.

ETTA: She was my friend!

JAMES: She was my friend, too ... I don't know what happened. She was supposed to meet me and I waited and waited and finally I just said ... fuck it. What am I supposed to do, Spencer [*Giggles.*], hang around, waiting for a ... a ... woman?

SPENCER: Where did you take her?

JAMES: Just a house.

SPENCER: JAMES!

JAMES: I took her to Ben.

SPENCER: Ben.

ETTA: I didn't know he was doing business.

JAMES: I dropped her off. She wanted to go. She asked me for a ride, that's all.

SPENCER: And then what?

JAMES: I went back to pick her up. Nobody was there, the house was empty. Nothing.

ETTA: Did you call Ben ?

JAMES: I don't know where he is.

ETTA: Bullshit!

JAMES: I don't know, he calls me, that's all ... I never know where he is.

SPENCER: You haven't talked to him since?

JAMES: [*Beat.*] Once.

SPENCER: And what did he say?!

JAMES: He says she disappeared.

ETTA: You mean like vanished?

JAMES: Like that's all he said!!

ETTA: He's lying!

SPENCER: I think you should vanish as well.

JAMES: Absolutely...

SPENCER: [*He hands him some money.*] Now.

ETTA: We're just gonna let him go?

JAMES: I can't split without my stash.

SPENCER: If you are determined to risk it, fine.

JAMES: Risk what?

ETTA: Spencer!

SPENCER: If you want to stay outside, I assume you do.

JAMES: You would give me up.

SPENCER: In a nanosecond.

ETTA: Shit!

SPENCER: [*To* JAMES.] What are you waiting for?

JAMES: [*Astonished.*] This is my home. All my friends are here. How long do I have to stay gone?

SPENCER: Forever.

JAMES: Is that necessary?

SPENCER: Get out of here, you scum-sucking leech, before I put the police on you myself.

JAMES: [*Beat. To* ETTA.] I'll get you for this.

[JAMES *exits.*]

SPENCER: [*Pause.*] Etta.

ETTA: Don't say it.

SPENCER: Sheri was a big girl. She knew what she was doing.

ETTA: Spencer... ?

SPENCER: I didn't kill her.

[*She stares at him a beat.*]

What do you want to do — get mad?

ETTA: I want to get even.

SPENCER: Oh, shit, Etta, grow up.

[*He moves off.* ETTA *looks out, she remains lit while the lights fade around her. She moves downstage. A light comes up on* DOLLY.]

SCENE 15

DOLLY *is wearing a loose wrapper. She holds a drink in one hand and a fan in the other. She's drunk.*

ETTA: You hear about Sheri?

DOLLY: Oh, Christ, is that what you came to talk about?

ETTA: I want to know where Ben is, Dolly.

DOLLY: Like, what? I'm supposed to help you? Screw off, Etta.

ETTA: What's the matter, Dolly, you getting old?

DOLLY: Maybe I think about the past a lot, things that happened, things that didn't work out. But I hold a grudge for you. Maybe that's not right, but I do.

ETTA: About Ben.

DOLLY: Ben and me had a good thing going.

ETTA: Ben was chewing you up and spitting you out a piece at a time.

DOLLY: Well ... it was good in the beginning.

ETTA: Everything is good in the beginning. It's only when they start to change, when their repuslive personal habits start to show up, that you have to wonder what you were thinking in the first place.

DOLLY: Yeah, we all change, but I don't like the way you've changed, so get out.

ETTA: They ever find your sister, Dolly?

DOLLY: Shut up.

ETTA: She was dating James for a while, and then all of a sudden she was nowhere to be found.

DOLLY: [*Beat.*] Ben says she's in Texas ... but ... I don't think she's anywhere, you know ... I just have that feeling. I can always tell when he's lying, that son of a bitch.

You know, in our business, you would have thought I'd meet a lot of men and that one of them would have meant something to me ... [*Beat.*] I get lonely, I brood. It's probably because of this that Ben begins to look good.

I went down to see him a few months ago. To see, you know, if there was anything there. He wanted it, too. [*Beat.*] I couldn't recognize him. I'm Mexican and in Mexico, I'm very psychic. When he met me at the airport and kissed me hello, I got this taste of dirt in my mouth.

He hugged me. I heard my bones crack and turn to dust and I saw us become this cloud of white powder blowing down the runway. I took a plane out of there so fast.

He's in Mexico City, Etta, he has a house near Chapultapec Park, he does business out of the hotel there. But don't go yourself. Send a man. I know somebody. I'll give you his name.

[*Lights fade.*]

SCENE 16

Lights come up on MAX. *He sits downstage at a small table.* ALEC *sits upstage on a barstool.*

    [ETTA *moves to* MAX. *Bar sounds come up. She takes the check and puts it on her side of the table, sits down.*]

MAX: Have you ever been to a funeral for a baby?

ETTA: I never have, no.

MAX: The box is so small. You wouldn't believe it. My sister's baby died. It tweaked her. She couldn't stop talking about it. What she'd be doing if she were alive ... you know, learning to crawl, teething ... all that.

ETTA: Interesting.

MAX: What about you, you want to have kids?

ETTA: I don't think about it. So maybe I don't.

MAX: You married?

ETTA: I didn't come to talk about myself.

MAX: You're not married. I know all about you, you're not even engaged.

ETTA: Nobody engages me.

MAX: [*Laughs.*] God, I love a woman who can make me laugh. You have no idea how many broads can't crack a joke.

ETTA: It's passive humor. I made a joke off of what you said. It's not like I'm funny, it's more like I'm quick.

MAX: It was a compliment.

ETTA: It was bullshit.

MAX: Have it your way.

ETTA: Twenty is your price.

MAX: Correct.

ETTA: That's high.

MAX: It's mid-range. Plus I have a partner. Safety in numbers, that's why policemen have partners, even if it's a dog. You like dogs?

ETTA: Not really.

MAX: That's too bad, 'cause I know a place in Hong Kong serves a very nice dog ... ever been to Hong Kong?

ETTA: No.

MAX: You want to go?

ETTA: I hate to fly.

MAX: We could take a boat.

ETTA: Look, I'm sure you're a very nice person, but ...

MAX: Wait a minute. Are you turning me down?

ETTA: Jesus ... look ... okay ... Forget it ... [*She stands.*]

MAX: No no no no wait ... sit down.

[*He takes her hand, pulls her down.*]
Your hands are freezing ...
[*He rubs her hands in his.*]
You want me to take this job?

ETTA: If you think you can do it.

MAX: If I think ... I'm taking it, okay?

ETTA: Fine.

MAX: Your hands aren't getting any warmer.

ETTA: I'll check my pulse ...

MAX: You should try a massage ...

ETTA: I have to go ...

MAX: What do you... wait ... what do you want, dating?

ETTA: Look, Max, I'm not interested.

MAX: [*He lets go.*] What are you, queer?

ETTA: Yeah, I'm queer, Max, okay?

MAX: No, you're not queer ... but I love a woman who lies ... they could get their stupid face slapped off lying to me but they don't care. Okay ... go. You want to go, go. I happen to know that I am a very attractive and interesting person ... I can talk to anybody.

ETTA: [*Beat.*] You know my business?

MAX: Frankly, it makes me uncomfortable. You're providing a public service for what I term nuisance individuals, lonely men who can't stop thinking about their cocks and also I'm a Catholic and I believe it undermines the stability of the family. I mean, these men are searching for some lost part of themselves — i.e. — the erotic, the animal, the beast, the devil — instead of spending the time with their wives and making sure their children are home instead of ripping off my fucking radio out of my brand new Porsche and ruining the console ... It'll probably cost me two, three thousand dollars to replace it ...

ETTA: I don't date people outside my business because they expect something that's not there.

MAX: Like what is it?

ETTA: A fantasy.

MAX: About sex?

ETTA: About people.

MAX: Maybe it was never there.

ETTA: It was. That's how I know it's gone.

MAX: Maybe that's why you got in the business.

ETTA: Max, when I look at you ... I don't see a human being any more. I see meat.

MAX: That's what I see when I look at everybody. I mean, if you think about it, that's good for me. Not that I had anything to do with it. I mean ... you know, I don't have a full set of human emotions. Poor parenting during the years between two and four? I'm not a psycho, like my partner, he really likes the work, but not me, I'm just sociopathic. I can still have a good time doing business, but it's an avocation rather than a calling, you see the difference?

ETTA: I hate sex.

MAX: Me, too. It's dirty.

ETTA: I don't want to have sex with you is what I'm saying.

MAX: I don't blame you — I have a disease.

ETTA: Okay, Max. You want to fall in love with me, do it — you probably deserve it.

MAX: Who said anything about love?

ETTA: I'll be in touch.

[*She moves down right and stands staring out. A moment later* ALEC *enters. He sits down, finishes* MAX's *drink.*]

ALEC: Is it on or is it off?

MAX: People crave love, Alec ... everywhere you look, hunger, yearning, people are starving for love.

ALEC: Is it on or is it off?

MAX: And yet when it's presented to them, boom, straightforward they duck, quack quack, they wag their head, they say, why me? Suspicious. Why is that?

ALEC: How would I know?

MAX: You ever been in love?

ALEC: Why should I?

MAX: Never mind ... Waiter?

[*Freeze.* MAX *and* ALEC *move upstage and stand facing up.*]

SCENE 17

Lights flicker across ETTA. BEN *enters a moment later. They are watching a movie.* ETTA *moves away, the movie ends. Lights up.* BEN *is a weird shade of green and is deadly calm.*

BEN: It is possible, but not probable. Because it's a particular type of commodity. The price, exorbitant. And you get what you pay for. People, clients, say they can tell the difference. You can't fake it, that moment the spirit departs the flesh, you could see for yourself, how intimate. It makes straight sex look like a kiss on the cheek.

ETTA: Jesus.

BEN: [*Sweetly.*] Don't use that tone of voice. I mean it.

ETTA: I don't like to think you're this kind of human being.

BEN: It's a market, Etta. You can't begrudge the market. You can't wage war on entrepreneurs, can you? You live by the sword and you die by the same sword, Etta. Wise up.

[*He hands her a drink.*]

You look green.

ETTA: I feel sick.

BEN: Wait till you get used to the water.

ETTA: I don't think that's it, water.

BEN: I myself hate philosophy, but if I were you, I'd either put up or shut up.

ETTA: I don't like myself.

BEN: I have felt that way for years, believe me. You will in time adjust.

ETTA: You did.

BEN: Yes.

ETTA: And you're happy.

BEN: [*Thoughtfully.*] Happiness is not destiny. You must be happy, no? Even the founding fathers wrote, "the PURSUIT of happiness." 'Cause they knew it was a crock. [*Smiles.*] They were not stupid like most people.

ETTA: If it weren't for you I wouldn't be in this business.

BEN: Oh, I don't know. All I did was exploit a situation to the mutual advantage of us both.

ETTA: You lied.

BEN: Lying is a tricky accusation, Etta. You can say I lied, I can say you believed the lie because deep down inside you didn't think you could make it. You see what I'm saying, Etta? It wasn't me that sold you out, it was you.

ETTA: No. It was you.

BEN: Think about it, Etta.

[*She watches him a beat, turns away.*]

BEN: [*Smiles.*] See, it doesn't pay to become circumspect.

ETTA: [*Beat.*] I think you used a friend of mine in a movie.

BEN: We've been using mainly Brazilian prostitutes we buy in bulk.

SHERI: James brought her in. She had a tattoo of a snake on her back.

BEN: A snake, with its shedding skin ...

ETTA: Her name was Sheri ...

BEN: I know Sheri.

ETTA: What happened to her?

BEN: We were making a movie. When what is visible becomes invisible. Her hair, skin, her eyes go transparent and she vanishes. Freaked my fucking film crew out of their gourds. I kept waiting for her to come back. But she never did. And then I noticed this smell, like gardenias, overpowering ... it seemed to hang in the air for hours.

[*He takes the flower from his lapel.*]

ETTA: Gardenias, Ben?

BEN: Yes.

ETTA: You like gardenias.

BEN: They're my favorite flower.

[*Beat. She lights a cigarette.*]

ETTA: I'll try and remember. The next time I see you I'll be sure to bring flowers. [*Beat.*] I have some vendors coming in from Seattle I want you to meet.

BEN: What are they vending?

ETTA: Runaways.

BEN: I have all I can use.

ETTA: We can talk.

BEN: I love to talk.

ETTA: They're very well educated. One of them studied at Yale. We'll have a nice dinner. You feel like eating, Ben?

BEN: Don't push me, Etta.

ETTA: Good. I'll see you at eight o'clock then.

BEN: Should I dress up or what?

ETTA: I think you should.

BEN: You do.

ETTA: Try and look your best.

BEN: [*Beat.*] All right. Eight o'clock. I'll see you.

[*Freeze.* ETTA *exits,* BEN *moves right,* MAX *and* ALEC *move down,* MAX *sits,* ALEC *stands up,* BEN *picks up a telephone and listens.*]

SCENE 18

MAX: First they had to tear the fence out to get the bulldozer in to dig the hole, right? The fucking idiots dug the hole so close to the property line they couldn't drive the dozer out again, can you believe the intelligence? So these guys put boards, like plywood, over the hole? Then they try and drive it out …

ALEC: Max, will you shut up.

MAX: They try and drive it out, right? The bulldozer weighs a million tons or something on these matchstick boards. Of course it falls in the hole, and they have to get a crane, coming over my house, it's twenty stories high and arrives in the middle of the night.

ALEC: Nobody's listening to you.

[BEN *hangs up, stares at the phone.*]

MAX: They take this fucking bulldozer up into the air and then suddenly it drops, straight down on my neighbor's car, a fucking Bentley, right? Antique? He just finished restoring the leather? We're talking about a hundred thousand dollar automobile, for Chrissakes!

[MAX *is doubled up laughing, the two men watch him, his laughter subsides.*]

BEN: I don't know where she could be.

ALEC: Is she always late?

BEN: No.

ALEC: I am starving.

BEN: Can I offer you a drink?

ALEC: I'm not drinking.

MAX: I don't trust a man who doesn't drink, do you, Ben?

BEN: I don't think about it.

MAX: Ben, why don't you have a drink? You need to relax.

BEN: It's eight-thirty. She should have been here.

MAX: She didn't call … ?

BEN: Maybe I should check her room.

ALEC: I don't think so.

MAX: I'll check ... oh, wait a minute.

ALEC: I wouldn't.

MAX: Yeah, absolutely. I don't think we should get involved with this ... missing person.

BEN: You don't think I should?

ALEC: I wouldn't.

[BEN *watches them,* MAX *and* ALEC *exchange looks.*]

MAX: Hey, you know ... I'm curious. Why don't you go ahead and check?

BEN: She could be sick, or something, it's better to know than not know.

[BEN *crosses to the door.*]

I'll be right back.

[*He exits.*]

MAX: Jesus, he's ugly.

ALEC: So where is she?

MAX: She's gone home.

ALEC: Oh.

MAX: She came down to make sure. She's very fair. She's a natural blond.

ALEC: What are you thinking of — selling her?

MAX: Weren't you?

ALEC: No. She's a very nice woman, a little stiff ... but ...

MAX: It was a joke. Fair, blond.

ALEC: God.

MAX: So ... you want to wait, eat first ...

ALEC: No, we don't wait! Eat, Jesus.

[MAX *moves around the room. He stares out downstage.*]

MAX: Gee, I'd love to see the museum while I'm here, you know? I've read they have this incredible archeological museum?

ALEC: I'm getting a headache.

MAX: You know the trouble with you? You can't relax, you can't talk, like normal people. Chitchat.

ALEC: Please, Max.

MAX: It's civilizing to be able to make small talk, Alec.

[BEN *enters.*]

BEN: She's gone.

MAX: How do you mean?

BEN: Like she was never there. The room is open, the bed is smooth, nothing.

MAX: Amazing. Alec, did you hear what Ben just said?

BEN: It's not like her. She says Yes, she says No, it means something.

MAX: So she turned. What are you gonna do — let it ruin your weekend? Shit, Ben, grow up.

BEN: I'm disappointed, that's all, to have poured so much of my time and talent into one individual and to be repaid in this way.

MAX: I think we know.

BEN: This is weird.

ALEC: What do you say we go get something to eat?

MAX: Yeah, let's go get some grub and do some business.

ALEC: A little food, you'll feel like a new man.

MAX: We thought we'd drive out to La Casita.

BEN: That's a long way to go.

ALEC: I only eat seafood.

BEN: They have a very good turbot right here at the hotel.

ALEC: I only eat shellfish.

BEN: I'm not very hungry.

ALEC: Why don't you just come along to keep us company?

BEN: No.

MAX: I wish you would, Ben, I sincerely do. I think it would do you a world of good. You don't have to eat, just come out to be social. Alec is no company at all, and I myself like to enjoy a good conversation with my meal. What do you say, Ben? Why don't you come with ...

BEN: Why don't you go fuck yourself?

MAX: [*To* ALEC.] That's not very nice, is it?

ALEC: No, it's not.

[*He makes a grab for the phone.*]

BEN: I swear to God, if you touch me I'm gonna scream my fucking head off!

[ALEC *detaches the phone cord from the receiver to the base.*]

MAX: Touch you, why would we touch you? What are we? Queers? I mean, Alec is queer, but so what ... He never forces himself on people, at least not ugly slobs like you, you're too old.

[ALEC *tosses the cord to* MAX.]

You have nothing to fear from Alec.

[*Blackout.*]

SCENE 19

Lights up on ETTA *downstage. She is cleaning out her briefcase in a deserted office.* SPENCER *stands watching her. He is very tense.*

SPENCER: Sheri was a zero, she was a thing.

ETTA: So was Ben.

SPENCER: Ben?! [*Snorts.*] I KNEW Ben. We went to school ... okay? I mean ... his mother knew my mother, we used to piss in the same toilet, for Chrissake!

Where are we when women decide it's time to get even? We're talking chaos, extreme situations, danger, danger ... danger!

ETTA: You can trust me.

SPENCER: Ben was my friend, Etta.

ETTA: I saw the films he made.

SPENCER: What are you — a critic? Nobody takes those films seriously, they're pictures.

ETTA: They're people.

SPENCER: They're self-hating greedbags who'll do anything for money.

ETTA: Like me.

SPENCER: Did I say you?

ETTA: You meant me ...

SPENCER: I meant other women ...

ETTA: I am other women.

SPENCER: It's in your heads, if it weren't we'd be out of business.

ETTA: I'm out.

SPENCER: Just like that?

ETTA: Exactly.

SPENCER: You killed Ben!

ETTA: What do you want me to say? I'm sorry? I'd like to feel sorry. I'd like to feel something. Relief. Revenge. I don't feel it. Except for this tast of dirt in my mouth, I could be dead. I'm not sorry, Spencer.

[*A loud knock*, MAX *enters.*]

MAX: I read all the magazines.

[*He moves to sit down.*]

Hi, Spencer.

SPENCER: Get him out of here.

ETTA: Wait outside.

MAX: What's so top secret?

ETTA: It's business.

[*He nuzzles her.*]

MAX: We've got a train to catch.

ETTA: Wait outside.

MAX: [*Stands, moves over, looks back at* SPENCER.] You ever been to Miami, Spencer? They got a hell of an ocean park down there. Dolphins? They're more than a fish.

[MAX *exits.*]

SPENCER: Don't you ever get sick of hanging out with scum?

ETTA: There's nothing wrong with Max that a lobotomy can't cure, but you, on the other hand, will have to wait for evolution.

SPENCER: I suppose if it's funny it's not a problem.

ETTA: It's not funny and I wasn't joking.

SPENCER: [*Beat.*] Are you threatening me?

ETTA: I don't know, am I?

SPENCER: Evolution, you think I don't know what that means? I know what that means, Etta. Dodo birds. Bald eagles. Endangered species ... extinction.

ETTA: Fly home, Spencer, your nest is on fire.

SPENCER: I'm not the only one, Etta.

[SPENCER *exits,* ETTA *stands, puts on her shoes.*]

[*A loud knock,* SHELLY *enters with an enormous suitcase.*]

SHELLY: Are you Emma Jenkins?

ETTA: I might be.

SHELLY: A friend said I could pick up some film work here.

ETTA: A friend.

SHELLY: She thought if I could do one or maybe two movies I could pay for my headshots and get an agent and put a few bucks by ...

ETTA: We're closed.

SHELLY: She said that you'd be very upfront and not screw me over. I went to these OTHER agencies run by these

PERSIAN assholes ...?

ETTA: Are you deaf or what?

SHELLY: She said she's a good friend of yours. She does these seminars on out of the body experience ...?

ETTA: [*Long pause.*] Dematerializing.

SHELLY: Yeah. I saw her do it in front of a bunch of people. She got real light, like you could see through her, and then ... poof. It teaches you how meaningless the body is and how it's never the thing you remember about people? [*Beat.*] Their bodies?

ETTA: Oh shit.

SHELLY: What? [*Beat.*] Hello? Hey!

ETTA: You know, I took this test when I was a kid ...

SHELLY: You mean like a screen test?

ETTA: It was a perception test. They show you a bunch of pictures, scenes of daily life, and they ask you what's happening. I can remember this one picture, of a woman, floating in the air, and this magician was pointing at her with his wand. They asked me what was happening. I said the woman is dead, she's floating to heaven, but my teacher shook her head and said, no, this is magic, this is a trick. But what if we were both wrong?

SHELLY: You know, I once read a book about a man who could bend a spoon with his brain.

ETTA: You know what kind of movies we make here?

SHELLY: Look, I think it's kind of a turn on to be naked in front of men, I mean ... they like me and I can make them think I like them. I do it all the time. Not that it's really possible to like them, 'cause they're, you know, maggots. But they don't know what I'm thinking, how I laugh at their sick needs. I'm already a great actress, you know what I mean? I bet you trip on this business.

ETTA: How old are you?

SHELLY: Eighteen, but like my stepdad "took me" when I was twelve so, you know, I'm not shy. How much do you think I could make, anyway?

ETTA: It depends.

SHELLY: Right.

[*She begins to undress.*]

My boyfriend used to cry when I'd take my blouse off. He would just stare at my tits and cry. He was really screwed up. Don't get shocked 'cause I'm wearing this leather shit underneath ... I just came from my other job, I'm a dominant. Listen, do you ever do whip movies? 'Cause I can really use a whip. I just about killed this guy the other night. I start wailin' and forget it's just action. Sometimes I think, how it would be to just ... well, you know? [*Laughs.*] Sometimes it won't go out of my head. It could be a public service. I bet the city would pay me. [*Beat.*] What do you think?

ETTA: I think you'll be able to make upwards of a thousand dollars a day. I think you could do a couple of films with no problem but any more than that and it will hurt your chances of straight film work. I think you have to be very honest with yourself.

[ETTA *pulls a card out of her briefcase, writes on it.*]

You have to see where you fit in the marketplace. Acting is hard work, not for everybody, it's a very tough business. However, in *this* busines, with your looks and your attitude, you could make a small fortune in two or three years, and with good investments, retire.

SHELLY: And do what?

ETTA: Drift.

[ETTA *hands the card to* SHELLY.]

SHELLY: That doesn't sound like much of a life.

ETTA: Think about it. The business, I mean. It's not for everybody.

SHELLY: Right.

[SHELLY *picks up her bag, exits. Lights fade out around* ETTA, *but as she speaks, she gets very bright; the suggestion of a train approaching can be heard faintly building.*]

ETTA: You have to like to travel. That's the trick to drifting. People you call friends become strangers — one day familiar, the next day better forgotten. You can't want anything, you can't keep anything because everything ... disappears.

[*The sound of the train comes faster and louder.* ETTA *seems to vanish as the lights go to black. A train whistle counds in the distance.*]

THE END

FIVE
IN THE
KILLING
ZONE

by

Lavonne Mueller

To Howard Stein

The following appears on a screen as the audience comes into the theatre:

"During the early years of the Viet Nam War, Congress authorized burial of an unknown soldier. Pathologists were so skillful at identifying even the most damaged body parts that it took nearly eight years before the military designated a set of remains it could not identify for the unknown soldier of Viet Nam."

—from a newspaper article in the Chicago Sun Time

CHARACTERS

    Captain Odom, black, age 35
    Sgt. Yarde, black, age 25
    Spec. 4 Tully, age 26
    Lt. Strobert, age 25
    Private Fudge, age 18

TIME
    1968

PLACE

A bombed out pagoda that serves as a lab and as a living quarters. The pagoda is set in the Dong Tien District, Viet Nam, which is bordered on the west by the wide, muddy MeKong River, and a few kilometers north of the Cambodian Border. This district stretches eastward out over vast flatlands known as the Plain of Reeds.

There is a large blackboard, a rack for hanging X-rays, and some machines for the analysis of blood and body parts. There is a large table for dissection. The pagoda is littered with religious statues, candles, joss sticks, test tubes, paraffin-lined bottles, string tags, adhesive tape, etc.

Army cots line the wall where the men sleep.

A cage with a mongoose is by the wall. A partial mud-brick wall is at one side of the pagoda along with a few sandbags. An exercise bike is by one of the cots.

AT RISE: *This is the first day in the Killing Zone. The men are getting the area ready.* ODOM *is doing some fine tuning on his microprobe.* FUDGE *is strumming his guitar outside the area of the men.* YARDE *briefly finishes placing some rocks and sandbags in position for a wall, then begins putting up green mosquito netting.* STROBERT *is setting up instruments on the table and alternately directing* YARDE *in hanging the netting.* TULLY *is trying to yank netting from* YARDE *to put around his pet mongoose. As* YARDE *and* TULLY *tussle over the netting, it falls over all the men. The tension of this situation makes* FUDGE *begin his song.*

FUDGE: Nothing on the table means ...

TULLY: Something on the collar .

YARDE: Give the man a dollar ...

YARDE/STROBERT/FUDGE/TULLY: Ah ah ah give the man a dollar.

STROBERT: Nothing on the table means ...
  something on the sleeve ...

FUDGE: Give the man a leave ...

YARDE/STROBERT/FUDGE/TULLY: Ah ah ah
  give the man a leave.

TULLY: We're Army
  working on the line ...

YARDE: We're Army
  with piece work from the mine.

STROBERT: Nothing on the table means ... [*Points to* ODOM. *Silence.*]

STROBERT: ... something on the sleeve ...

FUDGE: Give the man a leave ...

YARDE/STROBERT/FUDGE/TULLY: ah ah ah
  give the man a leave.

YARDE: Give the man a leave.

TULLY: Why we gotta sing that every damn morning?

YARDE: [*To* ODOM.] Why we gotta be in a free fire zone?

STROBERT: [*To* YARDE.] What would we do here without an artist? Fudge writes our songs. [*To* FUDGE.] You're Homer.

YARDE: Homer? The Cherry can't even swing a bat.

FUDGE: Why you gotta call me "Cherry"?

YARDE: Yer brand new, ain't ya?

FUDGE: I've been over here a month.

TULLY: One month! The dickhead's a regular Viet Nam Vet.

YARDE: Why we gotta be in a Killing Zone?

ODOM: That's our job, Yarde.

YARDE: Risking our lives ta get nothing?

ODOM: We were given an order, and I intend to see we carry it out.

YARDE: That's West Point bullshit, Cap'n.

ODOM: I'd like to remind you, Yarde, that you're talking to an officer.

YARDE: Now ... do I call you Cap'n Doctor ... or Doctor Cap'n?

ODOM: *Sir.*

YARDE: Sir. You moved us right into combat. How we gonna survive? Sir.

ODOM: We got Bravo Company.

YARDE: Bravo flies them rebel flags. You know where that fuckin' leaves you and me, Cap'n?

ODOM: I see the American Flag.

YARDE: A lotta "white" in that flag.

STROBERT: Yarde, keep it up and you'll find yourself with an Article 15.

YARDE: Ok ... ok ... don't wanna give you no extra paperwork, Lieutenant.

FUDGE: God. Our first day in a free fire zone.

YARDE: Lucky for us the Cong's ammo is worse'n ours and don't go off half the time.

TULLY: [*Feeding his pet mongoose.*] Come on, Ho Chi. Have some nice C-Ration pound cake. [*Pause.*] Sure fuckin' hot, already.

YARDE: It's always fuckin' hot.

STROBERT: That mongoose still kicking?

TULLY: Sonofabitch eats right off my fingers and looks at me real smart like my own dog at home.

STROBERT: You can't take that mongoose back to the States.

TULLY: The hell I can't, Lieutenant. [*Pause.*] Yer water's boiling, Yarde. [YARDE *goes to the camp stove and drops in the contents of a packet of C-Ration coffee.*]

YARDE: Now ... do I eat it or drink it?

FUDGE: God. First day in a free fire zone.

TULLY: In a bombed out pagoda.

STROBERT: I like it.

TULLY: Why?

STROBERT: Rather ironic, wouldn't you say, Odom?

ODOM: That occurred to me.

STROBERT: We're in a spiritual hospital.

YARDE: Shiiit. [*Pause.*] Come on, Cap'n. Let me go out there.

ODOM: We're doing a "Lazarus" here. Raising up souls to live again.

FUDGE: We're ... being God, sir?

ODOM: We're helping God.

YARDE: I don't believe in God. I belive in Baptists. [*Pause.*] You gonna let me go out?

ODOM: We're giving these men their names back.

FUDGE: Except the one we find that's unknown.

TULLY: We ain't gonna give *him* his name back.

ODOM: God will.

YARDE: Come on, Odom. I'm ready ... sir.

ODOM: You go out when I tell you to, Yarde.

FUDGE: [*To* ODOM.] You really think there are souls here, Captain?

YARDE: I've cut and shuffled everything there is inside a body. And I ain't found no soul. I ain't found nothin' lookin' anything like no fuckin'-A soul.

FUDGE: I kinda see what Cap'n Odom means.

TULLY: Get the Cherry up on the table.

YARDE: Yah. Let's find the Cherry's fuckin'-A soul.

[TULLY *and* YARDE *put* FUDGE *on the table.*]

FUDGE: Come on ... let me down ... I'm Catholic.

TULLY: A cat-licker in Buddha-City. [*Poking him.*] It's not here ... not here ...

YARDE: This is Buddhaville. His soul ain't here ... ain't here ...

STROBERT: For godsakes, Fudge. Your socks are all mildewed.

TULLY: A short dick. Hope that don't mean a short soul.

ODOM: Fudge, get going on the files.

FUDGE: How am I going to do that, sir? ... Ahhhhhhhh ... that hurts.

STROBERT: Didn't I tell you to roll your socks in your poncho? So the humidity ...

TULLY: Maybe his soul's in his socks.

FUDGE: Come on ... guys ...

TULLY: Yah ... there's his soul ... inna lot of fungus. [*Holds up* FUDGE*'s foot.*]

ODOM: Ok. That's enough rough-housing.

STROBERT: Cease the rough-housing.

YARDE: [*Lets go of* FUDGE.] Cease the bullshit rough-housing.

TULLY: [*Pushes* FUDGE *off the table.*] That, Cherry, is the fuckin' chain of command. [FUDGE *rolls off the table.*]

FUDGE: You guys zapped me. I'm dead ... I'm dead ... [FUDGE *falls against* STROBERT, *hanging on to him.*]

[STROBERT *turns abruptly from* FUDGE *and walks outside the pagoda.*]

TULLY: Now look what ya did, Fudge.

FUDGE: What'd I do?

ODOM: That's what happens when you men horse around.

FUDGE: What'd I do?

TULLY: Strobert's kid brother is missing in action.

FUDGE: You think ... me saying I was dead ...

YARDE: We don't think, Cherry. We know.

FUDGE: I was kidding.

TULLY: You sure the fuck know how ta kid around.

FUDGE: I didn't mean nothing.

TULLY: Think once in a while.

[STROBERT *comes in composed.*]

FUDGE: Lieutenant Strobert, I didn't know about your brother.

STROBERT: It's all right.

FUDGE: I'm sorry.

STROBERT: I said — forget it.

ODOM: 0800. I want everybody working.

YARDE: Send me out there, Cap'n.

ODOM: When I'm ready.

YARDE: Come on! [*Silence as* ODOM *continues adjusting microprobe.*]

YARDE: This place is a fuckin' soft target. [*Pause.*] Risking our lives to get him a pat on the head by some white general.

ODOM: What was that?

YARDE: You moved us here. Your orders. Right, Cap'n?

ODOM: I intend to accomplish the task at hand.

YARDE: Even if it kills us.

STROBERT: You are talking to an officer, Yarde.

YARDE: I know that.

STROBERT: "I know that—sir."

YARDE: I fuckin' know that. Sir.

ODOM: Back to work.

YARDE: [*To* TULLY.] He calls what we do ... work.

TULLY: [*To* YARDE.] Work is doing something.

ODOM: We are.

TULLY: Lookin' for nothin', Cap'n?

ODOM: Something is nothing.

YARDE: [*To* TULLY.] Officer's gotta say something like that.

TULLY: [*To* YARDE.] Lifer's always gonna say something like that.

YARDE: Day after day ... looking for blotto.

ODOM: It's the principal of science.

FUDGE: *Nothing* is, sir?

ODOM: Sometimes an idea comes serendipitously.

YARDE: Whatta we dippin' into on these tables?

STROBERT: *Inaction* sometimes works in medicine.

TULLY: [*To* YARDE.] The science teacher speaks.

STROBERT: Odom's trying to keep you men alive.

TULLY: With the help of dead troops.

ODOM: We're non-combative here.

TULLY: You believe that, Yarde?

ODOM: If replacements are brought in ... because this job's not getting done ... you'll all go right into action. I'm talking firefights in the Central Highlands.

YARDE: What about *you*, Cap'n?

ODOM: I'll get rear-eschelon. But you ... Fudge ... Tully ...

TULLY: Death City.

FUDGE: Even Lieutenant Strobert?

ODOM: [*Looking at* STROBERT.] Even Strobert.

STROBERT: Don't ... underestimate my abilities here on this table, Odom.

ODOM: [*Rapping his ring.*] Yarde ... the first body bags.

YARDE: Ok. I'm gone. [*He goes to door.*]

FUDGE: [*Goes to door.*] Me, too.

STROBERT: Not you, Fudge.

FUDGE: How am I gonna get any experience, sir?

STROBERT: This is our first day in a free fire zone. You're not "snow broken."

FUDGE: [*To* STROBERT.] What's that mean, Lieutenant? You're always saying I'm not "snow broken."

STROBERT: I'll tell you ... one of these days.

FUDGE: [*To* YARDE.] Come on, I wanna go out with you.

TULLY: [*To* FUDGE.] You nuts or something?

YARDE: Cherry, there ain't no place out there for a cherry. Hear?

STROBERT: The snipers will start when you get to the perimeter fence.

YARDE: I know all that. The Nam's got good elephant grass to crawl in.

FUDGE: Why's Yarde always have to go out?

YARDE: I want to, Cherry. You guys is fuckin' piss poor out there.

ODOM: Put your helmet on, Yarde.

YARDE: Ok ... ok, Cap'n. [*He puts on his helmet and exits.*]

[*Men go to the door and watch.*]

FUDGE: I don't see snipers.

TULLY: Jesus. Ya don't "see" 'em, Cherry. [*Pause.*] Think I'll just light me up one and watch the war.

ODOM: Don't stand there with a cigarette, Tully. There's V-C all around.

FUDGE: Good. [*Pause.*] If I could just talk to them.

STROBERT: I wouldn't talk to V-C, Fudge.

TULLY: [*Slowly putting out cigarette.*] Unless you want yer ass blowed off. [*Pause.*] Ten says it takes Yarde over five minutes to make it back.

STROBERT: It's bad luck to bet on a man in a free fire zone.

TULLY: I ain't betting on him. I'm betting on *time*. [*Pause.*] Who has a watch?

FUDGE: I got mine. It's under my gear.

STROBERT: We don't wear watches, Fudge. Yarde can't stand the ticking.

TULLY: He's gone now ... let it tick, Cherry. [FUDGE *gives watch to* TULLY.]

FUDGE: You do it.

TULLY: Ok, Cherry.

STROBERT: I ... think I just saw him. Yes. I saw him move.

FUDGE: You see him, Tully?

TULLY: Naw. He's too slick for me. [*Pause.*] Sixty seconds. [*Pause as they look out the door.*]

FUDGE: Look at that ... the peasants keep working the rice fields. Keep working in their gardens. Hanging up their clothes. Even with the war all around them.

STROBERT: You've got to wonder what's stronger ... their fear of hunger or their fear of death.

FUDGE: That mama-san over there could be my own mother. Hanging out the wash. Only her clothes is blowing dry, wet with blood.

TULLY: That ain't Illinois out there, Cherry. [*Pause.*] Two minutes.

FUDGE: God, sometimes I just miss listening to the television aerials creak in the wind. [*Pause.*] We have a button pear tree out in back of our house. Little pears. No bigger than walnuts. [*Pause.*] Something keeps that pear tree in my mind.

TULLY: Ain't gonna find yer fuckin' pear tree out there. Nothin' but shit out there.

STROBERT: Why the hell did you ever enlist, Tully?

TULLY: Del Monte shut down their Muscatine plant. There was nothin' else to do but join up.

ODOM: [*Looks up abruptly from microprobe.*] Sniping's started. [FUDGE *hunkers down fearfully.* TULLY *flattens himself on the ground.* STROBERT *stands hovered by door.* ODOM *calmly goes back to his microprobe.*]

[STROBERT *turns away and holds his mouth.*]

ODOM: I can pull that tooth, Strobert.

TULLY: Three minutes. [TULLY *goes to his exercise bike and pedals swiftly.*]

FUDGE: They shootin' at us?

TULLY: At Yarde, peckerhead.

FUDGE: Can't Bravo do something?

TULLY: How they gonna see snipers?

FUDGE: They're still shooting. That's good.

TULLY: Why?

FUDGE: Means they haven't got him.

TULLY: You're a dickhead. [*Pause.*] Three an a half minutes.

FUDGE: Well, doesn't it stand to reason ...

TULLY: I don't get Yarde. He struts around outside like he ain't got a worry in the world.

FUDGE: You see him yet, lieutenant?

TULLY: In here he's chickenshit.

FUDGE: You can't see him, sir?

STROBERT: Not yet.

TULLY: Is Yarde that combat smart or just fuckin' lucky?

ODOM: [*Looks up from microprobe.*] Yarde is absolutely uncanny in survival skills. I've never seen the likes of him.

TULLY: Four minutes.

FUDGE: Skills like what, sir?

ODOM: He knows that when the wind starts up, it will make the mortar rounds shift ... and he knows how many feet those rounds shift. He can tell what tree or bush can absorb grenade fragments that otherwise would explode in his stomach. He knows how much elephant grass can deflect a speeding bullet enough to send it harmlessly through his OD shirt.

STROBERT: The sniping's stopped. [*Pause.*] Here comes Yarde.

ODOM: [*To* TULLY.] Under five minutes, Tully! [TULLY *tosses watch to* FUDGE. FUDGE *stuffs watch in his pocket.*]

[YARDE *enters.*]

[TULLY *gets off his bike. Everybody stands.*]

YARDE: [*Carrying bags.*] First bag ... second bag ... third bag ...

FUDGE: What was it like out there?

YARDE: Man, I was crawling in tall grass. Saw me a couple of bamboo snakes. Couldn't kill 'em 'cause I'd give my position away. So I side-assed along real quiet 'n real tight like I was a fuckin' snake myself. And damn if I didn't crawl over a dead bat. Then I gets to the perimeter fence 'n seen me the body bags. I jumped up ta grab 'em and the sniping started. I had to creep out of there fast. Shiit ... it's like crawling through a live tunnel. It's like yer ceiling is alive ... like what the dead must hear all the time ... pop ... crack ...

ODOM: On the table, Yarde.

YARDE: Is that all you can say, Cap'n?

FUDGE: That was great, Yarde.

YARDE: I was talking to Odom.

ODOM: If you were as efficient in here as you are out there ...

YARDE: I'm free out there, Cap'n. Ain't nobody out there kicking my ass but the Cong. And he's color blind.

ODOM: You do the job in here, believe me, Yarde, you won't get flak. I don't care who you are.

YARDE: He don't care *who* I am.

ODOM: Just do the job.

YARDE: That's just it. What's the job? Sir. Nothing?

ODOM: Yarde, you're pushing me.

YARDE: I wouldn't wanna go'n do that ... Cap'n.

FUDGE: Yarde ... will you zip that bag for a minute?

TULLY: Yah. Nothin' stinks.

YARDE: Whattaya expect? It's one hundred percent pure U.S. Government inspected nothing.

FUDGE: A guy needs a gas mask for this.

TULLY: Least we get extra combat pay ta stink.

ODOM: Let's have the remains on the table.

YARDE: The Cherry was supposed to learn something useful in the Army. What's he gonna learn trying to draw a blank?

FUDGE: You said ... sir ... one day this week we'd do something medical.

TULLY: Yah.

YARDE: Ain't that what he said?

STROBERT: [*To* ODOM.] Why not today?

YARDE: You said, Cap'n, this sonofabitch week.

ODOM: Clean up your language.

YARDE: This ain't a livin' room, Doctor.

TULLY: It's *The Nam*..

ODOM: It's a medical detachment. We're a unit of older men — except for Fudge. We set an example for our new recruit ... and we show respect to each other and to these remains. Understand?

FUDGE: I don't want any examples set for me, sir.

TULLY: Cap'n, don't get sidetracked. How 'bout givin' us today?

STROBERT: Bravo Company says there're some sick friendlies.

TULLY: We got plenty of our own ta patch up.

YARDE: [*To* TULLY.] You'd do that to our side?

FUDGE: When Bravo goes on patrol, they could bring us back one Vietnamese.

STROBERT: We can handle more than that.

FUDGE: Just once I'd like to act like an Army Medic.

TULLY: A little carrot, Doc? Even Del Monte gave us that fuckin' much.

STROBERT: I know just the thing this situation calls for. A little incentive.

TULLY: [*To* YARDE.] That's what I fuckin' said.

STROBERT: [*To* ODOM.] I'm good with jungle rot. I treated that in Dong Tam before I was sent here.

YARDE: Just before I re-upped, I used to give blood transfusions.

FUDGE: I never even knew I had a pulse before ... till I made medic.

TULLY: I once cut off the leg of a blanket ass.

STROBERT: I don't want to hear you call Indians that.

TULLY: Everybody does, Lieutenant.

STROBERT: I said … I won't have it.

TULLY: In Basic, we always let 'em be the Chinks.

STROBERT: Tully, you're not talking like a good medic.

FUDGE: [*To* STROBERT.] Sir, give him some more practice, then. [*To* ODOM.] We're only asking for a few *real* hours. So I have something to write my folks.

YARDE: I promise to clean up my fuckin' language. If I can be a honest ta shit medic. [*Pause.*]

ODOM: Ok. This afternoon. [*The men cheer.*]

YARDE: Who tells Bravo?

ODOM: I'll tell Bravo. [*Pause.*] Bring the first body bag, Yarde. [YARDE *brings the bag.*]

YARDE: This nigger don't half-step. Him moves. [FUDGE *laughs at* YARDE.]

ODOM: Don't say "nigger." You know I don't like it.

YARDE: This here brillo-pad … him moves.

ODOM: Fudge, don't laugh at him.

FUDGE: I can't help it … sir.

YARDE: This here chocolate rabbit … him moves.

ODOM: Knock it off, Yarde.

YARDE: Don't like chocolate, Cap'n?

ODOM: This is the Army. Not Halstead Street in Chicago.

YARDE: I ain't from Halstead Street, Cap'n. That's too white for me. I'm from Independence Avenue.

STROBERT: Yarde — get the bag on the table.

YARDE: I don't live where it's all white.

ODOM: Do the job, Yarde.

YARDE: Yes, sir, Oreo, sir. [*Pause. To* TULLY.] Oreo Cookie. Black on the outside. White on the inside.

ODOM: What did you call me?

YARDE: I called you sir, sir.

STROBERT: Open the body bag, Yarde.

YARDE: [*Holds bag over table.*] Gentlemen, I give you A-mur-a-ca's finest.

STROBERT: Watch how you dump that. I don't want all splattered up. [*Silent pause.*]

TULLY: You know what … it's really dead in here.

FUDGE: Tully, don't the smell ever get to you?

TULLY: Thanks to Del Monte, I smell down anything. [*Holds up tooth.*] Your first patient today, Dr. Odom, and he's dead.

ODOM: Gum tissue connected?

TULLY: I'm taking it off. [*Pause.*] [*To tissue.*] I'm gonna cut but it ain't gonna hurt.

ODOM: Put it on a slide.

TULLY: Right. [*Cuts off tissue and hands tooth to YARDE.*]

YARDE: [*Looks at tooth under magnifying device.*] A left molar, Fudge. Bridge work. Anybody missing that had work done onna left molar?

FUDGE: [*Looking through cards.*] I'm looking … I'm looking …

STROBERT: [*To TULLY.*] You can give me that slide now. So I can stain it. [TULLY *gives* STROBERT *the slide.*]

FUDGE: Here's somebody had a filling on a molar. [TULLY *takes the record from* FUDGE.]

TULLY: [*Reading record.*] Naw. Lower front tooth. [*Gives record back to* FUDGE.]

ODOM: [*To* STROBERT.] A slide ready?

STROBERT: Ready. [*Hands slide to* ODOM.]

YARDE: This tooth's got some gold in it, too.

FUDGE: Here's somebody with a lot of work. [*Hands record to* TULLY.]

ODOM: You have a second slide on this?

STROBERT: Yes. I'll put it through the machine.

TULLY: [*Looking at record.*] Wisdom teeth, Cherry. That ain't molars.

FUDGE: Ok ... ok ... here's somebody. This looks good. Worked on at Soc Trang.

TULLY: Let me see. [*Takes record from* FUDGE.] Yah. A Private E-1. Williams. Milo.

STROBERT: Got his X-ray?

FUDGE: Attached to his record. [*Hands X-ray to* STROBERT.]

STROBERT: [*Looks at record.*] A fractured root.

FUDGE: [*Checks record.*] Right.

ODOM: Separated from the alveolus of the skull?

YARDE: Separated from everything.

ODOM: Bite registration?

FUDGE: Right here. [*Hands bite registration to* STROBERT.]

STROBERT: Photo of deceased?

FUDGE: Right here. [*Hands photo to* STROBERT.]

STROBERT: [*After a pause.*] There it is. Williams. Milo. 21.

YARDE: What kinda name's Milo?

FUDGE: [*Looking at record.*] Cicero, Illinois. That's not far from where I live in Earlville.

STROBERT: [*Looking at photo.*] He was eating a C-Ration candy bar when he got it. [YARDE *hands tooth to* ODOM.]

YARDE: Just a tooth. And C-Ration chocolate. I hope when I get it, man, I got me a mouth full of local el primo.

FUDGE: Wish we didn't find him.

TULLY: We find everybody.

FUDGE: Then ... it would be somebody from Illinios.

YARDE: If we don't find him, we don't know that.

TULLY: I'm going for Iowa.

YARDE: You find Iowa, and you ain't gonna know it's Iowa.

TULLY: I'm gonna know it's Iowa.

FUDGE: Yah?

TULLY: Iowa's God's country.

FUDGE: Illinois is God's country. Only we don't have to come out and say it 'cause everybody knows.

YARDE: Jesus. One fuckin' tooth.

TULLY: Little Milo's going home ... inna sandwich bag.

ODOM: Damn!

YARDE: What'sa matter, Cap'n? Ain't gonna make Major?

ODOM: I'll make Major, Yarde. [*Pause.*] Next remains.

TULLY: Legs and hands.

[STROBERT — *holding his jaw nervously* — *accidentally knocks over a vial of blood on the table.*]

TULLY: [*About spilled blood.*] Hey ... hey! Five bucks. Who's on? Who's on!

YARDE: I'm in.

FUDGE: Me, too.

ODOM: Now what are they betting on?

STROBERT: Which drop of blood will run off the table first.

[TULLY, YARDE, *and* FUDGE *are cheering.*]

ODOM: We don't have time to waste on gambling.

STROBERT: It lets off steam.

YARDE: Motherfucker! You won again.

FUDGE: God, Tully, you win at everything.

TULLY: Pay up! Pay up!

YARDE: Later, man.

TULLY: Now.

YARDE: Later. Dig me?

FUDGE: I don't have five. Can I give you my C-peaches?

YARDE: He don't pay either. Dig me?

FUDGE: Here. [*Hands peaches to* TULLY.] I don't like 'em all that much.

YARDE: [*To* FUDGE.] Why the fuck you go'n do that?

FUDGE: He won ... didn't he?

YARDE: Cherry ... from now on ... do what I fuckin' tell ya ta do. That gig was mammyfuckin' phony.

TULLY: "Blood racing" ain't phony.

YARDE: Who says?

STROBERT: Tully, what happened to that letter you wrote to the International Olympic Committee?

FUDGE: You really wrote 'em, Tully?

TULLY: I ain't heard from 'em yet. But I will.

YARDE: The dickhead wants "blood-running" included in Olympic competition.

TULLY: Why not?

STROBERT: I'd sure like to see their answer.

ODOM: Where's that report for calculating incomplete femur?

STROBERT: You mean the one by the French doctor? In Saigon?

ODOM: That one.

FUDGE: I ... tossed it somewhere, sir. [*He starts looking.*]

ODOM: Why?

FUDGE: It was written in French.

ODOM: French is worthless?

YARDE: If you don't read it, Cap'n.

ODOM: I read it. [*Silent pause.*]

FUDGE: I ... knew it was somewhere over here. [*He gets report.*]

ODOM: My mother made me speak French around the house.

YARDE: What for?

ODOM: It gave me a ... certain veneer.

STROBERT: [*To* YARDE.] Class.

ODOM: [*Reading report.*] "If a fragment of femur with an estimated age of 21 ... "

TULLY: He don't look a day over twenty.

ODOM: " ... measures 28.34 and 7.51 respectively, the pertinent equation is ... "

YARDE: Words is whores. Fucked over by any cat who pays.

STROBERT: God, Yarde, sometimes you talk like a genius.

YARDE: 'Specially French words. [*Pause.*] Where'd you go to school in Chicago, Cap'n?

ODOM: Latin Grammar School.

YARDE: [*To* TULLY.] I know that phony motherfucker. The only nigger ... only black *boy* who is went to a private high school.

ODOM: My mother taught there.

FUDGE: Where?

ODOM: The Latin Grammar School.

FUDGE: You studied Latin all the time, sir?

STROBERT: It's a prep school, Fudge.

FUDGE: [*To* YARDE.] I guess they had plenty of Latin music there.

YARDE: Don't study that crap and not have their boogie.

[YARDE *picks up the large jar of bones and rattles it like a maracas. He does a modified cha-cha.*]

YARDE: [*Shaking maracas and singing.*] Cha cha cha, cha cha mule, he has went to the Latin School, and drink him lava, that Latins call beer, and got a dose ... [*He claps his hands.*] of ven ... eer. Cha cha cha, cha cha mule, he has went to the Latin School, and saw some ...

YARDE: ... bull.

TULLY: ... and ate some beans.

FUDGE: Beans in Latin, ain't what they seems.

[YARDE, FUDGE, *and* TULLY *are now all dancing.*]

[TULLY *picks up mongoose cage and dances with Ho Chi.*]

YARDE: Naw, naw, naw, lava and beer, he got a dose ... [*Men all clap their hands.*]

TULLY/FUDGE/YARDE: ... of ven ... eer. Cha cha cha ...

[*As* TULLY *and* FUDGE *are dancing around* YARDE, YARDE *abruptly takes them each by the arm and smothers their voices into his chest. YARDE listens.*]

YARDE: [*He screams.*] Incoming!

[YARDE *pushes* TULLY *and* FUDGE *behind the partial brick wall.* TULLY *runs out briefly to get the mongoose and bring him back behind the wall.* STROBERT *throws himself on top of* FUDGE *behind the wall.* ODOM *protectively puts remains under him and falls to the floor by his desk.*]

[*After a pause there is quiet.*]

ODOM: [*Slowly gets up.*] Anybody hurt? [ODOM *is still holding his chest protectively where he shields remains.* TULLY *holds mongoose protectively.*]

YARDE: Look where you brought us. *Sir.* Right into the fuckin' front lines.

TULLY: Ho Chi's all right.

YARDE: Who the hell cares about the damn mongoose?

ODOM: You all right, Strobert? [*Pause.*] Where's Fudge?

TULLY: Under Strobert. [ODOM *looks at* STROBERT. TULLY *and* YARDE *turn over* STROBERT.]

FUDGE: What happened?

YARDE: Got yer first fuckin' incoming in the Killing Zone, Cherry.

STROBERT: You all right, Fudge?

FUDGE: What happened?

ODOM: Incoming.

YARDE: We ain't gonna last here a week.

TULLY: Bravo Company ain't even give us a fuckin' warning. [TULLY *goes to his bike and pedals furiously.*]

ODOM: The V-C caught them off guard. That's all. [*Pause. Listens. He hears firing.*] There. Outgoing.

YARDE: Yah. An hour after incoming.

FUDGE: I don't feel like I'm hit.

ODOM: You're ok.

YARDE: Sons-of-bitches! If anything happens to me ... and I end up hash, don't you guys do no work up on me! Dig?

ODOM: [*Looking over* STROBERT *but still with one hand holding tissue next to his chest.*] Far as I can see, you took a shard the size of a penny in your right ear. Just a nip of blood. A band-aid's all you need.

[FUDGE *puts a band-aid on* STROBERT's *ear.*]

ODOM: That's worth a Purple Heart.

YARDE: A what!?

FUDGE: All right!

STROBERT: Look, forget it.

YARDE: A fuckin' what?

STROBERT: It's not a big deal. Drop it, ok? As long as Fudge is all right.

FUDGE: You guys treat me like I'm some kind of stupid nerd.

TULLY: Well. [*Pause. Listens. Firing stops.*] Bravo's done.

YARDE: I personally build a fuckin' shelter. Out of my own pocket. Cost me good grass to pry loose sandbags from supply. I go out there in the free fire zone. And *he* gets decorated.

TULLY: What's those bricks supposed ta do, Yarde?

YARDE: I see you got yer ass behind them quick enough.

TULLY: Why don't you jist dig a tunnel?

YARDE: That's what the V-C do. I'm no Commie, man. [*Pause.*] We ain't gonna last fer shit here. We ain't gonna last to even find nothing.

ODOM: It's just the first day.

YARDE: I know that. How we gonna make it to tomorrow?

ODOM: I follow the standard five-paragraph field order ... which addresses situation, mission, and support we can expect.

YARDE: This ain't the Point, Cap'n.

STROBERT: We got perimeter wire around us.

YARDE: Some wire's gonna protect us? [*Pause.*] Tully, why the fuck you on that bike? We just got incoming. We just about got wasted.

TULLY: I'm gonna keep moving. [*Pause.*]   I see you guys sleep at night ... 'n you all look fuckin' zapped. Jesus, sometimes even the living look friggin' dead.

FUDGE: Why they shootin' at us? We're just medics.

YARDE: You walk down a street in Chicago, Cherry, 'n you're wearing black in a street that wears red ... yer gonna get yer ass kicked.

[ODOM *slowly takes his hands down from his chest. Some fleshy matter sticks to his uniform.*]

TULLY: Yer a mess, Cap'n.

ODOM: Cotton, Tully. [TULLY *gets off the bike and brings cotton to* ODOM. TULLY, ODOM, *and* STROBERT *dab carefully at* ODOM's *uniform.*]

[FUDGE *now tries to help* ODOM. *He impulsively and quickly tries brushing at* ODOM's *uniform.*]

[FUDGE *flicks matter out the door.*]

STROBERT: [*To* FUDGE.] You know what you just did? You just pitched some body out the door.

FUDGE: I ... wasn't thinking ...

STROBERT: Odom risked his life for that ... and you just flicked it out the door.

FUDGE: God, I'm sorry ...

ODOM: [*Dabbing at his chest.*] I have enough of him still here.

FUDGE: I'm sorry, sir.

ODOM: No harm done. It's all right, Fudge. [*Pause.*] Let's get back to work.

[YARDE *empties another bag of matter on the table.*]

[STROBERT *turns away holding his jaw.*]

STROBERT: Damnit to hell!

ODOM: I wish you'd let me take that tooth out.

TULLY: He won't even let me cut his hair ... Doc.

STROBERT: You ... stay away from my hair.

YARDE: Jesus, don't you ever cut yer fingernails, Lieutenant?

STROBERT: I don't have to. I wear gloves.

YARDE: Yer nails is pokin' through the gloves.

STROBERT: Lay off.

YARDE: Yer gettin' crap all underneath 'em.

STROBERT: I scrub up afterwards. More than some people I know. [STROBERT *puts on new gloves*.]

TULLY: Afraid something of you will end up on this table, L.T.?

YARDE: Shiiit. Roaches on the table again. [YARDE *reaches for a can of bug spray, but* STROBERT *angrily knocks the can out of his hand*.]

YARDE: What the ...

STROBERT: Don't ... kill ... with that stuff. You know I hate it.

ODOM: The palm print ... if you have time.

YARDE: [*To* STROBERT.] How am I gonna zap 'em?

STROBERT: There are some things in Nam we aren't going to kill with high power artillery.

YARDE: Bug spray is high power artillery?

STROBERT: Step on them! [*He brushes bugs to the floor*.]

[STROBERT *begins stepping on the bugs*.]

FUDGE: [*Steps on a bug*.] I kinda know what Strobert means. It's nice for once to zap something real simple.

YARDE: [*Steps on a bug*.] It's creepy.

ODOM: Killing roaches won't get us our objective.

STROBERT: Ok ... ok ... [STROBERT *delivers prints to* ODOM.]

FUDGE: [*Looking at some bugs*.] Look at that. Three of 'em is just stampeded themselves.

TULLY: Yah? I take the one in the middle. "Five" says he gets to the wall first.

FUDGE: I'm on. For the one on the right.

YARDE: The left one!

TULLY: Come on ... you ... come on you ... weird mother!

[YARDE, TULLY, *and* FUDGE *cheer. After a pause*:]

YARDE: Akkkkk!

FUDGE: How do you do it, Tully? How do you win all the time?

YARDE: I'd hate ta try'n fuckin' cheat on him with his wife.

STROBERT: Tully, you ought to go to college with smarts like that.

TULLY: Players ain't readers.

STROBERT: Don't you ever feel sorry for the people you beat?

TULLY: I let some guy slide once fer what he owed me. 'Cause his wife was sick. But he jist turned around 'n lost him my fuckin' money with somebody else.

YARDE: [*To* TULLY.] That's another thing. The way you throw dice. Next time I play with you, yer gonna blow them outta yer mouth. Dig?

ODOM: And I'm putting an end to these all night poker games. You men start work in the morning all hung over.

FUDGE: [To TULLY.] Why is it you never lose at poker?

YARDE: I find out yer dealing from the bottom, dealing seconds, using mirrors, marking cards ... I'll crack yer skull so it looks like the stuff we're working on.

TULLY: Yarde, you got so many tics — what we gamblers call "tells"... you'll never last fer shit in poker. [*Pause.*] You guys owe me five for last night's game. Ten from two days ago. And five from now.

YARDE: [YARDE *hands the bill to* TULLY.] A forty. My twenty plus his twenty.

TULLY: This is forty piasters.

YARDE: That's right.

TULLY: You peckerheads owe me forty thousand piasters.

FUDGE: You said forty.

TULLY: Serious gamblers always leave off the zeros. A five is five hundred. A ten is one thousand. A big dime is ten thousand.

ODOM: You men are dealing yourselves right into swamp patrol.

STROBERT: Think of it like this, Odom. Playing poker is good military training. Especially the bad games. You can win for months, but if you lose one day and go nuts and toss everything away ... you're dead.

TULLY: All right!

STROBERT: War is like freeze-out no limit poker. Both are crazy wild experiments in survival. At double time. No second chances. Any wrong move can be fatal. And — in the beginning — luck is a big part of both games and professionals know that. And it's only the amateurs who are dumb enough to enjoy themselves. [*Pause.*] You can count me in tonight, Tully. [*He hands* TULLY *a Q-Tip.*]

TULLY: What's this?

STROBERT: A chip.

TULLY: I don't take that shit.

STROBERT: The man who thought up poker was great. But the guy who invented chips was a genius. I'm going to freeze up tossing you a hundred dollars, Tully. But it doesn't hurt at all to hand you this. [*Pause.*] Take two.

ODOM: My God! [ODOM *stands and they all look at him.*] [*Holding up a slide.*] Flat cross sections. Continuous medulla. Fluctuations in diameter.

[*Pause as the men stare at* ODOM.]

FUDGE: So, what are you tellin' us?

ODOM: Pubic hair. [*Pause.*] Female.

TULLY: Big deal. Chink pussy hair.

ODOM: It's not ... Oriental.

FUDGE: How do you know, sir?

ODOM: Oriental hair has circular cross sections. Thick cuticles.

FUDGE: And that doesn't?

ODOM: No.

TULLY: So? [*Pause.*] Whattaya trying to tell us, Doc?

ODOM: This is ... pubic hair ... from a white woman. As yet ... unidentified. [*Silence as they stare at* ODOM.]

STROBERT: God, I love it. What if the unknown soldier is a

woman?

TULLY: Like hell. [STROBERT *chuckles*.] It ain't funny, L.T.

ODOM: What is the "chain of possession" of the remains?

FUDGE: [*Looking at record*.] Just a medic from Abel Company. And us, sir.

ODOM: Look through every profile printout, Fudge. A nurse missing?

TULLY: Fudge is blushing.

YARDE: Ain't you seen no nude woman before?

ODOM: Fudge, I asked you to go through the printouts.

FUDGE: I am ... I am ... sir.

ODOM: When was the last "missing" list called in?

FUDGE: 0500 this morning, sir.

TULLY: Fuckin' woke up Ho Chi.

ODOM: [*To* FUDGE.] You sure you entered the new data?

FUDGE: Sure I'm sure, sir.

YARDE: Show me.

FUDGE: See ... Ridleman, Sam ... Rucker, John ... Streeter, Timmy ... Westcott ...

YARDE: Wait. Wait a fuckin'-A minute. [*Pause*.] Streeter, Timmy?

FUDGE: Yah.

YARDE: It's a woman. Checked *F*. Female.

FUDGE: Timmy Streeter's a girl?

YARDE: You filed it under men, Cherry. [*To* ODOM.] And she's a doc, Doc.

ODOM: Ok. Let's check her out.

STROBERT: Right.

ODOM: Make some slides of the surrounding genital tissue. And put the stomach particles through the machine. [STROBERT, TULLY, YARDE *prepare slides*.] Fudge, check her records for ABO blood.

FUDGE: God. A woman.

YARDE: Hey. The Cherry's still shook up.

TULLY: [*Holds up slide.*] This could be Joey Heatherton.

YARDE: Man, if she is, she ain't got no boobs.

TULLY: Yah. It ain't Joey Heatherton.

FUDGE: Timmy Streeter?

TULLY: It's Star Fingerhunt. I saw her at this special show. Put on by our Chink allies. They flew her over from the states.

FUDGE: Wow!

ODOM: I'm waiting for the first slide, Tully.

TULLY: She was wearing a mini skirt.

YARDE: Yah?

TULLY: And a tiny little pink blouse.

FUDGE: God!

TULLY: We hadn't seen nothin' but slant eyes fer six months. There she was ... slowly taking off her earrings ... [*He takes a tweezer and picks off matter to put on the slide.*] ... her scarf ... [*Picks off the matter for the slide.*] ... first one side of her blouse ... then the other ... [*Picks off matter for slide.*]

YARDE: Yah?

ODOM: Damn it, I'm waiting, Tully.

TULLY: And there we was, sir. Lookin' at 'em. Two beautiful melons. I'm talkin' fuckin' Iowa melons. [TULLY *hands first slide to* ODOM *who takes it excitedly to examine it.*]

YARDE: Yah?

TULLY: I'm talkin' Muscatine home grown melons.

YARDE: Will you get the fuck on with it?

STROBERT: Yarde. Pay attention. We've got remains in this machine.

TULLY: So she slips her hands down to the belt of her skirt ...

YARDE: Yah?

TULLY: She takes the belt off. [*Picks matter off for slide.*] Throws it out to us.

STROBERT: Tully, watch it. I don't want to have to redo those slides.

TULLY: Then ... steps out of her skirt real dainty. [*Takes off more matter for slide.*] She's in black lace panties. [*Hands second slide to* ODOM.]

FUDGE: God!

TULLY: We could see her muff through the pants.

YARDE: Yah?

TULLY: I'm talking good Iowa muff. Not hairless Chink pussy.

YARDE: Ok ... ok ...

TULLY: I'm talking Muscatine home grown muffs.

YARDE: Will you get the fuck on with it?

TULLY: [*Hovers tweezers over slide.*] So she stands there. And we're screaming: Star ... Star ... take it off. Take it *all* off. There must have been five thousand of us sitting out in the hills. Just back from the river. Mud all over us. Thousands of us yelling ... finish it ... finish it ... please ... [*He stops. He suddenly sniffs, holding back emotion.*] She wouldn't go no more. Stopped at her pants. [*He tosses the tweezer on the table.*] We was all fuckin' crying by now. Tears was rolling down our cheeks ... right over the delta mud. Thousands of us ... crying ... begging ... bawling like little babies. I ain't never seen anything so pitiful. [*He wipes his eyes on his sleeve.*] Shit. I ain't even got over it yet. We was in mourning for weeks. This fuckin' gyp war. [TULLY *hands slide to* ODOM.]

ODOM: [*Takes slide and holds it out to* STROBERT.] Stain this one, Strobert.

STROBERT: [*Takes slide.*] Right.

YARDE: The only decent war was that one Strobert told us about.

STROBERT: Which one was that?

YARDE: The one fought over good cunt.

STROBERT: You mean the Trojan War?

TULLY: Maybe she wasn't even clean, either.

YARDE: She was clean. If all them countries was fightin' over her.

TULLY: You some kinds expert on women, Yarde?

YARDE: I walk down Tu Do Street. In Saigon. All the boom-te-boom girls is after me.

TULLY: Why?

YARDE: 'Cause of Buddha.

TULLY: How's that?

YARDE: Buddha's black.

TULLY: Yer crazy.

YARDE: Here. take a look for yourself. [*Takes Buddha image from wall.*] He's got thick lips and kinky hair.

FUDGE: Yah. He does ... sorta.

YARDE: What did I tell you?

TULLY: So who the hell cares what color Buddha is?

YARDE: They care. The Chinks. You wanna get it on with somebody that looks like yer god.

ODOM: [*Rapping his ring on the table.*] Yarde, get me a paraffin-lined bottle.

FUDGE: You ever think of women, Lieutenant Strobert?

ODOM: [*Rapping his ring.*] Yarde! The paraffin-lined bottle.

YARDE: There he goes again ... rapping that West Point ring at me. [YARDE *hands the bottle to* ODOM.]

FUDGE: What about your wife? Don't you think about her, Lieutenant?

STROBERT: Sure I do.

FUDGE: So? Whattaya think about?

STROBERT: I ... grind my teeth in my sleep.

TULLY: We can hear you on the other side of the pagoda.

STROBERT: And ... she always puts her finger ...

TULLY: Yah ...

STROBERT: She always puts her finger ... gently to my lips. To stop me.

TULLY: That's it, L. T.?

STROBERT: I miss ... feeling her finger on my lips. In the darkness.

TULLY: [*Shaking his head over* STROBERT.] Jesus!

FUDGE: I understand that.

YARDE: What about you, Cap'n Odom?

ODOM: [*Holds out his hand without looking up from his microprobe.*] The infrared.

[STROBERT *hands a bottle to* ODOM *and then* STROBERT *goes back to the table.*]

YARDE: Cap'n?

ODOM: Not now, Yarde.

FUDGE: Don't you think about yer wife, Captain?

ODOM: I do. [*He is arranging material under his microprobe.*]

YARDE: So? Whattaya think?

FUDGE: You can tell us, sir.

YARDE: [*To* TULLY *and* FUDGE.] Maybe he don't think nothing. Maybe he don't feel nothing.

FUDGE: You can tell us, sir.

YARDE: I'll even cover my fuckin' ears so you can tell Fudge.

ODOM: All the positions of love-making ...

YARDE: Yah?

ODOM: ... simulate the act of murder.

TULLY: What the fuck's that mean?

YARDE: You into Voodoo, Cap'n?

ODOM: [*Looking up.*] It's ... Timmy Streeter.

STROBERT: Damn. Damn. [*He takes a drink from his beer bottle.*]

TULLY: Don't bust a gut, L. T.

STROBERT: A woman could have meant something.

TULLY: What?

STROBERT: I tell you, it would have meant something.

TULLY: I'm saying ... what?

STROBERT: A woman is not a warrior.

YARDE: The hell she ain't, Lieutenant.

TULLY: My old lady's beat up on me enough.

ODOM: This is an honor no matter who gets it.

STROBERT: Honor? Come on, Odom. You're too smart for that. The Unknown Soldier glorifies war.

ODOM: I don't believe that. It's the Army's way to glorify ... everyman.

FUDGE: I kinda know what Cap'n Odom means. That flame going all the time ... it's kinda ... music. Music that belongs to everybody.

STROBERT: You believe that, Fudge, and you'll burn for them.

ODOM: We've been over this before.

STROBERT: Macho crap.

ODOM: What the hell do you want to find on this table, Strobert?

STROBERT: You tell me, Odom.

ODOM: Don't you belittle these remains.

STROBERT: The Unknown Soldier belittles these remains ... by saying death in battle is worthwhile.

TULLY: Yah. Ain't it fuckin' wonderful ta die for your country? What about gettin' honored for *livin'* for yer country?

STROBERT: [*Picks up slide of Timmy Streeter.*] Timmy Streeter is the real casualty of war. Because we didn't expect her to be. That's what war is, Odom. Casualties you don't expect. Casualties that aren't supposed to happen. Women ... children ... brothers.

TULLY: Yah. that's what our "nothing" should be. Somebody you don't expect.

YARDE: [*Drums on the table and sings.*] Nothin' on the table ... mean ... something on the collar. Ahh ah ahhh ...

TULLY: Got a Kool on you, Yarde?

FUDGE: I got a "Rubby Queen."

TULLY: Yer gonna fuckin' ruin yer body smoking Chink cigarettes.

YARDE: Ain't a nigger ... black *boy* ... in the Nam ... outside of Doctor-Cap'n who don't have hisself Kools. [YARDE *gives a Kool to* TULLY.]

[*Field radio comes on.*]

RADIO: Eagle One to Eagle Two ... Eagle One to Eagle Two ... do you read me? Do you read me? Over?

[ODOM *picks up radio.*]

ODOM: [*Into radio.*] Eagle Two to Eagle One ... Eagle Two to Eagle One. Loud and clear. Over.

[*Muffled sounds as* ODOM *listens. Then* ODOM *puts the radio down abruptly and stands.*]

[*Points in back of the pagoda.*] Bravo ... has sighted something moving out in back of us.

[*Tenseness as the men freeze.*]

[STROBERT *holds out his hand to the men to signal he will handle it. Tully picks up the mongoose cage protectively.* STROBERT *exits with an M-16.*]

[FUDGE, TULLY, *and* YARDE *hunker down by the wall taking hold of their guns.*]

[ODOM *calmly reaches down for his gun by his desk, attaches a bayonet to his gun, and puts the gun on top of his desk as he continues to work.*]

FUDGE: [*Whispers.*] Who do you think it is?

TULLY: [*Harsh whisper.*] Three guesses, Cherry.

FUDGE: V-C?

YARDE: Ain't yer mama, Cherry.

TULLY: You wanna talk ta V-C, Fudge. Go on out there 'n have a nice fuckin' chat with 'em.

FUDGE: I don't wanna talk to no V-C anymore.

ODOM: [*Harsh whisper.*] Keep it quiet in here.

[*After a few seconds, a shot is heard.* STROBERT *returns.*]

STROBERT: I zapped him.

ODOM: V-C?

STROBERT: How do I know?

ODOM: Not a civilian, Strobert?

STROBERT: I didn't have time to ask for any papers.

ODOM: Tully, bring him around front. We've got to bury him. The Geneva Code. [ODOM *goes back to looking in his microprobe.*]

TULLY: Fuck the Geneva Code, Cap'n.

YARDE: I'll go. No big fuckin' deal. [YARDE *exits.*]

FUDGE: [*To* STROBERT.] Weren't you scared, Lieutenant?

STROBERT: Sure. A soldier has to be. It keeps him alert. So he won't do stupid things.

FUDGE: Then I'm sure a good soldier. Look at me ... my pick hand's shaking. I thought we were goners.

STROBERT: You were mortared the night you joined our unit. You came to us crawling on your hands and knees.

FUDGE: I know ... but now it's like they're getting closer 'n closer.

TULLY: Everybody's gettin' the shit kicked out of 'em. Charley's saving us fer last 'cause we're just a bunch of medics and we're cut off.

ODOM: [*Holds up X-ray.*] Strobert, did you print this?

STROBERT: [*Goes to* ODOM.] That's my writing.

ODOM: You labeled it "spleen."

STROBERT: It's a spleen.

ODOM: Don't tell me what remains are. It gives me "bias."

STROBERT: We're working on bodies. You know that.

ODOM: I want to handle remains as an unknown.

STROBERT: How the hell can you do that?

ODOM: Science: substituting fact for appearance.

STROBERT: Whose science is that, Odom? [*Pause.*]

[STROBERT *grabs some cards from* FUDGE, *shuffles them, and starts laying them out on the table.*]

STROBERT: A Master Sergeant with one eye. Appearance. Pal him up with a Private with one lung. Appearance. For a whole body. Fact. We'll start a new standard of very simple and happy socialism, too.

FUDGE: Hey ... I had those alphabetized.

STROBERT: Half of them wrong. "V" comes before "W", Fudge. Do it again. Correctly. [STROBERT *walks away from the cards on the table as* FUDGE *collects the cards and puts them back in order. After* FUDGE *collects the cards, he stares at the back of the area.*]

FUDGE: How do you think he got right up on us?

ODOM: We've got to tighten security. [YARDE *comes in.*]

YARDE: Jesus! It's a cow. [STROBERT *laughs.*]

ODOM: [*Looks up from work.*] You sure?

YARDE: Scrawny ... filthy ... runt of a cow. [ODOM *exits still looking at the X-ray.*]

TULLY: Why the fuck you shoot a defenseless dumb animal?

STROBERT: I didn't have time to find out what it was.

TULLY: Don't you have fuckin' eyes? [ODOM *comes in slapping the X-ray at his side.*]

ODOM: Dead cow, all right.

RADIO: Eagle One to Eagle Two. Eagle One to Eagle Two. Do you read me? Over.

ODOM: That's Bravo. Checking to see what happened. Tully, drag the body in the brush. Yarde, let's have the heavy stuff. [TULLY *exits carrying an Army blanket.* ODOM *goes to radio.*]

ODOM: [*Into radio.*] Eagle Two to Eagle One. Eagle Two to Eagle One. Read you loud and clear. All is clear. Splinter is gone. Over. [*Pause. To men.*] Now, back to work. [YARDE *goes to the side of the room and looks at a very large heavy bag. But there's another smaller bag on top.*]

ODOM: [*To* YARDE.] What's that?

YARDE: A mine job. [*Reads a tag on the bag.*] He got it by a Claymore. Electricity in the air set off the blasting cap.

FUDGE: Another one who didn't get it by the V-C.

YARDE: What difference does it make?

STROBERT: [*Being ironic.*] [*Looking at remains.*] Beheaded ... amputated ... disemboweled. I ask you, is it moral anymore to be in one piece?

YARDE: [*As he sorts through body parts.*] Will ya look at that. Blown ta bits ... and here's a picture of his girl ... and it ain't even torn or bent.

[STROBERT *takes out a rotor blade and puts it on the table.* STROBERT *begins to work exclusively on the rotor blade.*]

FUDGE: Let me see her. [FUDGE *goes to* YARDE.]

YARDE: She ain't bad. Wanna see, Lieutenant?

[STROBERT *is so intent on his work on the rotor blade he ignores* YARDE.]

[TULLY *drags the cow in on a blanket.*]

TULLY: It ain't dead yet.

YARDE: Get it outta here, man. I've been attacked by water boo. The Cong use 'em.

TULLY: This one ain't big enough ta do shit.

FUDGE: I thought you killed it, Lieutenant.

STROBERT: I did.

TULLY: I tell ya, it ain't dead.

STROBERT: It's zapped.

TULLY: It moved. I saw it. [ODOM *goes to cow.*]

ODOM: This ... cow's pregnant. [*Pause.*] Looks like you brought on labor, Strobert. [*He throws off his jacket and rolls up his sleeves.*]

FUDGE: Yah ... now I see. It's sides are pulsing.

ODOM: Sterilize a knife.

YARDE: Sterilize, Odom? Fer a cow?

TULLY: You heard him, fuckhead. [*He dabs some cool water on the cow's head.*]

YARDE: Ok ... ok ... [YARDE *gets a knife. He pours hot coffee over the knife.*]

ODOM: [*At back of cow.*] Fudge, over here! [*Pause.*]   Ok … see if you can push down and get the contractions working again.

FUDGE: [*Pushing.*] Nothing's happening.

YARDE: [*Backs away.*] God. It's all diseased.

FUDGE: [*Backing away.*] It's got fleas.

ODOM: This is a hospital. Push harder.

TULLY: He said … push! [*Fans cow's head.*]

FUDGE: I am. [*Pause. To* TULLY.] The cow ain't feeling that, Tully.

ODOM: Give me the knife, Yarde.

YARDE: What the hell's that on your arm, Cap'n?

TULLY: [*To* FUDGE.] You still ain't pushing hard enough.

FUDGE: I'm trying … I'm trying …

ODOM: The knife, Yarde. [*Pause.*] Tully, it's not doing any good to attend to the mother.

TULLY: She deserves a little peace. For once.

[YARDE *gives* ODOM *the knife.*]

TULLY: Yer gonna cut?

ODOM: The animal's dead, Tully. Without sensation. We got to get in there to the baby. [*To* TULLY.] You help Fudge push.

STROBERT: You want me to cut, too?

ODOM: Better get another knife.

[STROBERT *gets another knife.*]

YARDE: What happened to your arms, Doc?

TULLY: We're pushing.

FUDGE: Looks like the stomach muscles is paralyzed.

TULLY: Work 'em loose, Fudge.

FUDGE: It's jist … bones 'n lice.

ODOM: Throw on some water.

[FUDGE *takes his canteen and pours liquid over the cow's stomach.*]

TULLY: Jesus. Not grape Kool-Aid, fuckhead.

YARDE: Nothing's happening.

TULLY: Get the damn flies off of her.

ODOM: I'm going to make a bigger incision.

STROBERT: Easy … easy …

ODOM: I am.

STROBERT: A lot of blood is coming out. I can't see.

ODOM: We've got to make the incision larger.

STROBERT: Ok … ok … I can't tell what I'm doing with all the blood.

FUDGE: I'll mop up.

YARDE: Take my shirt. [*He rips it off.*]

TULLY: It ain't clean.

YARDE: It don't matter, jerk-off.

FUDGE: [*With* YARDE's *shirt.*] This is soaking it up.

STROBERT: Better … better. Keep at it, Fudge.

ODOM: Somebody wipe my forehead. [STROBERT *wipes* ODOM's *forehead with his sleeve.*] More water. [YARDE *pours his canteen on the animal's stomach.*]

TULLY: [*To* FUDGE.] Ok … ok … that's good. Now you're doing it.

STROBERT: I think the incision's long enough.

ODOM: We'll just lift it out.

TULLY: Easy … easy …

YARDE: Watch it, man … fuckin' watch it …

TULLY: I can see the head.

FUDGE: Yah. Look at that.

TULLY: I can see the little ears.

FUDGE: It's … perfect … it's … so perfect.

STROBERT: I think I've got it … yah … I've got it. [*Pause.*] Now pull.

YARDE: I ain't gonna pull.

ODOM: Pull!

YARDE: Ok. I'm pullin'.

TULLY: I got a leg.

STROBERT: Pull.

ODOM: That's it ... that's it. [ODOM *lifts out the calf*.]

YARDE: Cherry ... yer fuckin' dream is come true. You jist delivered a baby.

FUDGE: My God! [*Pause as they look*.]

TULLY: It's alone inna bag of blood. You gotta wonder ... was there anything between it and the scrawny mother ... it coming out all right and her dead? Is it all just fuckin' aimless?

YARDE: Now whatta we gonna do?

STROBERT: It can't live without the mother.

ODOM: That's right.

TULLY: The fuck it can't.

FUDGE: We're not ... just gonna turn it loose?

TULLY: I can feed it.

STROBERT: It'll starve to death.

ODOM: That's right.

STROBERT: We'll do the merciful thing.

FUDGE: What's that, Lieutenant?

TULLY: I can feed it with a test tube. I'll make a nipple with one of L. T.'s gloves.

STROBERT: It'll starve to death.

TULLY: Yer a broken record, L. T.

ODOM: We have no room here for an ailing animal.

TULLY: It ain't sick, Doc.

YARDE: We can't even fuckin' take care of ourselves.

STROBERT: We have to do the merciful thing.

ODOM: No pain, Strobert.

[STROBERT *lifts the gun and shoots the calf.*]

FUDGE: Lieutenant ... you killed it. [STROBERT *drops the gun slowly on the floor.*]

ODOM: It's ... regrettable ... nobody wants to kill a baby.

FUDGE: We shouldn't have shot a pregnant cow. [*He turns away and begins to cry.*]

STROBERT: How the hell did I know?

ODOM: [*To* FUDGE.] Nobody wants to end a new life.

TULLY: Then ... why the fuck we do it?

FUDGE: Why ... we go 'n give it life in the first place?

YARDE: The Cherry's got a point.

ODOM: All living things have a right to be born.

TULLY: Yah!

YARDE: I ... kinda see why the Cherry's freaked.

STROBERT: There was no alternative.

ODOM: Pull yourself together, Fudge. You're an Army man. None of us wanted this to happen.

FUDGE: It was so ... perfect.

STROBERT: We had to.

ODOM: For the good of this unit.

TULLY: Fuck this unit. [TULLY *goes for* STROBERT *angrily, but* YARDE *holds him back.*]

ODOM: Tully, for Godsakes. Don't strike an officer.

TULLY: [*To* STROBERT.] Fuckin' monster.

YARDE: There ain't no monsters, Tully. Just wars. [YARDE *lets go his hold of* TULLY.]

FUDGE: [*To* TULLY.] It's nobody's fault.

TULLY: Don't fuckin' tell me, Fudge.

ODOM: Come on. It's all over. [*Pause.*] Tully, take "them" out in the brush. [*Pause.*] Yarde, let's get on to the heavy work..

[TULLY *drags the cow and calf outside and comes back in.*]

[YARDE *dumps out the contents of a bag.*]

ODOM: [*To* TULLY.] Now don't you hold this against Strobert.

YARDE: Yah, didn't he pull strings ta get you that bike from Saigon?

ODOM: We have to work together here.

TULLY: I'm ... ok.

ODOM: Sure?

TULLY: I'm ok. [STROBERT *walks back to his work area.* TULLY *goes to the bike, picks it up and throws it out of the hootch and then goes back to work.*]

FUDGE: Why'd ya go and do that?

TULLY: The speedometer's Chink. I fuckin' hate that. [TULLY *abruptly moves around to* STROBERT *and grabs his pony tail and starts to cut* STROBERT*'s pony tail off.*]

STROBERT: You cut ... and so help me to God, Tully, I'll shoot that fuckin' mongoose to Kingdom Come. [*There is a tense pause.* TULLY *freezes, the knife still poised.* ODOM *goes to them.*] Stay away, Odom. [*Pause.*] You can't watch me twenty four hours, Tully. I'll waste it. You know I will.

ODOM: Tully, I'll give you one minute to drop that knife. [*Pause.*] I'm talking Court Martial.

[TULLY *drops the knife, then* TULLY *suddenly flips* STROBERT *to the floor with a flip of his foot — pinning* STROBERT *to the floor.*]

ODOM: Let him go, Tully. That's an order.

TULLY: [*Sings to* STROBERT *as he pins him to the floor.*] I'm gonna shoot me a human bird not a hummin' bird ... I'm gonna shoot me a human bird ...

ODOM: Court Martial, Tully. Stripped of your rank. Five years in the stockade. No allotment to your family. Dishonorable discharge.

[ODOM *picks up* STROBERT*'s gun from the floor.*]

[ODOM *flicks the M-16 to fire position.*]

YARDE: [*To* ODOM.] Whattaya going to do?

ODOM: [*To* YARDE.] Stay out of this.

YARDE: You gonna kill him?

ODOM: I intend to execute him ... for treason ... if he doesn't release Strobert.

YARDE: He ain't even armed.

ODOM: Stay outta this.

YARDE: [*Puts his hands on* ODOM'*s shoulders to restrain him.*] Get away from him.

[TULLY *lets go of* STROBERT.]

[ODOM *turns abruptly to* YARDE. ODOM *places the muzzle of his weapon — still cocked in the fire position — in the cavity of the underside of* YARDE'*s chin.*]

ODOM: I give the orders here. Don't you try and stop me again. Don't you *ever* put a hand on me again.

[YARDE *goes up on his toes as* ODOM *increases the pressure of the rifle barrel, lifting it up against the bottom of* YARDE'*s head.*]

Interfere ... with ... my orders again ... Yarde ... [ODOM *slowly rotates* YARDE *as he says the above.* YARDE *stretches to keep his toes touching the ground.*] and ... you'll ... be one ... dead black man. [ODOM *keeps* YARDE *like this a few seconds. Then slowly,* ODOM *lowers* YARDE *off the barrel and flicks the weapon back to safe.* ODOM *turns abruptly to* TULLY.] Tully, you assaulted an officer.

TULLY: He tripped, Cap'n. It's an accident. I got me witnesses. Ain't that right, Yarde? [*Pause.*] Yarde!

STROBERT: It's all right, Odom. It ... was an accident.

TULLY: See? What did I tell you?

YARDE: Yah. Just an accident.

FUDGE: You all right, Strobert?

STROBERT: I'm fine.

FUDGE: You never should of killed a pregnant cow. That's all. It's nobody's fault.

ODOM: This will not happen again!

STROBERT: We're all uptight, Odom. That's all. It's not going to happen again.

ODOM: Tully!

TULLY: Yah ... yah ... Cap'n.

ODOM: I want everyone in their areas. Now! [*Raps his ring.*] Next ... [*Holds out his hand.*] [*Men go back to work.*] [YARDE *hands* ODOM *a bone.*] You disarticulated this bone leaving marks.

YARDE: You try cutting a bone without no saw lines, Doctor.

TULLY: [*Mocking* ODOM's *tone of voice:*] Yarde, I want you to take the remains more seriously. [*Addressing remains as if he were* ODOM:] Ok, you scattered guts — single file. Keep your intervals. Blood, this is a test analysis, not a hootnanny. [YARDE *can't help but give a begrudging grin.*] [*Mocking* ODOM's *tone of voice:*] Yarde, this is no laughing matter.

YARDE: I ain't laughing.

TULLY: [*Mocking* ODOM's *tone of voice:*] This is a medical detachment, not a joke.

YARDE: [*To* ODOM:] [*Sullen.*] This unit ain't no joke. Not in the Killing Zone. I'm the first one that knows that. Who else makes their way through snipers? Who brings in the hash? [*Pause.*] I go out there 'cause it's no different than Chicago. I don't go out there for no ... Doctor-Captain.

[ODOM *and* YARDE *stare at each other.*]

ODOM: Back to work.

[ODOM *raps his ring.*]

[STROBERT *carries a rotor blade to a machine.*]

FUDGE: "Hey, hey, infantry boys ... infantry boys ... " God, I'm blocked ... I can't think of nothing else.

TULLY: How 'bout some peace 'n fuckin' quiet then, Cherry.

FUDGE: Hey ... hey ... infantry boys ... infantry boys ...

ODOM: Not now, Fudge, we have work.

FUDGE: [*Stops strumming.*] God, I'm blocked.

STROBERT: [*Suddenly whistles in awe.*] This ... is it. [*Pause. Yells:*] Goddamn ... this *is* it.

[*Men freeze and look at* STROBERT.]

[*Looking at copter rotor blade.*] His copter was probably shot down ... and dropped on a gasoline storage unit. He melted right into the rotor blade. I can't lift any body samples.

ODOM: Did you diffuse on the monochromatic X-radiation?

STROBERT: The machine won't take it. Negative.

ODOM: Where's the findings?

YARDE: On your left, Cap'n.

ODOM: [*Looks at report on table.*] Ring test?

STROBERT: No soluble proteins. Anywhere.

FUDGE: You don't have no data — I can't give you no profile print-out, sir.

STROBERT: [*Holds up the rotor blade.*] Odom, we don't know who this is.

END OF ACT ONE

ACT TWO

ODOM: Is that … all of him? You sure?

STROBERT: That's all. [*Pause.*] He just needs your final check and signature.

[STROBERT *hands the blade to* ODOM.]

YARDE: Fuckin' way to end up.

TULLY: We all end up like that more or less.

YARDE: I'd rather be more than less.

YARDE: Real feather in your hat, Cap'n Odom.

ODOM: It's a feather for all of us. [Pause.] I'll just … re-check … then sign the report.

FUDGE: A three day pass. Saigon!

YARDE: Gonna get yourself *Major*, Cap'n.

STROBERT: We'll all get a promotion.

YARDE: [*To* TULLY.] Senior Officer's gonna get *his* first. Then the rest of us they won't remember fer shit.

ODOM: I wouldn't do that to my men. [*Pause.*] A record of all pilots missing, Fudge.

YARDE: Might find yerself forgetting ... in all your glory. Sir.

FUDGE: Captain Odom wouldn't do that. [*Pause.*] Here they are. Ten, sir.

TULLY: Maybe they'll send us into combat anyway.

ODOM: They're not going to send national heroes into combat. [*Pause.*] Give me the area the copter blade was found.

TULLY: You believe that, Yarde?

ODOM: We'll be like Medal of Honor winners. We'll be the Army's pride. On display. In the States.

FUDGE: The blade was found in the Sampan Valley area, sir.

STROBERT: We're all going to ride the Freedom Bird. We're all walking up those eighteen steps to freedom.

ODOM: Do a work-up on the metal frame, Strobert.

STROBERT: I already did. It's from 8th Army.

ODOM: Do a second reading.

STROBERT: Right. [*Pause.*] Maybe they'll make us diplomats.

TULLY: What's so fuckin' great about that, L. T.?

STROBERT: Immunity. They can't give you detention.

TULLY: Nobody can?

STROBERT: That's right.

ODOM: Astronauts were made diplomats. They went to outer space. We went to inner space. [*Pause.*] Any ground matter with the blade, Yarde?

YARDE: Twenty centimeters of marsh grass. [*Pause.*] Shiiit. Everybody thought we was just military backwater. We were jokes in Saigon bars.

FUDGE: Five pilots are missing in the Sampan Valley this week.

YARDE: Tully will get hisself a stripe. Me — Master Sergeant. The Cherry — Spec. 4. [*Pause.*] I'll put the marsh grass in the analyzer.

FUDGE: A three day pass. Right, sir?

ODOM: Anywhere you want. [*Pause.*] Check for paint splinters, Tully.

FUDGE: This time I'm even looking in the women's file. To see if there's a man.

TULLY: Maybe there's a fuckin' Marion John Wayne.

ODOM: We'll all have our pictures in the paper.

YARDE: They gonna put *us* in the paper? Or *you*, Cap'n?

STROBERT: We did this together.

ODOM: That's right. [*Pause.*] Paint chips, Tully?

TULLY: Type 640. From Supply. In Dong Tam.

TULLY: Well, you got what you wanted, L. T. That rotor blade ain't what we expected. Not for no fuckin' unknown soldier.

YARDE: Honor guards is gonna march back and forth to a metal corpse.

STROBERT: It makes this war different. That's the important thing.

FUDGE: You think it will change how people think, Lieutenant?

STROBERT: A shock can do that. This war has to be the one that stops all wars.

TULLY: Fuckin' nothin' aint' gonna stop nothin'.

YARDE: At least it's gonna get us a three day pass.

FUDGE: God. We're somebodies.

TULLY: Thanks to nobody.

FUDGE: Saigon!!

YARDE: You ain't going to Saigon and get the clap, Fudge. [*Pause.*] This marsh grass checks out to type 001. Sampan Valley.

ODOM: Good.

FUDGE: I'm not stupid. I don't want the clap. Some way ... I'm gonna find a nice clean virgin.

YARDE: I almost got the clap from a virgin. [*A beat as all the men look at* YARDE.] In Cam Ranh Bay. She was all in white. Head to toe. White dress. Little white purse. White shoes. White nylons just like a nurse. Her old pimp with no teeth stood behind her whining: No V-C, no V-D. No V-C, no V-D.

FUDGE: I still don't wanna just play ping-pong.

YARDE: We do ping-pong. I'll fix you up in Chicago.

FUDGE: Think we'll be going back home right away?

STROBERT: Right after a three-day pass.

FUDGE: Then ... Earlville.

TULLY: Went home on leave when the last kid was coming. Me bein' a medic, they let me in the operating room. I was glad when the baby was born all right. But I fuckin' took a quick look at the afterbirth ta see it was ok.

FUDGE: I'd come home from church on Sunday ... polish my car all day long. In Earlville, they'd polish the air if they could. [*Pause.*] God, I really miss the States.

YARDE: You ain't been gone that long, Cherry.

FUDGE: My sister 'n me used to walk to the liquor store every day after school — for Mounds Bars and corn chips. [*Pause.*] It's like loneliness is come right inside my body like a long road in Illinois.

ODOM: [*Looking at slide.*] Yes. This is what I love about a cell. It's true. A cell doesn't sham disorder. A cell doesn't simulate disease.

STROBERT: Second reading of metal frame. Negative.

ODOM: Good.

[STROBERT *rubs his jaw, then takes a last drop from a beer bottle.*]

STROBERT: I'm out of beer.

YARDE: You'll be hurting, Lieutenant.

TULLY: I got one "33" put away. [TULLY *gets the beer from under his bunk and gives it to* STROBERT.]

ODOM: I could save you a lot of pain.

STROBERT: [*To* ODOM.] Maybe tonight I'll let you pull the damn thing.

TULLY: All right! He's finally letting go.

ODOM: Style code on the endplate, Yarde?

YARDE: Negative.

ODOM: I have my thoughts about home, too.

FUDGE: Whattaya think about?

YARDE: This oughta be good.

ODOM: Well ... I want to enroll in a refresher course, for the new techniques of typing blood.

YARDE: Jesus.

ODOM: Of course I'll take my wife and kids on a little vacation first.

YARDE: To Ranger School at Fort Bragg, no doubt. The family that shoots together toots together.

ODOM: Some people relax in different ways, Yarde.

YARDE: You're too Army, Cap'n. That ain't gonna happen to me. I'm not re-upping this time. They ain't gonna wave no bonus check under this black nose again.

ODOM: No more missing pilots, Fudge?

FUDGE: No, sir.

ODOM: Now ... other personnel.

FUDGE: Right, sir. [*Pause.*] You just gonna keep on living in Chicago, Yarde?

YARDE: Sure.

FUDGE: Even though you ain't got no family?

YARDE: Just the Baptist orphanage I lived in. And it ain't even there no more.

FUDGE: You got nobody?

YARDE: I like this one cat. He runs a nice hamburger place on Diversey Street and ... He gave me my first job when I was fourteen. Cleanin' off tables. [*Pause.*] I was the lowest guy in the joint. And he wouldn't call me bus-boy. He made everybody call me bus-man.

TULLY: So big deal.

YARDE: [*To* TULLY.] Nobody ... ever ... was that good to me!

TULLY: Ok ...ok ...

STROBERT: I'm really counting on you to visit me in New York,

Yarde.

YARDE: Me? Goin' in one of those fancy buildings?

STROBERT: I've never had a friend from Chicago.

YARDE: Naw. You come to Chicago. You, too ... Tully ... Fudge. I'll show you the good time.

FUDGE: What about Odom?

YARDE: He'll be in fuckin' school.

TULLY: Shiiit. I haven't been outta Iowa. 'Cept for The Nam.

STROBERT: Tully, I'm going to change that. [*Pause.*] When we get back to the States, I want to invite you and your wife and three children to visit me in New York City. [TULLY *stares at* STROBERT.]

STROBERT: Your children need to see a big city. They ought to know what it's like.

[*Silence as* TULLY *stares at* STROBERT.]

Ok ... ok ... so it's kind of a phony way of life. We live on the twentieth floor. An apartment with a doorman. Little trees outside in iron fences. [*Pause.*] Diane will probably feed the kids omelettes instead of hot dogs. [*Pause.*] Ok. Boring. You don't have to come. Put the kids on the train. I'll pick them up myself at the station.

TULLY: You'd ... you'd ... do that?

STROBERT: Why not?

TULLY: You're ... an officer ... and ... you'd do that for a Spec. 4 ... from Muscatine.

FUDGE: Sergeant, now.

STROBERT: Why not?

TULLY: You'd ... [TULLY *abruptly turns away. He goes just outside the pagoda. Silence.*]

FUDGE: Aren't ya gonna do nothin'?

[*Silence.*] [*Then* FUDGE *goes to look at* TULLY.]

The man's destroyed.

[*Silence.* FUDGE *nervously goes in and out of the doorway.*]

The man's destroyed.

[ODOM *goes out and looks at* TULLY. *He comes in.*]

ODOM: He's all right.

STROBERT: I didn't mean to upset him.

YARDE: Maybe the cat's trippin'.

FUDGE: He only had one Kool.

ODOM: He's overwhelmed, that's all. [*Pause.*] I'm just about done here. Did you check off all the remaining personnel?

FUDGE: Yes sir. [*Pause.*] I hate to see him out there all alone like that.

ODOM: Let the man have his privacy.

STROBERT: I was going to invite everybody, but after that response ...

[TULLY *comes in carrying the exercise bike. He puts the bike in it's old place and then goes back to the table.*]

FUDGE: We're getting a three-day pass. For anywhere! Think of it.

STROBERT: I was in Paris, once.

YARDE: What did ya do, Strobert?

STROBERT: One night in Paris.

FUDGE: You were in Paris?

STROBERT: I was nineteen years old ... in Paris ... and I didn't know what the hell to do.

YARDE: I'm glad I'm no First Looey. Look at him. It's mindblowing.

TULLY: Saigon. That's for me.

STROBERT: I was in Saigon once.

FUDGE: What happened?

YARDE: He didn't know what to do.

[TULLY *laughs.*]

ODOM: No pigment in the metal interstices, right, Strobert?

STROBERT: I don't think so.

ODOM: What do you mean, you don't think so?

STROBERT: I saw only air spaces. Molecular absorption is minus.

ODOM: Didn't you put this through heat radiation?

STROBERT: Why?

ODOM: Why?! Because sometimes you find visible red regions of pigment granules.

STROBERT: Less than a five percent chance.

ODOM: You send this out to Command Headquarters, and eventually they'll check that out.

STROBERT: Ok ... ok ...

ODOM: Getting everybody all psyched up. Without final proof. [ODOM *has a slight facial twitch*.]

TULLY: Back to abnormal.

ODOM: Damnit to hell. You don't get people's hopes up until you're sure. [*Pause*.] I hate sloppy work.

STROBERT: What are you implying, Odom?

ODOM: I asked for a medical officer as my second in command. Not a science teacher.

STROBERT: I keep up with you pretty well, Odom.

FUDGE: Cap'n Odom didn't mean anything.

STROBERT: You think I don't want to get this thing over with?

ODOM: You can do your part by being thorough.

[ODOM *works on the copter blade at the machine*.]

STROBERT: I'm as anxious as you. I've got a big investment here. I've got parents back home who want to know what the hell kind of war this is that killed their son.

ODOM: Just as I thought. I found pigment, Strobert. [ODOM*'s face begins to twitch*.]

STROBERT: Ok ... ok ... so I jumped the gun. It looked so ...

ODOM: Don't you pull that on us again.

STROBERT: I'm sorry, for Godsakes.

ODOM: Tissue fluid. Blood type A. Prior anemia. No Barr

bodies present in the cells.

FUDGE: [*Reading record.*] Benson. Oscar. Acute anemia prior to enlistment. Blood type A. Neutron activation analysis checks out, sir.

ODOM: Tag him.

[ODOM *puts his head in his hands for a moment. Twitching stops.* ODOM *goes back to work.*]

Next.

YARDE: Cherry! you motherfucker! Ahhhhhhhhhh [YARDE *makes angry animal sounds and rushes to* FUDGE *and picks him up and shakes him.*] Where is it? I know you got it!

TULLY: Five says it's in his front pocket.

YARDE: Back pocket!

FUDGE: Let me down!

TULLY: You'll get an Airborne patch for that, Fudge.

STROBERT: Don't act like a caveman.

ODOM: You're showing where your ancestors came from, Yarde.

YARDE: My people don't come from caves. They come from Africa.

FUDGE: Yarde ... come on ... let me down.

YARDE: You drop it, Cherry. Or you die.

[FUDGE *drops his watch on the floor.* YARDE *puts* FUDGE *down.*]

I just ... can't stand ... no ticking.

ODOM: I'm waiting for remains, Yarde.

TULLY: None of us wear watches. Yarde can't stand it. You know that, Fudge.

FUDGE: How can he hear it?

YARDE: I ... hear it.

TULLY: I put five on the front.

STROBERT: You're a genius, Tully. You ought to go to college.

TULLY: I told ya ... players ain't readers.

[ODOM *taps his ring for order.*]

FUDGE: My mother gave me that watch.

YARDE: I don't care who gave it to you. Get it outta here.

FUDGE: Ok ... ok ...

YARDE: Now!

TULLY: You intend to pay up?

FUDGE: [*Looks to* YARDE *proudly.*] Later. Dig?

YARDE: When I was a kid, all I wanted was a Mickey watch. Later on ... a ten dollar watch. Then a big Rolex. When I joined the Army, man, I realized the biggest luxury was not to know the fuckin' time.

[FUDGE *puts his watch in a metal box. Just before* STROBERT *puts the box in a drawer,* YARDE *stops him.*]

Wait! [YARDE *listens. He can't hear.*] Ok.

[STROBERT *puts the box away.*]

ODOM: [*Raps his ring.*] Back to work ... back to work.

[*The men begin working.*]

TULLY: Back to abnormal!

STROBERT: [*About remains.*] Here's part of the groin and what looks like semen in the trouser leg.

TULLY: Fresh semen.

ODOM: Alkaline odor?

TULLY: Yah.

ODOM: Old semen's mucous crystalline incrustations.

TULLY: This is new. It'll test out good. [*He puts it back down on the table.*]

YARDE: Why is it yer dick goes off when ya get hit?

STROBERT: Maybe it's exciting.

YARDE: Ta get blowed up, Lieutenant?

ODOM: Put it on a slide.

YARDE: Joey Heatherton could come in here right now and drop her fuckin' pants under his nose, and he'd say ...

TULLY/YARDE: [*Together.*] ... put it on a slide!

FUDGE: [*Sings and strums:*] Hey, hey, infantry boys ... 'specially youse ... that come from Ill ... a ... noise.

ODOM: Not now, Fudge. We have work.

TULLY: There's shit mixed up with this semen.

ODOM: Fecal matter can reveal parasites.

TULLY: I know ... I know ... we gotta record on every soldier with the runs.

YARDE: Ya get hit ... and yer bowels and dick spill out. Jesus, the only two things that do anything for you when ya die.

FUDGE: Yarde, I'm trying to work on some new music.

YARDE: About time. I'm tired of singing yer old half-assed songs.

STROBERT: Those old songs are good.

FUDGE: You mean that?

YARDE: No. He don't.

FUDGE: I'm blocked. Think I'll be ok?

TULLY: You got plenty of time to find out. We ain't gonna find nothing.

ODOM: I don't want to hear that kind of talk.

YARDE: Cap'n, we ain't "gonna find nothin' " is good talk. [*He sings:*] "Nothing on the table means ... something on the collar ..."

ODOM: We have a good job here. Better than some have it.

TULLY: Why we the only unit, sir, in the whole Army living and sleeping and working with friggin' guts all day long. [*Pause.*] L. T., yer fingernails is all poked through them gloves again. Time ta powder 'n change.

STROBERT: I'll change gloves when I'm ready.

TULLY: Might break off yer nail ... L. T. [TULLY *looks carefully on table.*] Yah ... there it is.

YARDE: Where?

TULLY: Here.

YARDE: Yah. Now I see it. A officer's fingernail.

TULLY: Officer Strobert?

YARDE: Yah.

TULLY: Send him home in a baggie.

STROBERT: You bastards.

FUDGE: It's just a joke, Lieutenant.

ODOM: Are you two harassing an officer?

TULLY/YARDE: Article Fifteen!

ODOM: I want an apology. Now.

FUDGE: It was just a joke, sir.

ODOM: Stay out of this, Fudge. [*Pause.*] Apologize.

YARDE: [*To* STROBERT.] Like Fudge said. A joke. That's all, Lieutenant.

TULLY: [*To* STROBERT.] Nothin' personal, sir.

STROBERT: I don't like jokes like that. [*Pause.*] Fudge, write the ridge details on the blackboard.

[FUDGE *goes to blackboard.*]

FUDGE: You hear something?

TULLY: Yah. The usual shit.

FUDGE: No. This is different.

[*They listen.*]

YARDE: Jesus. Sounds like the Sky Raiders.

[*They go to the door.*]

TULLY: Look at'em. Our fuckin' Air Force. Layin' eggs all over the V-C.

STROBERT: That's a pretty awesome sight.

TULLY: Think I'll just light me one up 'n' watch the war.

ODOM: Ok. Back to work. Back to work.

FUDGE: Sounds closer.

YARDE: It's always gonna sound closer.

TULLY: Just our luck, they'll drop the bomb when we're over here.

FUDGE: [*Writing on blackboard.*] They wouldn't do that.

TULLY: Why not, Cherry?

FUDGE: Not with yer U. S. Troops here. [*Pause.*] What blows ya up 'n jist leaves "pinkies"?

YARDE: It'd be one way they could waste a lot of niggers.

STROBERT: You're talkin' like a Commie.

YARDE: I'm talkin' like a nigger, Lieutenant.

FUDGE: You're not talking for Cap'n Odom.

YARDE: *I'm* the only "black" man in here?

FUDGE: Odom is ... a doctor.

YARDE: I know ... from the way he opens a C-Ration can.

ODOM: They're not going to drop the bomb anywhere. [*Pause.*] I want slides on these. Double time. [*Pause.*] You're responsible for this, Strobert. Getting the men's hopes up. Breaking down moral with sloppy work.

STROBERT: I didn't break down anything that wasn't broken down to start with.

ODOM: I asked for a medical officer. [*Face begins to twitch.*]

STROBERT: You got one.

ODOM: I got a teacher. If you were medically thorough, we wouldn't have all this disruption.

STROBERT: How many times do I have to say I'm sorry, For Godsakes.

YARDE: The Doc's so thorough that last week we identified five water buffalo ribs.

FUDGE: It's not Captain Odom's fault. Animals is always wandering around over here.

STROBERT: [*Angrily.*] We logged in ... Two rat tibia, six sheep thoracic vertebrae ... one dog sacrum/humerus ...

FUDGE: ... and the skull of a monkey.

STROBERT: What can you expect from a veterinarian?

TULLY: [*Laughs.*] Yah. You could be a vet, Cap'n.

STROBERT: Odom *is* a veterinarian.

YARDE: What was that?

[ODOM *hurriedly goes back to his desk and gets very busy.*]

STROBERT: Nothing.

YARDE: I asked you, Lieutenant, ta tell me what you said Odom is.

STROBERT: He's a veterinarian.

YARDE: [*To* ODOM.] Is it true?

ODOM: Let's get on with the rest of the heavy stuff.

YARDE: Odom ... is it true?

STROBERT: Didn't you see how he operated on the cow?

ODOM: Sample from that quonset door.

[TULLY *scrapes off matter from the quonset door and puts it on a slide and hands it to* ODOM. ODOM *studies it under his microprobe.*]

YARDE: Cap-tain! I'm talking ta you! [*Pause.*] Is it true?

ODOM: [*Pause. His voice weakens.*] You don't have a chance, the Dean told me. Medical school's ... restricted. There's a tight quota. It's controlled. Regulated. It's ... exclusive. [*Pause.*] Tully, a clean slide.

[ODOM'*s hands begin to shake. He can't take the slide.*]

YARDE: I'm waiting fer your answer.

[TULLY *puts slide on* ODOM'*s table.* ODOM *puts his hands — one under each armpit — to stop them from shaking.*]

ODOM: Go into veterinary medicine, my West Point C.O. told me. The quota's more lax there ... more ... accessible ... for people like you. And you get the same kind of training. You're a doctor in the end. [*Pause.*] Look, boy, we gave you the Point. You can't have everything. [*Pause.*]

STROBERT: I'm sorry, Odom.

ODOM: For telling the truth?

STROBERT: Christ, I'm sorry.

ODOM: It's all right.

YARDE: [*Less hostile but firm:*] Whitie gave you the Point, Cap'n.

[ODOM *stares at* YARDE *for a moment. Then* ODOM *takes off his dress coat and rolls up his sleeves.* ODOM *reveals an arm of pockmarks and permanent bruises.*]

FUDGE: Is that why you always wear full dress, sir?

ODOM: There are more civilized ways to get a nigger, Yarde. Officer ways. [*Pause.*] My official shots record kept getting lost. I had to undergo the full battery of inoculations ... over and over ... 'till my arms ended up looking like this.

[*Nervous pause as the men all stare at* ODOM.]

TULLY: [*Takes out his canteen.*] Here. Some PX whiskey. Yer nerves is shot ta hell, Cap'n.

[ODOM *knocks the canteen out of* TULLY's *hand and it falls on the floor.*]

ODOM: [*To* YARDE.] Let me tell you something, nigger. It will get you through prep school. It will get you through West Point. It will get you through life. [*Pause.*] When you get up in the morning, and look at yourself in the mirror, make sure you see nothing. Make sure what's looking back at you is an empty face. Empty. Like the mask the Aztec dead wear. A mask that doesn't haunt the living. [*Pause.*] Put your shirt on every morning, sleeve by silent sleeve. Keep inside yourself like a hidden friend. There's a trick to the lips dreaming. [*Pause.*] Live the days ... here! [*Hits his chest.*] Days that come unknown with secret hands. [*Pause.*] It doesn't take long to find you're just an ugly bird — a hundred dreams a year like feathers falling off — that won't grow back. [*Pause.*] Yes, I'm a veterinarian. [*Pause as the men look at* ODOM. *Then:*]

YARDE: [*To* ODOM.] Ok ... brother. Ok! [*To others:*] I found myself a brother. [*To* ODOM.] Why the fuck didn't you tell me before? O ... k!

[*With much ceremony* YARDE *puts a package of Kools on* ODOM's *desk.*]

[ODOM *angrily shoves Kools on floor.*]

[*The men go back to work,* YARDE *smiles happily.* ODOM *lowers his head over his microprobe in intensive work.*]

FUDGE: I'm glad.

TULLY: 'Bout what?

FUDGE: I'm glad Captain Odom ain't no tight-assed doctor.

STROBERT: Me, too.

FUDGE: Really, Lieutenant?

STROBERT: Really.

YARDE: That there brother is been to West Point.

FUDGE: People don't deserve Odom.

YARDE: What people?

FUDGE: Tight-assed people.

YARDE: Ok.

TULLY: It always used to make me mad.

YARDE: What?

TULLY: Those ... funny little dead animals all over Plank Road. In the summer. Rabbits and 'coons and squirrels. With tire-lines for faces. With headlights stamped down their backs.

FUDGE: Yah. Lotta guys in Earlville made a game of it. Trying to run over animals on the highway. I wouldn't do that.

TULLY: My dog Barney is smarter 'n a lot of people.

FUDGE: Yah?

TULLY: Clocks went out once from a storm ... 'n' Barney put up a yell 'till we fixed them.

FUDGE: Yah? You believe that, Captain?

[ODOM *doesn't answer. He works silently.*]

TULLY: It's true. Animals is smart.

FUDGE: Captain Odom probably knows that better than us.

[*Pause.*]

Hey, I just thought of something. [*He picks up his guitar and sings:*]

FUDGE: [*Singing:*] In Nam
of all the guys I met ...
only one's
a vet vet.

[*Pause as they all look a* ODOM. ODOM *looks up from his work and stares at* FUDGE. *Pause.*]

ODOM: I'm ... immunized ... to the degree ... of protecting a bull-elephant from heat rash. [*He smiles.*] I'm a veteran ... veterinarian. [*The tension is broken and the men laugh.*]

FUDGE: [*Strumming and singing:*]
I think you know him,
Cap ... tin Odom.
a vet
from the Tet
and
Sampan Valley
An Khe
Bien Hoa
Dong Tam
Cu Chi
Cam Ranh Bay ...
hey
hey ...
He's a vet
from the Tet
the only guy I ever met ...

TULLY/STROBERT/YARDE/FUDGE: Who's a vet vet.

ODOM: I'm a vet ... vet.

FUDGE: We all know him ...

FUDGE/TULLY/YARDE/STROBERT: Cap ... tin Odom.

[*They all laugh.*]

TULLY: Look's like yer writer's block is over, Fudge.

FUDGE: I'm hot again.

STROBERT: You know what, Fudge ... I think it's time I taught you some real poetry.

FUDGE: Yah?

STROBERT: What do you think, Odom?

ODOM: [*Looks up from his microprobe.*] I think Fudge has a nice natural sensibility.

STROBERT: Wouldn't hurt him to have a little "unnatural" sensibility.

YARDE: [*Walking to* ODOM.] Section of culvert pipe. With scalp
samples.

[YARDE *puts the pipe on* ODOM'*s desk.*]

ODOM: [*To* FUDGE.] You know anything about Robert Frost?

YARDE: I know Jack Frost.

FUDGE: He's a poet!

YARDE: [*To* ODOM.] Ain't ya gonna do a "infrared" on the pipe,
Cap'n?

STROBERT: Frost is a New England poet. And one day ... he
sees this little horse as he is driving down the road.

TULLY: What road?

ODOM: Doesn't matter what road.

TULLY: The hell it don't.

STROBERT: Ok ... ok ... let's say ... Plank Road.

TULLY: Ain't no horses on Plank Road.

YARDE: Just ... make up a road.

FUDGE: How about Roosevelt Road? That goes right by
Earlville.

STROBERT: It's snowing. And he's driving down Roosevelt
Road.

YARDE: Got hisself good snow tires, right?

STROBERT: And he sees this little colt ... out in the snow. And
the colt's scared.

TULLY: Where's its mother?

STROBERT: That's just it. The mother's not there.

TULLY: The mother's gonna be there.

ODOM: The point is ... the mother isn't.

TULLY: I ain't buying it.

FUDGE: Let him go on.

STROBERT: So Frost says that "the little fellow isn't snow
broken."

[*Silent pause.*]

FUDGE: So that's what it means.

TULLY: He ain't ... "snow broken"?

ODOM: It's his first winter.

FUDGE: I like that.

TULLY: The first winter, none of us is snow broken.

STROBERT: That's the point.

YARDE: So... why doesn't he just say that?

STROBERT: It wouldn't be poetry.

FUDGE: Will you let him go on?

STROBERT: Well, Frost just ends it by saying something like ... whoever left him out like that ... ought to be told to go and take him in.

YARDE: That's it? [*Silent pause.*]

FUDGE: I like it.

YARDE: There ain't ... nothin' else?

FUDGE: I ... like it.

YARDE: Cherry, you need me!

FUDGE: I don't know ... I guess if I just read it, I'd probably hate it. But it's the way Lieutenant Strobert tells you.

ODOM: The mark of a good teacher. [*Pause.*] I'll take that pipe now, Yarde.

[YARDE *gives the pipe to* ODOM.]

FUDGE: If I could get me a teacher like Lieutenant Strobert, I'd go back to school.

ODOM: There's the G.I. Bill, Fudge. Ought to take advantage of that.

[ODOM *begins to prepare a slide from matter on the pipe.*]

STROBERT: Listen to Odom. [*He begins to scrape matter off a jeep steering wheel.*]

ODOM: Yarde, that goes for you and Tullly, too.

TULLY/YARDE: Players ain't readers! Sir!

ODOM: A gas chromatograph on this, Strobert.

[ODOM *holds out a slide.* STROBERT *takes the slide to a machine and puts it in and waits.*]

[FUDGE *begins scribbling as the men are working.*]

TULLY: 'Least animals don't get the clap.

FUDGE: Yah?

YARDE: How do you know?

TULLY: I got me so many infections over here ...

YARDE: You take it home to your woman?

TULLY: I always get me fixed up 'fore I go home. [*Pause.*] This doctor at Ban Me Thuot ... he drained my balls and stitched them up. A little line on the right one. Little frown line on the left one.

STROBERT: Tully carries around his own theater.

TULLY: Wanna see?

YARDE: Save it for the boom-te-boom club.

[STROBERT *takes the slide out of the machine and gives it back to* ODOM.]

FUDGE: I'm really over my writer's block now.

ODOM: How about finishing up those cards, too.

TULLY: This job is ... bor ... ing. And we ain't never gonna find nothin', Cap'n.

ODOM: Yes, we will.

YARDE: You really believe that, brother?

ODOM: [*Ignores* YARDE *and looks down at a slide.*] No cortical surfaces on this. [*To* STROBERT.] Put it in the glass-jet separator.

RADIO: Eagle One to Eagle Two. Eagle One to Eagle Two. Do You read me? Over.

YARDE: It's Bravo.

ODOM: [*Into Radio.*] Eagle Two to Eagle One. Eagle Two to Eagle One. Loud and clear. Over. [ODOM *listens, then turns to men.*] A short run today. Across the paddy. Sky Raiders were out this morning. They got a V-C patrol. Unfortunately, they think ... some of Bravo Company was hit, too, by the LZ.

TULLY: Our own men wasted by us again.

ODOM: A mistake, Tully.

YARDE: [*To* ODOM.] Just ... check out the LZ? For hash, brother?

ODOM: For remains, *Yarde*!

YARDE: You sure Sky Raiders ain't coming back?

ODOM: *Sir.*

YARDE: I ain't gettin' myself zapped by no U. S. Air Force. Sir.

ODOM: We're nearly out of remains. This trip is necessary. I've been assured it's all clear.

YARDE: Who goes with me? I can't carry a big load by myself.

FUDGE: I go.

STROBERT: No way.

YARDE: Here we go again.

FUDGE: I'm going.

STROBERT: I outrank you, Fudge. And you're not going. [*Pause.*] I'll go.

ODOM: You went out last time, Strobert. Not twice in a row. Regulations.

YARDE: Come on, I ain't gonna wait all day.

TULLY: I'll go.

FUDGE: No!

YARDE: Let the Cherry go.

FUDGE: I want "snow broken."

YARDE: You ain't doin' him no favors, Lieutenant. Yer gonna get him kilt actin' like this.

ODOM: He's got to get experience. Or he won't know how to protect himself.

YARDE: You heard what the brother said.

TULLY: Yarde ain't got any of us wasted yet.

YARDE: I know this place. I don't go on no trails or paths. That way we ain't gonna step on any punji sticks or get ambushed.

TULLY: Yarde brings us back.

YARDE: That's right.

ODOM: Just a short one today. Across the paddy to the LZ and back. It won't take them any longer than fifteen minutes.

FUDGE: Fifteen lousy minutes.

YARDE: With the best jungle rat in 6th Army.

TULLY: Come on. The Cherry went out before. And he come back all right.

STROBERT: He didn't go out in a Killing Zone.

YARDE: You can't keep him in here forever, Lieutenant.

STROBERT: Odom?

ODOM: [*After a pause:*] Let the boy go.

[FUDGE, YARDE, *and* TULLY *cheer.*] [*After the cheers:*]

FUDGE: God, I'm lucky. Me ... a private ... put with the best jungle rat in 6th Army.

STROBERT: Fifteen minutes, Yarde. Not a second more.

YARDE: Right, Lieutenant.

STROBERT: I'm taking out my watch!

YARDE: Don't take out no watch! Sir.

STROBERT: Be careful of mines.

YARDE: I'm not stupid, Lieutenant.

STROBERT: Watch *ours.* Bravo lays some of them outside the pattern — to fool the V-C who sneak in to cut the wires.

YARDE: I know all that.

STROBERT: Keep a look out for V-C zapper squads.

YARDE: Man, yer insultin' me. Sir.

STROBERT: Don't fire unless you have to. Muzzle flash will give your position away.

YARDE: He's the Cherry. Not me. [*Pause.*] Now move back. I'm dressin' fer the occasion. [*Pause.*] I've been giving this a lotta thought. [*Pause.*] Jungle fatigues is worthless, man. They're fine when you don't move. Move ... and yer a target. [*Pause.*] I ask you ... do chinks wear them? [*He points to his fatigues.*]

Hell, no. Chinks wear black. [*Pause.*] I'm chuckin' fatigues. These here is chains of slavery. [*He rips off his fatigues.*] I'm puttin' on a suit. The salesman to Robert Hall where I bought this on Halstead Street said I could bowl in it ... sleep in it ... even let a convoy run over me in it ... and it wouldn't wrinkle.

[YARDE *puts on a pink shirt, brown suit, black sunglasses and a papa-san hat. Then he puts on a gun and radio.*]

YARDE: One last thing. My Ho Chi Minh sandals. [*He puts them on.*] Well? [*There is quiet as they all look at* YARDE.]

TULLY: You're a cool dude, Yarde.

[YARDE *and* FUDGE *exit.*]

[STROBERT *goes to* ODOM's *desk to get his watch from the metal box.* STROBERT *winds his watch.*]

ODOM: Now's a good time to get everything finished up. Before the new remains come in.

STROBERT: I give them fifteen minutes.

TULLY: Then what?

STROBERT: I'm sending Bravo Company out after them.

[TULLY *goes to his exercise bike and pedals.* STROBERT *paces and steps on bugs.*]

[*Silent pause.*]

STROBERT: You hear anything, Odom?

ODOM: Even the mosquitoes here don't make a sound.

STROBERT: Tully?

TULLY: I ain't heard nothin', L. T. [*Pause.*] Wait!

STROBERT: What?

[*Silent pause.*]

TULLY: Yarde's right. You can hear that watch ticking.

STROBERT: Tully!

TULLY: Ok ... ok ... don't blow a fuse, L. T.

[*Silent pause.* STROBERT *begins to pace and step on bugs.*]

ODOM: Will you get that slide from the glass-jet separator? It should be done.

STROBERT: This light isn't on. It's not ready.

[STROBERT *continues to pace and to step on bugs.*]

ODOM: Sort some slides. The time will go faster.

TULLY: Best fuckin' thing is to keep movin'.

[STROBERT *still paces and steps on bugs.*]

ODOM: Is that a steering wheel over there, Strobert?

[STROBERT *paces silently.*]

Tully, we can use some help.

TULLY: Ok ... ok ... L. T. [*He gets off the bike.*]

ODOM: I'd like to see the wheel.

TULLY: It's routine. Blood. Skin. Saliva. Perspiration. You fuckin' name it, L. T.

STROBERT: I can identify that guy fifty times over.

[ODOM *looks at some matter from the wheel under his microprobe.*]

ODOM: Hmmmmmm.

[ODOM *gets up from looking at microprobe and walks to* FUDGE's *records.*] You're right. Easy. [*Pause.*] William Laturette. Blood checks. Prints check. [*Pause.*] Now what do you know? His folks live in Nassau. [*Pause.*] My parents were born on the islands.

TULLY: Yah?

ODOM: Martinique. [*Pause.*] You know who was born in Martinique?

TULLY: If it ain't Joey Heatherton, I don't give a fuck, Cap'n.

ODOM: Josephine.

TULLY: Josephine who?

ODOM: Napoleon's wife. [*Pause.*] Did you know that, Strobert? [STROBERT *stops pacing, mildly curious.*] That's right. [STROBERT *starts pacing again.*] [STROBERT *rubs his sore jaw.*] When I was a kid, I watched my old grandmother in her garden. She always carried the watering can on her head. [*Pause.*] I used to think ... nothing is as beautiful as my grandmother ... walking in the irises ... with a watering can on her head. [*Pause.*] Later, I was ashamed of her.

[ODOM *goes to the table for a cup of coffee.*]

ODOM: You want a cup, Tully? Strobert?

TULLY: This is really something, Odom. You ... taking a coffee break.

[STROBERT *continues pacing and stepping on bugs and rubbing his jaw.*]

[ODOM *stands by the coffee table drinking.*]

My grandma died when I was eight.

ODOM: In Muscatine?

TULLY: She died in Harvey. She was the best cook in Harvey, Iowa. She had a skillet reached across all four burners. I always used ta say: I'm gonna fuckin' buy me a house right next to grandma's kitchen. [*Pause.*] When she died, I was sittin' on the side of her bed. And she ... kinda leaned over. And I'll never forget her last words.

ODOM: What did she say?

TULLY: She kinda pulled at my shirt ... 'n she put her face next to my ear ... 'n she said: "Shake the casserole."

[*Silent pause.*]

ODOM: That's what she said?

TULLY: "Shake the casserole"

[*Silent pause.* STROBERT *is still pacing and stepping on bugs.*]

STROBERT: Where are they!?

ODOM: It's too soon. [*He goes back to his desk to work.*]

STROBERT: If they really double-timed, they could be back.

ODOM: It's too soon. [*Pause.*] Want to tag this, Tully?

[TULLY *gets the steering wheel from* ODOM's *desk and puts it in a bag.*]

STROBERT: They're going to take every damn minute.

TULLY: That's right.

STROBERT: Not one second early.

TULLY: That's right, L. T.

STROBERT: [*To* TULLY.] Will you shut up?

TULLY: I was only trying to fuckin' agree with you, sir.

ODOM: [*To* TULLY.] Laturette's print-out is on Fudge's desk. [*Pause.*] When I entered West Point, I used to spell my name with an "e" on the end. O-d-o-m-e.

TULLY: [*As he gets print-out from* FUDGE's *desk and staples it to the bag*:] Why?

ODOM: So people would think I was French. [*Pause.*] A glass photographic plate, Strobert.

[STROBERT *goes to a machine, takes the plate out of it, and hands it to* ODOM.]

STROBERT: Somebody sent my kid brother out there.

ODOM: First time I saw a cotton field, I was eight years old. I thought it was summer snow.

STROBERT: What's a kid doing out there in a Killing Zone?

ODOM: Pretty funny, don't you think? Considering I'm from people who are experts on cotton. [*Pause.*] We need to stain this plate.

STROBERT: The way he writes those songs ... he's got a real gift.

ODOM: Some acid, Strobert.

STROBERT: [*As* STROBERT *hands acid to* ODOM:] You heard him. With the Frost poem. He understood.

ODOM: Let's have that grille section.

[TULLY *takes the grille section from the table and hands it to* ODOM.]

STROBERT: I got him thinking about school.

ODOM: [*Scraping material from the grille.*] Now ... I'll put some of this on the photographic plate ...

STROBERT: Then I go and let him take off out there.

ODOM: You can't be around every minute to protect him.

STROBERT: I could have protected him — this time. That's something.

ODOM: I could use a Globar tube. [*Pause.*] Don't confuse Fudge with your brother.

STROBERT: What are you talking about?

ODOM: Don't use him.

STROBERT: I'm not using him.

ODOM: I know you want to protect the boy's future. What about his past? That's got to be protected, too. He has to look back and know he did what he felt he had to.

STROBERT: My brother, Odom, can't look back. He's missing in action. He's nowhere. He's in limbo.

ODOM: Don't love too much.

STROBERT: Nothing … nothing in this Goddamn world is loved too much. [*Pause.*] Tully, go outside. Get up on the roof. See if you can spot them.

ODOM: The Globar tube.

[STROBERT *ignores* ODOM.]

[ODOM *gets up and goes to a cabinet to get the Globar tube. He returns to his desk.*]

STROBERT: [*To* TULLY.] Move!

[TULLY *exits.*]

[ODOM *works silently.* STROBERT *paces, stepping on an occasional bug. After a few seconds,* TULLY *comes back in.*]

TULLY: Nothin'.

STROBERT: You sure?

TULLY: Yah, I'm sure, L. T.

[TULLY *goes back outside to watch.*]

STROBERT: [*Pacing.*] "Whoever left him out … whoever left him out … ought to be told to go and take him in."

[STROBERT *looks at the work table.*] My God … look at that. Rust streaks running down the table legs. Everything bleeds here.

ODOM: Can you check the glass-jet separator for me?

STROBERT: Now! They should be back … now!

ODOM: If you'd find something productive to do ...

STROBERT: I'll give it a few more minutes. Then I'm calling *Bravo*.

[ODOM *gets up to go to the jet separator machine and takes out a slide. As* ODOM *goes back to his desk, He takes a nervous moment to look out the door.*]

They ought to be back. Right?

ODOM: Don't panic ... [*He walks to his desk.*] ... it ... doesn't do anybody any good to panic.

[STROBERT *walks to the radio.*]

STROBERT: [*Tapping the radio.*] Odom?

ODOM: Give it a few more minutes. Then we'll call Bravo.

[ODOM *goes back to looking in his microprobe.* STROBERT *stands by the radio tapping it nervously.*]

TULLY: Hey! [*He whistles like a bird.*]

[STROBERT *and* ODOM *look to the door tensely.*]

I think I see 'em. [*Pause.*] Yah!

STROBERT: Thank God.

TULLY: Yah ... I can see 'em.

ODOM: [*To* STROBERT.] Calm down. Don't let Fudge see you all worked up. It will only embarrass him. [*Pause.*] Here, take this slide. Run it through the GC/MS.

STROBERT: I'm ok now. I'm ok.

[*He goes to the machine with the slide.*]

[ODOM *goes back to working on his microprobe.*]

[*Suddenly, mortar rounds are heard.*]

TULLY: Incoming! Yah ... here they come.

[ODOM *and* STROBERT *jump up.*]

I ... can see Fudge.

ODOM: [*To* STROBERT.] Get down.

TULLY: Incoming, for Christsakes.

ODOM: Where the hell's Bravo?

STROBERT: I'm going out to help Yarde. [TULLY *runs in*.]

ODOM: Stay down.

[TULLY *and* ODOM *grab* STROBERT *and they all hit the floor*.]

STROBERT: Let me go.

ODOM: Outgoing. Thank God. Bravo's firing.

TULLY: [*Trying to keep* STROBERT *down*.] Keep down.

ODOM: They'll make it. I tell you, They'll make it.

[*Suddenly* FUDGE *appears. The men help* FUDGE *pull* YARDE *inside the pagoda*. FUDGE *is pulling* YARDE *on a poncho*.]

FUDGE: Napalm strike. Sky Raiders. You told us they weren't coming back.

ODOM: Bravo said it was all clear.

FUDGE: It was *napalm*, Odom.

[FUDGE *talks as men get* YARDE *settled on a cot*.]

We were walking about a half a mile from the LZ. Without any warning, Yarde shoves me to the ground and says: "Don't get out of my sight." And he up and disappears. [*Pause*.] Next thing I know, he comes outta nowhere on fire.

[*The men all hunker down around* YARDE *at a particularly close mortar shell*.] Yarde ... Yarde ... can you hear me? [*Pause*.] You tell me not to get outta yer sight ... then all of a sudden, I can't find you. [*Pause*.] Odom, do something. He's ... still burning.

ODOM: You call a dust-off?

FUDGE: They can't come in.

STROBERT: They've got to come in.

FUDGE: The LZ's hot. Yarde ...Yarde ... can you hear me?

ODOM: I'll give him a shot.

TULLY: You think he feels anything?

ODOM: Just in case.

FUDGE: This is my fault.

ODOM: Don't blame yourself. [*Pause*.] I had no right sending him out all the time.

TULLY: He wanted to.

ODOM: I had no right.

STROBERT: Yarde ... can you hear me?

FUDGE: [FUDGE *goes into a rage so that* ODOM *has to pick him up and hold him by the waist to calm him.*] Yarde, I really wasted two V-C. Stitched 'em right down their stinkin' yellow Chink bellies. I'm going back and cut off their ears. I'm gonna string their ears on my dog tags. Hear me, Yarde?

ODOM: Fudge, you're not helping Yarde this way. Do you hear me ... you're not helping him.

[ODOM *sets* FUDGE *down.*]

Strobert, give him a shot. [*Rolls up* YARDE'*s sleeve.*]

TULLY: I'll get the needle.

ODOM: [*To* TULLY.] Sterilize it.

TULLY: Right.

ODOM: Fudge, over here. Get something under his head.

FUDGE: My OD shirt?

ODOM: Good.

FUDGE: I'll roll it up. [*Rolls up shirt.*]

STROBERT: [*Giving* YARDE *a shot.*] I'll be easy ... easy ...

TULLY: God, he's still on fire.

FUDGE: He's burning.

[*Puts OD shirt under* YARDE'*s head.*]

ODOM: This is a hospital. Don't just stand there. Get some blankets.

FUDGE: Right. [*Goes to get blankets.*]

[TULLY *fans* YARDE'*s head and face.*]

ODOM: I'm afraid he won't feel that, Tully.

TULLY: He deserves a little air. For once.

[FUDGE *puts blankets on* YARDE.]

ODOM: [*To* FUDGE.] Easy ... easy ...

TULLY: Careful, for Christsakes.

FUDGE: I'm being as careful as I can.

[*Finishes putting blankets on* YARDE.]

TULLY: Get the damn flies off of him.

ODOM: He needs a blood transfusion.

STROBERT: We don't have any blood.

ODOM: Ok ... ok ... give him some water, then.

FUDGE: [*Puts his canteen up to* YARDE's *lips.*] Come on, Yarde.

TULLY: [*Still fanning* YARDE.] He ain't drinking nothing.

STROBERT: That water cool?

FUDGE: How am I gonna get cool water?

TULLY: He ain't drinking.

STROBERT: Moisten his lips.

FUDGE: Ok ... ok ...

TULLY: Gently, Fudge ... gently ...

ODOM: That's enough. Let him rest.

TULLY: Put some fuckin' mosquito netting over him.

FUDGE: Right.

[*They all put green mosquito netting around* YARDE *and hunker down around him.*]

TULLY: He's got a chance. Right, Doc?

STROBERT: Of course he's got a chance.

FUDGE: We were safe. Then he ... just ... disappeared.

ODOM: It's not your fault.

FUDGE: We coulda come in safe.

STROBERT: It's not your fault.

ODOM: It's mine.

STROBERT: Odom, you're not to blame.

ODOM: I want him quiet now. [*Pause.*] There's nothing to do but wait for the mortars to stop. So the dust-off can come in. [*Pause.*] I want everybody quiet. So he can rest.

[*The mortars whine outside. The lights change to signify passage of time. The green netting around* YARDE *hides his body and as the lights change for passage of time,* YARDE'*s body disappears from view.*]

[*Suddenly the mortars stop.* ODOM *stands.* STROBERT, TULLY, FUDGE *are hunched over in grief.*]

[ODOM *abruptly pulls* STROBERT *up from his hunched position.*]

ODOM: There was nothing we could do. White phosphorus embers deep in the tissue ... where it smoulders ... long after the external burning.

[STROBERT *moans softly.*]

It's ... an ignominious death. [*Pause.*] I look out there ... the last place he walked, and I can't even see the birds. The sky's blank. It's like this Godforsaken place knows enough to keep them away. It's the earth getting back at us. [*Pause.*] Well, wherever he is ... now ... I wish him robins, and sparrows, and humming birds. [*Pause.*] Lieutenant Strobert, I want you to listen up. [*Pause.*] I don't know why a young man like you, from New York City, is here. In this hell. At the end of his ropes. With nothing but a Private E-1, a Spec. 4 canner from Muscatine. And a nigger veterinarian. [*Pause.*] But that's how it is. [*Pause.*] You're an officer. And you're going to set an example for these men. [*Pause.*] I've never been the best at giving commands. When I was a cadet a West Point, I had to walk to the Hudson and shout orders across the water. That's how somebody like me had to practice commands, you see. [*Pause.*] But I want it made clear, Lieutenant, I'm an officer and a gentleman. By an act of Congress. [*Silent pause.*] A dust-off will be coming in soon. And strangers will take what's left of our friend. But before they do, this detachment is going to say goodbye with honor, dignity, and bravery. [*Pause.*] Is that understood?

[ODOM *pulls* STROBERT *to his chest for a manly hug.*]

You love too much.

[*He pulls away from* STROBERT.] We both would have been all right ... in another time. [*Pause.*] Prepare the men for services.

[STROBERT *stares at* ODOM *blankly.*] That's an order, Lieutenant.

[STROBERT *slowly turns and goes to* FUDGE *and* TULLY. *He nudges them gently.*]

STROBERT: Fudge ... Tully ... stand up.

FUDGE: We ... let him die.

TULLY: A fuckin' dust-off didn't even take him to a decent hospital.

FUDGE: Yarde's dead. There's nothin' left of him ...

ODOM: Call the men to order.

STROBERT: A ... ten ... shut.

FUDGE: What's going on here? What kind of unit is this?

ODOM: [*To* FUDGE.] You were given a command, soldier. Snap to!

[FUDGE *and* TULLY *stand at attention, along with* STROBERT.]

ODOM: Men, I'm ... deeply sorry to report ... that Sergeant. Yarde has been killed in action. A napalm casualty. [*Pause.*] At ease.

[TULLY, FUDGE, *and* STROBERT *stand at ease.*] My friends ... please ... sit down.

[*The men sit on the floor.*] I'd like to take a minute to discuss something important with you. Something concerning Sergeant Yarde.

FUDGE: We ... let him die ...

ODOM: I ... want to ask you ... if ... we couldn't do something special in his memory.

TULLY: He was the best man out there.

STROBERT: The best.

FUDGE: How am I ... gonna get along without him?

STROBERT: What kind of special thing for Yarde were you thinking about, Odom?

ODOM: One soldier can get out of this war without being tainted.

TULLY: Whataya mean?

ODOM: Somebody ... can escape the infamy of Viet Nam.

STROBERT: The Unknown Soldier.

ODOM: Whoever's in that tomb ... won't have his name connected to this hell. [*Pause.*] Why not Yarde?

STROBERT: You're talking mutiny, Odom.

ODOM: I know that.

STROBERT: You're ... a lifer.

ODOM: From now on, I'm wearing my sleeves rolled up.

STROBERT: There will be careful checking ... investigations.

ODOM: I can handle that.

STROBERT: And your career?

ODOM: It's time a man like me thinks of his brother first.

STROBERT: You sure?

ODOM: I'm sure.

STROBERT: I'm with you.

TULLY: Me, too.

FUDGE: Me, too.

ODOM: We'll destroy Yarde's records.

FUDGE: I can do that. I know everybody in records.

TULLY: Yarde's gonna have himself the eternal flame.

ODOM: I submit this unit has met it's military purpose.

STROBERT: We have new remains that can't be analyzed.

ODOM: Right.

TULLY: Them ... new remains have no bones to disarticulate.

STROBERT: No blood.

FUDGE: Can't match no ID printout to nothing.

ODOM: No need to submit my microprobe.

STROBERT: Sergeant Yarde's ashes are without question non-verifiable.

ODOM: .Forward information!

STROBERT: Relay to IV Corps.

TULLY: IV Corps to Saigon.

FUDGE: Saigon to Washington.

TULLY/FUDGE/STROBERT: Yes, sir!

ODOM: Objective accomplished.

STROBERT: A ... ten ... shut.

[STROBERT, TULLY, *and* FUDGE *stand at attention.*]

ODOM: We have a napalm casualty. Only remains — cinders. [*Pause.*]

This medical detachment has found the Unknown Soldier.

MEN: Yes, sir.

ODOM: I can't hear you.

MEN: Yes, sir.

[ODOM *gets* FUDGE's *guitar and hands it to* FUDGE.]

STROBERT: Pa ... rade, rest.

[*The men now stand at parade rest.*]

ODOM: Fudge, lead the men in services.

[FUDGE *strikes a chord on the guitar.*]

STROBERT: [*Sings:*] Nothin' on the table
mean ...

ODOM: Something on the collar.

TULLY: Give the man a dollar
ah ah ah
give the man a dollar.

FUDGE: Nothin' on the table
mean
somethin' on the sleeve ...

TULLY: Give the man a leave
ah ah ah
give the man a leave.

ODOM: We're Army
working on the line ...

STROBERT: We're Army
with piecework from the mine.

FUDGE/TULLY/STROBERT/ODOM: Nothin' on the table

mean
somethin' on the sleeve.
Give the man a leave
ah ah ah
give the man a leave ...
[*Softly*:] ... give the man a leave.

[*Lights fade to darkness*.]

THE END

MILL
FIRE

by

Sally Nemeth

CHARACTERS

Marlene, 25 years old, high school education, office worker.

Champ, late 20's, Marlene's husband. Steel worker.

Sunny, mid-to-late 30's. Marlene's sister-in-law. Does not work.

Bo, pushing 40, beginning to thicken. Marlene's brother. Steel mill foreman, Vietnam vet.

Jemison, also around 40. A substantial black man. Also a foreman.

Minister, mid 30's. Alabama Baptist, but not sanctimonious. The minister doubles as the OSHA investigator.

Widow 1, 2, 3. Even though the widows speak as a sort of collective consciousness and are dressed alike, they should be as distinct physically as possible. They should be of different age, race, height, etc. They are not the same woman.

NOTES ON STAGING

The play will work under a variety of circumstances — proscenium, thrust, 3/4, or 2/3. It is important, however, to clearly delineate areas of the stage as CHAMP *and* MARLENE's *bedroom,* SUNNY *and* BO's *kitchen, the mill, the church area, to help clarify for the audience where and when we are in the play.*

ACT ONE

Late 1970's. Birmingham, Alabama. The stage should be divided into various areas, not necessarily by scenery, but often with lights. Distinctions need to be made between the following areas: MARLENE *and* CHAMP's *bed,* SUNNY *and* BO's *kitchen, the mill, the church. It is helpful to have levels on the stage — a catwalk or scaffolding — and staircases leading to the upper level. At the top of the play, the* WIDOWS *sit downstage, veiled in tulle and dressed in black, sipping from white coffee cups. The bed is draped in a sooty tarp. The* WIDOWS *go to the bed and remove the tarp, revealing* MARLENE, *lying on the bed in a slip.*

MARLENE: In the hottest part of a hot July day, I lie on the bed, a fan oscillating over me, a tall glass of tea on the bedside table. Beads forming on the glass, sweat beads, running down its sides. A ring of water, ruining the finish on the table top. My skin still hot after my second shower of the day. Hot to the touch. My arms and legs arranged so as to leave space between. Breathing space. Space to let my hot skin breathe. You know what I mean? How that is?

CHAMP: [CHAMP *appears, standing at the head of the bed in a full steelworker's heat-reflective suit, hardhat, safety glasses and gloves.*] Yeah.

MARLENE: And hot as I am, with my limbs arranged to avoid contact with one another, I want you next to me. In that heat I want you there. I think you there. And there you are. I start to feel good. The heat doesn't bother me. It all goes away. Everything goes away except you and me and the bed. Sometimes in the afternoon there's a thunderstorm.

CHAMP: Sometimes.

MARLENE: Sometimes there is. The curtains start to blow and my head starts to clear like all the worry in the world will never be mine. And when the rain comes pouring over the sills we don't get up and close the windows. We let it pour over the sills, soaking the rug, warping the floorboards. Because none of those things are there. Nothing is there except you and me and the bed.

CHAMP: Nothing's there.

MARLENE: Not a thing. You, me, and the bed. [CHAMP *disappears.*] Nothing. No thing, no body.

SUNNY: [*Knocks at door.*] Marlene? Marlene honey, wake up.

MARLENE: I'm not asleep.

SUNNY: [*Entering room. She is dressed in dark clothing and carries a black dress and panty hose over her shoulder.*] You're not?

MARLENE: No, I'm not.

SUNNY: Well, you're not now, but you were then.

MARLENE: How do you know?

SUNNY: You were talking up a storm.

MARLENE: So?

SUNNY: I guess you were talking in your sleep.

MARLENE: You guess.

SUNNY: Ok. You were talking to yourself and now we all got to worry about you.

MARLENE: Why?

SUNNY: Evertbody's going to think you're a crazy lady.

MARLENE: Don't they already?

SUNNY: Maybe you'd like them to.

   [*Takes dress and stockings off her shoulder and lays them on the bed.*]

MARLENE: What is that?

SUNNY: What does it look like?

MARLENE: I'm not wearing that.

SUNNY: Marlene.

MARLENE: I threw that in the Goodwill bag.

SUNNY: And I took it out.

MARLENE: It's not touching my skin.

SUNNY: Well, what are you going to wear?

MARLENE: Not that. [*Hurls dress to the floor.*]

SUNNY: It's the only dark thing you've got.

MARLENE: Oh, for Christ's sake. I'm not going to do that. I'm not going to make everybody else comfortable because I'm behaving appropriately.

SUNNY: I don't see any point in that.

   [*Retrieves dress, lays it out.*]

MARLENE: You don't.

SUNNY: No, I don't.

MARLENE: That doesn't surprise me. Where's Bo?

SUNNY: Coming from the mill with the rest of the shift.

MARLENE: Showing in numbers.

SUNNY: What did you expect? They're going to stay away?

MARLENE: That wouldn't be appropriate.

SUNNY: Goes a little deeper than that.

MARLENE: Can't tempt fate.

SUNNY: Marlene, you are full of shit, you know that?

MARLENE: I've never known more superstitious men than steelworkers. Have you?

SUNNY: That's shit. How can you even think things like that — especially about your own Goddamn brother. And how do you think I feel when you say things like that about Bo?

MARLENE: You tell me.

SUNNY: He's my husband. That's how I feel when you say things like that. I mean, I've let a lot of things slide.

MARLENE: Oh. Well.

SUNNY: Listen, anniversaries are hard. Bringing it all back up again. But lay off Bo. He feels awful. They all do.

MARLENE: They can feel as awful as they want. And the anniversary is no harder than the day to day. Can't bring anything back up again that never went away.

SUNNY: Give it time.

MARLENE: Oh, Sunny, that's some fine advice. I think I'll take it to heart.

SUNNY: Wear what you want. We'll be leaving for the church in half an hour.

MARLENE: I don't need an escort. Tell Bo.

SUNNY: You tell him. Half an hour.

[*Exits.* MARLENE *dresses in a very colorful dress. The* WIDOWS *enter, unveiled, and will move to an observer's position on the upper level.*]

WIDOW 1: They'd swung over to graveyard shift a day or two before. He never could sleep those first couple days after the shift had changed.

WIDOW 2: Never could sleep. Went to work tired. Came home tired. Then the sun would come out and it didn't matter if the drapes were drawn or the kids were quiet.

WIDOW 3: It was never quiet enough or dark enough.

WIDOW 1: And I'd slip around the house.

WIDOW 3: Getting the kids ready for school. Myself ready for work. And he'd toss.

WIDOW 2: Rolling back and forth on the bed. The sound of the mill still in his ears.

WIDOW 1: And the kids would be ready and I'd be ready and I'd unplug the phone and lock the door behind me.

WIDOW 2: Come home at three with the kids to find him up having a beer.

WIDOW 1: Couldn't ever sleep. Too light. Too loud.

WIDOW 3: Even those two days before. When it rained and rained.

WIDOW 2: That sound of rain. That lulling sound. On the roof. Dripping from the gutters.

WIDOW 1: Even that didn't do it. I'd come home that day to find him up.

WIDOW 2: Having a beer and a sandwich.

WIDOW 3: I said I'd fix him something hot to eat but he said he didn't want it.

WIDOW 1: It didn't feel like it was time to eat something hot. It wasn't just the sleep. It was food, too.

WIDOW 3: He said he never knew when he was coming or going. Never knew.

[SUNNY *enters the kitchen with a bag of groceries. She takes a pint bottle of whiskey from the bag and puts it in her purse. She replaces the receiver of the wall phone back on the cradle, and starts to put things away, calling up the stairs to* BO. *It is night and it is raining.*]

SUNNY: Bo, Bo honey, wake up.

BO: Yeah.

SUNNY: It's time to get up.

BO: What time is it?

[BO *comes down the stairs in his underwear and takes a seat at the table.* SUNNY *sets a place before him.*]

SUNNY: Nine.

BO: First time I've slept straight through in the past couple of days.

SUNNY: It's the rain. Makes it cooler. Darker.

BO: I guess.

SUNNY: Jemison called from the mill, but I told him I wasn't going to wake you until nine.

BO: Sunny — you know to wake me.

SUNNY: First time you've slept in days.

BO: What did he want?

SUNNY: Creek's up.

BO: Into the mill?

SUNNY: Part of it. He said one furnace is out.

BO: Shit.

SUNNY: He just wants you to call him.

BO: [BO *heads up the stairs.*] You should have just woken me up.

SUNNY: Yeah, we've been through that. What do you want to eat?

BO: I don't know. What did you have?

SUNNY: Tuna casserole.

BO: No. Why don't you just fix me some eggs.

SUNNY: How do you want them?

BO: Surprise me.

MARLENE: [CHAMP *is in bed asleep.* MARLENE *enters.*] Champ! Baby, it's nine o'clock.

CHAMP: So?

MARLENE: So get up. Your shift rolled over two days ago.

CHAMP: I know.

MARLENE: And you left me a note to come get you at nine.

CHAMP: Well, come on, girl. Come and get me.

MARLENE: What time you got to be there?

CHAMP: Eleven thirty or so. We won't do shit out there with this rain. Just sit around and collect pay.

MARLENE: Best kind of work to have.

CHAMP: Come here.

MARLENE: I'm here.

[*Gets into bed and curls up against* CHAMP. *Shift over to the kitchen, where the phone is ringing.* BO *runs down the stairs to get it, more or less dressed in mill clothes. He will button, tie, zip, etc. as he talks.*]

BO: Yeah, I got your message.

[*Pause, laughs.*]

Well, she knows what happens when she don't let me sleep. So, what have we got? Uh huh. Well, I can't do much with that. I know that. Yeah. I know.

[*Pause.*]

Well, my shift ain't the only one's not up to quota ... yeah, I know you know.

[*Pause.*]

How many heats? With one furnace out? That's ridiculous. I mean I guess we can do it we keep the other two fired all night.

[*Pause.*]

When I have a choice. All right, man. I'll be down right away.

[*Hangs up. Begins to tie his shoes, remembers* CHAMP, *and redials the phone.*]

Champ, you awake? Well, why didn't you let Marlene answer?

[SUNNY *enters in a robe with a cup of coffee.*]

Oh. Well, anyway I won't be able to give you a ride in tonight. I got to go early. Unless you want to go when I do.

[*Pause.*]

Didn't think so. All right. See you before midnight.

[*Hangs up.* SUNNY *comes in with a cup of coffee.*]

You fix them eggs yet?

SUNNY: I was waiting for you to come down.

[*Hands him coffee.*]

BO: Well don't. I got to be off now.

SUNNY: How long are a couple of eggs going to take?

BO: You got to cook them then I got to sit and eat them and I hate to shovel my food.

SUNNY: Then don't. Sit down and eat like a human being. They can wait another half hour.

BO: I said I'd be right down.

SUNNY: I haven't seen you to say boo to in some time.

BO: Well I'm not going to make conversation sitting and shoveling eggs.

SUNNY: Fine. You're just going to shovel doughnuts or some shit when you get to the mill, anyway.

BO: Then fix some damn eggs.

SUNNY: Fix them yourself.

[SUNNY *heads up the stairs*, BO *grabs his jacket and exits the house. Shift over to* MARLENE *and* CHAMP *in be*d.]

MARLENE: What did he want?

CHAMP: He's going in early. Can't give me a ride.

MARLENE: Something wrong?

CHAMP: I don't know. I guess, if he's going in early. You need the car?

MARLENE: Not till morning.

CHAMP: I hate to leave you without a car.

MARLENE: I'm not going anywhere. Except to bed.

CHAMP: You're already there.

MARLENE: Yeah, I know it. Damn Bo.

CHAMP: Why?

MARLENE: I don't know. Since it's raining and all I kind of

thought I might could talk you into maybe calling in sick.

CHAMP: Well, I can't do that now I've talked with him.

MARLENE: Maybe we could have car trouble.

CHAMP: That's pushing it.

MARLENE: I guess. But you know how I get when it rains.

CHAMP: I know how you get.

MARLENE: Come on. Car died. What do you think?

CHAMP: Girl, you're crazy.

MARLENE: You love it.

CHAMP: Don't I though.

　　[CHAMP *exits*.]

MARLENE: Champ!

　　[*Chases after him.*]

　　[*Shift over to* BO *and* JEMISON *in the mill area.*]

BO: Wouldn't you know. The thirty ton furnace is the one to go out.

JEMISON: It's nearest the creek.

BO: Fucking poor planning.

JEMISON: You said it.

BO: So what's the story?

JEMISON: We're way behind.

BO: Like I don't know it. Everyone's been crawling up my butt all week.

JEMISON: Mine, too.

BO: So we need to make at least five heats on each furnace of seventy grade. That's it, right?

JEMISON: You got it.

BO: It can be done. If we don't lose another furnace.

JEMISON: Never happen.

BO: Bullshit.

JEMISON: [*Pulls cigarettes out of his front pocket. They are soaked.*]

Shit. These are all wet. You got a smoke?

BO: [*Pulls a pack of Lucky Strikes out of his pocket.*] Always do. [*They light up.*] So what's the big fucking hurry on this seventy grade?

JEMISON: Big highway project up north.

BO: Yeah?

JEMISON: Yeah. Construction company swung over to us after the mill supplying them went on strike. So they cleaned up out of our inventory and want more. Yesterday. You know.

BO: Nice to get a contract like that.

JEMISON: Sure, if we can do it. And you know, front office will say anything. A million tons tomorrow? No problem.

BO: I'm just as glad.

JEMISON: Yeah.

BO: The way things are going and all. It's good to have orders coming in.

JEMISON: So long as we deliver. I mean, we fuck up on this, and another might not come our way.

BO: Don't I know it.

JEMISON: Did you hear about U. S.?

BO: What — they striking again?

JEMISON: Hell, no. They got no leverage at all. Here's what I heard. They're closing down their rolling mill.

BO: No.

JEMISON: Yeah. Just keeping the melt shop open, then taking the steel elsewhere to mill it.

BO: Jesus.

JEMISON: They'll be laying off a couple thousand men.

BO: Shit. Where'd you hear that?

JEMISON: It's been flying around for a while.

BO: How come I didn't hear that?

JEMISON: I don't know.

BO: Well, I've got some time to kill here. Is there any coffee on?

JEMISON: Been on for a while. You might want to make some fresh.

BO: I'll do that.

JEMISON: There's some doughnuts in there, too. Help yourself.

[*They exit. The* WIDOWS *enter with* MARLENE, *and sit in chairs with their coffee cups.* MARLENE *lights a cigarette.*]

WIDOW 1: It cleared that morning. Cleared and the sun came out hot and bright.

WIDOW 2: Everything got steamy. All that wet ground. Oversoaked and steaming.

WIDOW 3: I wanted the rain back again. Wanted the dark, the gloom of it. It seemed that was more in keeping with everything else.

WIDOW 2: Wanted that sound. To hear water rolling off the roof.

WIDOW 1: The cicadas came out to dry their wings. Thousands of them. Millions. Setting up that buzz.

WIDOW 3: The buzz came in waves, like they planned when they were going to get loud. When they were going to get softer.

WIDOW 2: And I listened to that. The cicadas. Let it wash over me. Let it roll off the roof.

WIDOW 1: The bugs buzzing and the house full of people, relatives, friends, buzzing.

[*The* MINISTER *enters and pours a cup of coffee.*]

WIDOW 3: The kids crying. Not really sure what was going on, but crying because everyone else was.

MARLENE: Except me. I was listening to the buzz. Going right through me.

MINISTER: Mrs. Hotchkiss? Mrs. Hotchkiss — would you like some coffee?

MARLENE: Coffee?

MINISTER: Would you like some?

MARLENE: No. No coffee. Thank you.

MINISTER: Well, if you're sure.

[*No response.*]

Well, it's good to see you again, though of course I wish the circumstances were different.

MARLENE: You said that last year.

WIDOW 1: Marlene.

MARLENE: What?

WIDOW 1: Don't start. Please. Not tonight.

MARLENE: I don't see what's so damn different about tonight. 365 days. Each one of them the same.

WIDOW 2: I hear you.

MINISTER: Marlene — may I call you Marlene?

MARLENE: Everyone else does.

MINISTER: I believe that — I believe that what we're here to do tonight is a healing thing. It was a senseless accident that took your husbands. Folks need to work it out. They need to bring it up again so it doesn't stay down deep inside them.

MARLENE: Oh, I don't think this has gone too far below the surface.

WIDOW 1: Marlene, why are you here?

WIDOW 3: Can't we just be a —

WIDOW 1: No, I can't. Marlene here has yanked us around but good.

WIDOW 2: I don't think she did what she did to yank anybody around.

WIDOW 1: You were talking something different back when the mill was ready to yank the settlement.

WIDOW 2: Well, I've had some time now to think about it.

WIDOW 1: So have I. So why are you here, Marlene?

MARLENE: I'm here to heal. How about you?

[*They exit. Shift over to* SUNNY, *who comes to the kitchen table and pours herself a drink from her bottle. She has had a few. She opens a magazine and leafs through it briskly, then notices the placesetting* BO *left behind.*]

SUNNY: Fuck you Bo, fuck you Bo, fuck you.

[*She clears the placesetting, then goes back to her magazine. The phone rings three or four times before she answers it.*]

What? No, Marlene, he's already gone. Uh huh. Well, I'm sorry to hear that but I'm going to be using my car tonight. Yeah. Well, sounds like all you need is a jump. Right. Well, he's got to be there by now — he left like a house afire. Have Champ call him there. 'Bye.

[*Hangs up. Freshens her drink.*]

I'm going out tonight. Sure. Gonna have me a good time.

[*Takes phone off the hook and goes upstairs. Shift over to* MARLENE *and* CHAMP's *bedroom. They enter.*]

CHAMP: Why did you ask her for the car?

MARLENE: I knew she'd say no.

CHAMP: How'd you know that?

MARLENE: I just knew.

CHAMP: Is she drunk?

MARLENE: [*Gets into bed.*] Champ.

CHAMP: Is she?

MARLENE: On her way there.

CHAMP: Well, that pretty much settles it.

MARLENE: What?

CHAMP: [*Gets into bed with her.*] I got to go in tonight.

MARLENE: Aw, Champ.

CHAMP: Bo's a son of a bitch when Sunny's hitting it.

MARLENE: He can be.

CHAMP: He is. You've seen it.

MARLENE: Yeah.

CHAMP: Sometimes I don't see it — the two of them.

MARLENE: You don't.

CHAMP: Not at all.

MARLENE: He loves the fucking steel mill and all she does is drive him there.

CHAMP: What does she get out of it?

MARLENE: What do you think she gets out of it?

CHAMP: I'm asking you.

MARLENE: She gets to be "poor Sunny."

CHAMP: Poor Sunny.

MARLENE: Poor Sunny. No kids and that man who don't pay her no attention.

CHAMP: Bo's lacking in some of the finer points.

MARLENE: That ain't all he's lacking.

CHAMP: That's not fair.

MARLENE: Fair or not, you know that's what it is and what it's about.

CHAMP: Wasn't nothing she didn't know about.

MARLENE: They were married before he went.

CHAMP: So?

MARLENE: So, you don't divorce no fucking Purple Heart. Not in Sunny's book.

CHAMP: What time's it getting to be?

MARLENE: Around ten.

CHAMP: You want to fix me something to eat?

MARLENE: [*Getting amorous.*] No I don't want to fix you something to eat.

CHAMP: You don't?

MARLENE: No.

CHAMP: Why not?

MARLENE: Because I want you to eat me.

CHAMP: Fix me something to eat first.

MARLENE: I don't want to.

CHAMP: I'll faint. Pass out cold. Everything's starting to go — dark.

[*He slumps over, not to be roused.*]

MARLENE: Champ. Champ, come on. Champ. Shit.

[*Gets out of bed.*]

How do you want your eggs?

[*He grabs at her feet as she exits. Shift over to* BO, *munching on a doughnut with a styrofoam cup of coffee in his hand in the mill area.* JEMISON *holds a clipboard.*]

BO: What kind of scrap we got?

JEMISON: Automotive.

BO: Shit.

JEMISON: Yeah, it's pretty wet.

BO: Holds water like a sponge.

JEMISON: Some of it's under cover, but you'll go through it pretty quick.

BO: We'll just use the wet stuff for the first melt and charge the heats with the drier stuff.

JEMISON: Yeah. I been doing that.

BO: Ain't you smart.

JEMISON: Not too. I started off throwing anything in before I knew how wet it was.

BO: Kaboom.

JEMISON: Yeah. You know. The furnace is capped off. You know it, and the guys know it but it still scares the shit out of them.

BO: Oh yeah.

JEMISON: A couple guys dove for cover.

BO: Who?

JEMISON: Pritchett and Turner.

BO: Yeah?

JEMISON: And you know with all the other noise I'm surprised anyone hears it. It don't make that big a bang.

BO: It's big enough.

JEMISON: You're going to run out of dry scrap. Maybe mid shift.

BO: I run out, I'll figure it out. You know.

JEMISON: [*Hands over clipboard.*] I know.

[*Shift to* MARLENE *and* MINISTER.]

MARLENE: [*Entering with the* MINISTER.] What?

MINISTER: Marlene —

MARLENE: What?

MINISTER: Look. This isn't easy for any of them, either.

MARLENE: You don't think I know that?

MINISTER: I wasn't sure.

MARLENE: I do. Real well. Real well.

MINISTER: May I ask you something?

MARLENE: You can ask.

MINISTER: How old are you?

MARLENE: Shit. I thought it was going to be something important.

MINISTER: Important?

MARLENE: Yeah. So solemn. "May I ask you something?"

MINISTER: Well?

MARLENE: Twenty-five. Now you going to tell me I got my whole life ahead of me?

MINISTER: No.

MARLENE: No?

MINISTER: Not exactly.

MARLENE: But something along those lines.

MINISTER: You're just — you're awfully hard for a woman of twenty-five.

MARLENE: You got any better ideas?

MINISTER: I don't understand.

MARLENE: On how to behave. You got any ideas for me? Do you? Because I'm open to ideas. But I don't know a whole lot of twenty-five year old widows and I don't know a whole lot of other ways to get myself to tomorrow and the next day and the next day —

[*Begins to break a little bit.*]

MINISTER: Marlene —

[*Reaches to her and places his hand on her shoulder.*]

I didn't mean to upset you.

MARLENE: Yes you did.

MINISTER: Yes I did.

MARLENE: Hold me.

MINISTER: Marlene, I —

MARLENE: Please, just do it.

[*He holds her. Very stiffly. He is totally uncomfortable. She holds him and tries to get relaxed into him. He still doesn't relax. She pulls away.*]

MINISTER: I'm sorry. I've never — I've been asked for all kinds of solace, but I've never had a parishoner ask to be physically comforted.

MARLENE: I'm not a parishoner. I'm a twenty-five year old widow.

[*Pause.*]

I haven't been held in a year.

MINISTER: Marlene I'm sorry. I — you're a twenty-five year old widow.

MARLENE: With a hard edge.

MINISTER: No.

MARLENE: Are you a Methodist?

MINISTER: Baptist.

MARLENE: You hug like you've got a corncob up your butt.

[*They look at one another for a moment, then laugh. They exit. The* WIDOWS *appear above.*]

WIDOW 3: The children are quite a comfort to me.

WIDOW 2: Quite a comfort.

WIDOW 1: The youngest still crawls up into my lap when I'm watching the TV at night.

WIDOW 2: Leans into me and falls asleep.

WIDOW 1: I carry him upstairs and put him to bed. Tuck him between cartoon sheets.

WIDOW 3: Brush the hair away from his father's forehead.

WIDOW 1: His father's face.

WIDOW 2: My big boy is getting too old to be held.

WIDOW 3: That's what he says.

[*Shift over to* CHAMP *in bed, asleep.* MARLENE *enters.*]

MARLENE: Get up.

CHAMP: I'm up.

MARLENE: No, you're not.

CHAMP: Well I am now.

MARLENE: You want some eggs or don't you?

CHAMP: I want some.

MARLENE: You got to be awake to eat them.

CHAMP: I'm awake.

MARLENE: You always do this.

CHAMP: Well, girl, you wear me out.

MARLENE: No I don't.

CHAMP: Yeah you do.

MARLENE: I do?

CHAMP: Yeah.

MARLENE: Shit.

CHAMP: I'm not complaining.

MARLENE: Good.

CHAMP: What time is it?

MARLENE: Eleven.

CHAMP: [*Gets out of bed.*] Were you going to let me oversleep?

MARLENE: I thought about it.

CHAMP: Good choice.

MARLENE: [*Gets into bed.*] Says you.

CHAMP: Well, I'll be back in eight hours. Then you can call in sick.

MARLENE: Maybe I will.

CHAMP: Maybe.

MARLENE: I got a whole eight hours to sleep on it.

[CHAMP *exits. Shift up to the* WIDOWS, *still above.*]

WIDOW 2: This is what I liked. Right where his butt went in. That indentation that men have and women don't. Boy, I liked that.

WIDOW 3: His hands were amazing. They were always being banged up at work. His right hand ring finger went every which way. Scars all over from burns and cuts. But the way he moved them. They looked almost pretty.

WIDOW 1: My man was definitely packing it on. Right across the middle. Getting stretch marks on his lower back. All the other men in his family were spindly. He got a kick out of it. He loved his little gut.

[*Shift to the mill.*]

JEMISON: Bo. Hey. Your wife's on the phone.

BO: What does she want?

JEMISON: Didn't ask.

BO: All right.

[BO *gets on the mill phone, while* SUNNY *is on the kitchen phone.*]

BO: Yeah.

SUNNY: I want you home now. I want you home.

BO: Sunny — I can't do that. I'm at work.

SUNNY: I don't care.

BO: I'm up to my neck in water and I can't —

SUNNY: Oh, it's always a crisis. Always a fucking crisis.

BO: Sunny, you don't seem to understand.

SUNNY: I understand fine. I just don't care. You hear me? I just don't care.

BO: I hear you.

SUNNY: You hear me.

BO: Sunny, listen, I'll be home in the morning. We can talk then.

SUNNY: Yeah, we can. But we won't.

BO: I swear to you, honey.

SUNNY: Because I won't be here in the morning.

[*She hangs up and exits. Shift over to* MARLENE *and* CHAMP. *Phone rings.*]

MARLENE: Hello? Hang on, he's just getting ready to head out.

[*Covers receiver and hollers.*]

Champ! Honey! It's Bo!

[*Back to phone.*]

Why you at work so early? Yeah. Uh-huh. That doesn't sound good.

[CHAMP *enters.*] Here's Champ. Oh, ok. Yeah, I talked to her not too long ago.

[*Pause.*]

Listen, don't worry about it. No, don't. You got enough to worry about tonight.

[*Pause.*]

Hey, Bo, I'm sorry. I know you know. Yeah. 'Bye.

[*Hangs up.*]

CHAMP: What was that about?

MARLENE: He wants you to go over to his house and take Sunny's car keys away.

CHAMP: What?

MARLENE: You heard me.

CHAMP: Why?

MARLENE: Said she called him, loaded, and told him she was taking off.

CHAMP: Well, that's something new.

MARLENE: Yeah, it is.

CHAMP: Shit.

MARLENE: I'm sorry, baby, it's just —

CHAMP: No, it's ok.

MARLENE: You know he doesn't like to drag you into this.

CHAMP: I'm family.

MARLENE: Not blood.

CHAMP: I'm still family.

MARLENE: Well, you know Bo.

CHAMP: Yeah, I know Bo

> [*Pause.*]

> I better get.

MARLENE: Yeah.

CHAMP: Hey, you want to come with me?

MARLENE: No.

CHAMP: I could just take Sunny's car and you could keep ours.

MARLENE: No.

CHAMP: Come on.

MARLENE: You know how it goes. I get over there I'll never get out.

CHAMP: It was worth a try.

MARLENE: It's always worth a try.

CHAMP: Yeah.

> [*Kisses her.*]

> See you in the morning.

MARLENE: Drive careful.

> [*He exits. Shift over to* BO *at the mill. He takes a pill bottle out of his shirt pocket and takes two.* JEMISON *approaches him.*]

JEMISON: Jeff Smyer called while you were on the other line.

BO: To say what?

JEMISON: He ain't comin' in.

BO: What?

JEMISON: He ain't comin' in.

BO: Why not?

JEMISON: His cellar flooded and a wall's caved in.

BO: He ain't going to change that by being there.

JEMISON: No, he ain't.

BO: Shit. If it was me I'd come to work. I wouldn't stand around like no asshole and watch my house go down.

JEMISON: [Goes to a locker, takes off his mill jacket and changes into a street jacket.] My old place? I'd stand there and cheer it on.

BO: Yeah?

JEMISON: Yeah. I'd love to see it go down. Collect insurance. Build me a brand new house. New wiring, plumbing. I'd love to see that happen.

BO: Them old houses are built.

JEMISON: Yeah.

BO: Make it through a tornado.

JEMISON: Yeah.

BO: There's something to be said for that.

JEMISON: I don't know what. Hey, man, I'm out of here.

BO: [Heading him off] Listen, can you hang on until Champ gets here?

JEMISON: Aw, man, I'm beat.

BO: I know, but Smyer's out and Champ's running late. I just need another body.

JEMISON: [Returning to his locker resignedly and changing back into his mill jacket.] All right, but Champ better hurry his ass.

BO: He's on his way.

[SUNNY enters with a suitcase, which she opens and puts on a kitchen chair. She exits and returns with a pile of laundry.]

CHAMP: [Enters tentatively.] Sunny?

SUNNY: Oh, Jesus.

CHAMP: I'm sorry, did I scare you?

SUNNY: Champ?

CHAMP: Yeah.

SUNNY: What are you doing here?

CHAMP: I'm here to see if you're all right.

SUNNY: [*Sorting out* BO's *laundry and packing her own in the suitcase, sloppily.*] If I'm all right.

CHAMP: Yeah. Bo was worried about you. He asked me to look in on you on my way to work.

SUNNY: He did.

CHAMP: Yeah.

SUNNY: Well, isn't that something.

CHAMP: So I'm looking in on you.

SUNNY: Do I look all right?

CHAMP: Fine.

SUNNY: All right, then.

CHAMP: Sunny — I need —

SUNNY: What do you need?

CHAMP: I need your keys. To borrow your car.

SUNNY: Didn't I tell Marlene —

CHAMP: Marlene's waiting out in our car and I need to borrow yours so she can have ours.

SUNNY: Marlene's in the car? Well, why don't she come in?

[*Heads over to window and hollers out.*]

Marlene! Hey, Marlene. Get the hell in here, girl.

[*She turns from window.*]

Champ, honey, I hate to tell you this, but Marlene ain't in your car.

CHAMP: I know.

SUNNY: And she ain't in the house.

CHAMP: Ok. Bo asked me to get your keys.

SUNNY: He did.

CHAMP: Yeah.

SUNNY: Well, you can't have them.

CHAMP: Come on, Sunny.

SUNNY: No.

CHAMP: You shouldn't be driving.

SUNNY: I shouldn't.

CHAMP: No. The roads are awful.

SUNNY: Oh. You're concerned for my safety. I see. Well, that's different.

CHAMP: Where are your keys?

SUNNY: Nowhere.

CHAMP: [*Picks up her purse.*] Are they in here?

SUNNY: You stay out of my bag.

CHAMP: Are they in here?

SUNNY: You stay out of that.

[*He reaches in the bag.*] Stay out of that.

[*Launches herself at him. He comes up with the keys. She hits at him.*]

You son of a bitch.

CHAMP: [*He restrains her.*] Sunny.

SUNNY: Son of a bitch.

CHAMP: Sunny. Sunny. Shhh. Shhh.

[*He holds her from behind, pinning her arms down to her sides. He rocks her.*]

That's right. That's right.

SUNNY: [*Begins to cry.*] You know. I've had a bad day. A real bad day.

CHAMP: I know. I know.

SUNNY: No you don't. You don't know.

CHAMP: I know.

SUNNY: You don't.

[*Struggles in his hold.*]

CHAMP: Sunny!

[*Restrains her.*]

SUNNY: Oh shit.

[*Long pause.*]

Listen to that. Listen to that rain.

[*She gets sexual in the hold. He releases her.*]

CHAMP: It's coming down hard.

SUNNY: Off and on like that. All day. At that house catty-corner there was a kid sitting on the porch playing "Swanee River" over and over on his harmonica. Badly. Over and over. Rain pouring over the eaves like a curtain. And this kid. Probably driving his mama crazy so she sent him outside to drive the rest of us nuts. And there's Bo asleep upstairs. "Swanee River" over and over. Banging into my head. Thinking Bo's gonna wake up. That's going to wake him up. I pull my coat over my head and start across the street to talk to this boy's mama. I don't know these people. They're new on the street. They don't know most folks in the neighborhood work swing shifts. I need to tell them. I need to represent my community. Today I am civic minded. I get over to the porch and I look at this kid. His eyes are way too far apart. His mouth is funny. He smiles. So big. Hollers, "MamaMamaCompanyMama!". And now I don't know what to say. What can I say? Your idiot child is making me crazy?

CHAMP: Sunny, if you're all right now I'll —

SUNNY: I got down on my knees and that child threw his arms around me and I held on. Held on so the ground wouldn't open up underneath me. His mama come to the door and I said to her, "He's a wonderful boy." And she said, "Yes, he is."

CHAMP: Sunny. I'm gonna be late now. You ok?

SUNNY: Ok? Yeah, I'm —

CHAMP: [*Pause.*] All right then.

SUNNY: Hey, Champ.

CHAMP: [*He pauses.*] Yeah?

SUNNY: I don't know. I thought I married well. What do you think?

CHAMP: Good night, Sunny.

[*Exits.*]

SUNNY: [*Pauses, then yells.*] I asked you a question!

[*She heads upstairs.* MARLENE *enters, smoking a cigarette.* WIDOW 1 *approaches her.*]

WIDOW 1: You and the Reverend have a nice talk?

MARLENE: We talked.

WIDOW 1: Uh-huh. [*Pause.*] You got another cigarette?

MARLENE: Sure.

[*Takes a pack from her pocket and hands it over.*]

WIDOW 1: [*Takes cigarette out of pack, hands the pack back.*] You got a light?

MARLENE: [*Hands over her own cigarette.*] You'll have to jump start. I'm out of matches.

WIDOW 1: [*Jumps her cigarette. Hands lit cigarette back to* MARLENE.] I'm smoking a lot these days.

MARLENE: I always smoked a lot.

WIDOW 1: I try not to with the kids. Don't want them smoking.

MARLENE: They probably won't if you do. They got to be different.

WIDOW 1: I suppose that's true. My folks didn't smoke. My daddy chewed some.

MARLENE: I think that's worse.

WIDOW 1: Yeah. With the spitting and all.

[*Pause.*]

Mind if I ask you something?

MARLENE: Everybody's full of questions tonight.

WIDOW 1: That letter you got from the mill —

MARLENE: I signed it.

WIDOW 1: I know you signed it.

MARLENE: All right then.

WIDOW 1: Was it for real, or are you going to change your mind and take the mill to court?

MARLENE: No.

WIDOW 1: Which one?

MARLENE: Which one what?

WIDOW 1: Which one no? Wasn't a yes or no question.

MARLENE: No, I'm not going to get into this.

WIDOW 1: You can't blame me for wondering why you turned that money down.

MARLENE: My reasons were mine. You got what you wanted.

WIDOW 1: No, baby, the one thing I wanted was the one thing I can't have back again. And you can feel mighty as you want for refusing blood money. But some of us got kids. Thanks for the smoke.

[*They exit in opposite directions. Shift over to* BO *in the mill.* CHAMP *approaches him, reaches into his pocket and tosses him* SUNNY's *keys.*]

CHAMP: Here you go.

BO: Thank you.

[*Takes keys.*] You know I don't like to — [*Pause.*] Well, it's nothing you don't know about.

CHAMP: [CHAMP *changes into mill jacket and hard hat from his locker.*] No.

BO: No big secret.

[*Pause.*]

Did she fuss about the keys?

CHAMP: Not at all.

BO: I figured she wasn't going anywhere, but I felt better knowing she couldn't.

CHAMP: I don't blame you.

JEMISON: [*Approaching*.] All right. Quitting time.

CHAMP: What are you doing here still?

JEMISON: Waiting on your ass to get here.

CHAMP: Why is my ass so special?

JEMISON: Just because it is.

BO: Jeff Smyer ain't coming in.

CHAMP: Bet his ass is grass.

BO: He's got good reason. I'm going to have to put you down on the furnace, though.

CHAMP: Aw, man.

BO: Got to. I can't be short there tonight.

CHAMP: I fucking hate the furnace.

JEMISON: Got to keep them fired all night. Got to be fast.

CHAMP: I ain't feeling fast.

JEMISON: You ain't looking fast, either.

CHAMP: Come on, Bo. Send someone else. I ain't been on furnace in months.

BO: Everybody's at it already. Don't want to shuffle people around now.

CHAMP: Hey, man, why am I late? Do me a favor. You owe me.

BO: I know, I know. I'll pay up some other night.

CHAMP: Shit.

JEMISON: Night always goes by fast on the furnace.

CHAMP: For you, maybe.

JEMISON: And my night's fast gone. I'm taking off. Pray for a sunny morning.

BO: Then I won't sleep none.

JEMISON: Got to give a little to get a little.

BO: Yeah, why don't you get a little?

JEMISON: I'm on my way home to do just that.

CHAMP: Get some for me.

JEMISON: You look like you had more than you can handle, sweet son.

BO: Don't talk about my sister like that.

CHAMP: Get you home, Jemison.

JEMISON: I'm out of here.

CHAMP: 'Night.

JEMISON: [*Shakes hands with* BO.] 'Night.

BO: 'Night.

[JEMISON *exits*.]

Well, let's go. We got a lot of heats to fire tonight.

CHAMP: Who's taking my place on the caster?

BO: I am.

CHAMP: *You* are. Why don't you go on the furnace?

BO: My back's fucked up.

CHAMP: Aw, that's a load of shit.

BO: God's truth.

CHAMP: How did you fuck up your back?

BO: Old football injury.

CHAMP: Man, that's my excuse.

BO: It works for you.

CHAMP: That's because I really did play football.

BO: No, I'm really having some problems with it.

CHAMP: You are?

BO: Yeah.

CHAMP: Bad?

BO: Yeah. I'm taking these muscle relaxers.

[*Pats his shirt pocket*.]

CHAMP: Those will fuck you up good.

BO: I know. Not supposed to take them before work.

CHAMP: Give them to me. I'll take them for you.

BO: Too late now. Come on. Let's move. We got a lot of work tonight.

CHAMP: I'm moving.

BO: Not near fast enough.

CHAMP: Faster than you, old man.

[*They exit. The* WIDOWS *appear down front.*]

WIDOW 2: It's always that way, when something bad happens. People always say they felt it.

WIDOW 3: They felt something bad in the air.

WIDOW 1: Had a premonition. Were overly concerned.

WIDOW 2: More concerned than usual.

WIDOW 3: Had a funny feeling.

WIDOW 1: Said goodbye like they meant it.

WIDOW 3: See you in the morning.

WIDOW 2: Drive careful.

[*Lights up on* MARLENE *in the bed. The phone rings three or four times.* MARLENE *wakes, startled, and answers.*]

MARLENE: Hello.

[*Lights flash up fast and bright, freeze-framing* MARLENE *in the "hello." Lights fade out. Blackout.*]

END ACT ONE

ACT TWO

The WIDOWS *escort* MARLENE *on stage, dressed in lab coats over their black dresses. One* WIDOW *takes a pack of cigarettes from* MARLENE'*s pocket, hands one to her and returns the pack to* MARLENE'*s pocket. Another* WIDOW *lights the cigarette for* MARLENE. MARLENE *accepts these ministrations, but does not acknowledge them. The* WIDOWS *exit.* JEMISON *enters into the area that will be the hospital, carrying two styrofoam cups of coffee.*

JEMISON: Marlene. Hey. I brought you some coffee.

MARLENE: What?

JEMISON: I got a cup of coffee here for you.

[*She takes it.*]

That's a girl.

MARLENE: Yeah, I'm a good girl.

JEMISON: Doing real good.

MARLENE: Not for long if they don't fucking let me in there.

JEMISON: Doctor says that —

MARLENE: Bo's been in there.

JEMISON: Bo rode in the ambulance.

MARLENE: I don't see what —

JEMISON: His hands got burned.

MARLENE: Did they?

JEMISON: So I hear.

MARLENE: Where was his gloves?

JEMISON: I don't know.

MARLENE: Don't he wear gloves? Fireproof gloves?

JEMISON: Everybody does.

MARLENE: Fireproof suit. Safety glasses. Hard hat. Steel-toed boots.

JEMISON: Marlene.

MARLENE: To keep him safe.

JEMISON: Nothing going to do that.

MARLENE: Yeah?

JEMISON: Nothing going to keep you safe.

[*Shift to the* WIDOWS, *entering above. While they speak,* SUNNY *will enter, dressed in a robe and looking ragged.*]

WIDOW 2:   It's usually a wrong number. That call that comes at 2 A.M.

WIDOW 3:   Make you jump out of your skin.

WIDOW 1: Count your children.

WIDOW 3: Count your blessings.

WIDOW 1: Count ten, breathe deep, pick it up. Cradle it against your cheek.

WIDOW 2: Cradle the receiver, rock it like a baby. Nice baby, good baby.

WIDOW 3: Don't cry. Don't cry.

SUNNY: Bo! Bo! You home, Bo? Bo!

[*No answer.*]

Shit!

[*She considers replacing the phone on the cradle, but lays it back down on the table and exits.*]

[*Shift back to the hospital.* JEMISON *and* MARLENE *sit.* BO *approaches still in mill clothes, his hands bandaged in gauze.*]

MARLENE: Bo.

JEMISON: Hey, Bo.

BO: Hey, y'all.

MARLENE: Get me in there now, Bo.

BO: In a minute.

MARLENE: Now.

BO: Jemison.

MARLENE: Bo!

BO: You called Sunny?

JEMISON: Last I called it was still busy.

BO: Well, call her again, and if she don't answer, go get her for me.

JEMISON: All right.

[*Starts off.*]

BO: Wait — [*Digs in his pocket.*] Here's her keys. She can bring herself.

JEMISON: You sure you don't want me to bring her? I'm coming back anyway.

BO: Just give her the keys.

JEMISON: Ok. I'll be back soon.

[*Exits.*]

BO: Marlene.

MARLENE: Enough of this bullshit, Bo. Nobody's telling me nothing. I'm so scared. I never been so scared.

BO: They're going to let you see him now.

MARLENE: Oh God.

BO: And they wanted me to tell you —

MARLENE: Tell me.

BO: They wanted —

MARLENE: Shut up.

BO: Marlene —

MARLENE: Just shut up. Where is he?

BO: Room I just came out of.

[BO *takes* MARLENE *toward a door, but is met by the* WIDOWS. *He exits as* WIDOW 1 *takes* MARLENE *downstage, while the other two* WIDOWS *enter, flanking* CHAMP. CHAMP *stands in front of the bed.* WIDOWS 2 *and* 3 *will cut a pair of mill pants and a T-shirt from him as they speak, with the calm/efficient bustle of nurses.*]

WIDOW 1: We just want you to be prepared.

WIDOW 3: So your expectations will be realistic.

WIDOW 2: We don't mean to scare you.

WIDOW 3: We don't mean to discourage you.

WIDOW 1: This is what we know about this sort of thing.

WIDOW 2: When a patient is burned over eighty percent of his body.

WIDOW 1: With burns of second and third degree.

WIDOW 2: There are factors in the recovery.

WIDOW 3: The skin is the largest organ of the body.

WIDOW 1: The rest of the body must work very hard to

compensate for the injury.

WIDOW 3: Obviously dehydration is a factor.

WIDOW 2: There is a great deal of danger from bacterial infection.

WIDOW 3: A great deal of danger.

WIDOW 1: There is bacteria in the air we breathe.

WIDOW 2: In the sterile bed.

WIDOW 3: In the human touch.

WIDOW 1: Wear this.

[*Ties a surgical mask on* MARLENE.]

WIDOW 2: He's heavily sedated now.

WIDOW 3: Heavily sedated.

WIDOW 2: We have him on painkillers.

WIDOW 1: Antibiotics. For any possible infection.

WIDOW 3: We don't mean to frighten you.

WIDOW 1: We only want you to be prepared.

[CHAMP *is now naked before her.* WIDOWS 2 *and* 3 *lay him on the bed, spreading his legs and arms apart.* WIDOW 1 *leads* MARLENE *to the bed. The* WIDOWS *stand away, apart from the action.*]

MARLENE: Champ. Champ.

[*She removes the mask, reaches towards him, then pulls back.*]

Champ.

CHAMP: Come to bed. It's time to go to bed.

MARLENE: Champ.

[*She gingerly climbs onto the bed, and touches him at the hollow of the throat.*]

CHAMP: That's good. That feels so good.

[*She kisses the hollow of his throat.*]

WIDOW 1: What the hell are you doing?

[WIDOW 1 *yanks* MARLENE *from the bed and drags her downstage.* CHAMP *rises and exits as the other two* WIDOWS *strip the bed bare.* WIDOW 1 *and* MARLENE *struggle with one another downstage.*]

MARLENE: I'm just —

WIDOW 1:   Do you realize —

MARLENE: I'm trying to tell you —

WIDOW 1:   I think you ought to —

MARLENE: Let go of me!

WIDOW 1:   Help me! Orderly! I need some help here!

MARLENE: Get off of me!

[BO *enters and grabs* MARLENE *from behind.*]

WIDOW 1:   Calm down! I need some help here.

MARLENE: Get this bitch off of me!

[MARLENE *manages to get a hand free and slaps* WIDOW 1 *across the face.*]

Get off of me!

[*They all leave the stage, and* MARLENE *is alone, downstage center. She pauses, collects herself, reaches in her pocket and takes out a pack of cigarettes. She pats her pockets for matches. The* MINISTER *approaches her.*]

MINISTER: Church is filling up.

MARLENE: Is it?

MINISTER: It is.

MARLENE: You got a light?

MINISTER: I don't smoke. Sorry.

MARLENE: That's good you don't smoke.

MINISTER: I used to.

MARLENE: No vices now.

MINISTER: I got my bad habits.

MARLENE: No.

MINISTER: Yeah, I do.

MARLENE: Like what?

MINISTER: This is a bad one.

MARLENE: I can't imagine.

MINISTER: At least I always feel bad about it.

MARLENE: How bad can it be?

MINISTER: I have a habit of eavesdropping.

MARLENE: Eavesdropping.

MINISTER: Yes.

MARLENE: Well, if that don't beat all.

MINISTER: Did she shake you up some?

MARLENE: Her? No.

MINISTER: You seem —

MARLENE: I'm tired of being scrutinized.

MINISTER: I'm sorry if I —

MARLENE: Marlene, why you acting like this, Marlene why'd you do that. I'm tired of everybody in my face.

MINISTER: Why'd you do it? Why did you sign your money away?

MARLENE: Jesus.

[*Pause.*]

You want to know?

MINISTER: I'd like to know.

MARLENE: I didn't want it.

MINISTER: That's it?

MARLENE: That's it. I just didn't want it. I didn't want them to feel better. To feel like they'd done their part. Give the sad little widow her sad little compensation. Pat her on the head. Send her off satisfied.

MINISTER: It was a good deal of money.

MARLENE: Not near enough. Not even close.

MINISTER: You wanted more?

MARLENE: You're not listening, son. I did not want it. Not even a little bit. Because what is it, really? What is that money they offer me? What is that?

MINISTER: It's your due.

MARLENE: It's bullshit. And every month of my life for the rest of my life there it would be in a brown envelope sitting in my mailbox. Every month of my life. You understand?

MINISTER: To a degree.

MARLENE: I got to go find me a light.

[MARLENE *and the* MINISTER *exit in opposite directions.* MARLENE *is met by* BO *and* WIDOW 1. *She collapses into their arms, as though sedated.* WIDOW 1 *helps* BO *get her into a chair, then he sits beside her, holding her.* WIDOW 1 *exits.* SUNNY *comes running on.*]

BO: Sunny.

SUNNY: You all right?

BO: I'm all right.

SUNNY: Jemison told me.

BO: Told you what?

SUNNY: Furnace exploded last night around two. Three men already dead. Champ —

BO: Champ's dying.

SUNNY: He is?

BO: He will.

SUNNY: Oh no.

BO: Bad as he's burned he better hope he does.

SUNNY: How's Marlene?

BO: They knocked her out.

SUNNY: Why?

BO: She got hysterical. Tried to get in bed with Champ. Hit a nurse.

SUNNY: She did?

BO: She did.

SUNNY: Where's Champ?

BO: Last room on the left. You going to go see him?

SUNNY: No.

BO: I think you should.

SUNNY: Will he know any different?

BO: I don't think so.

SUNNY: Then I don't think I will.

BO: Sunny —

SUNNY: What.

BO: I want you to.

SUNNY: Why?

BO: I just do.

SUNNY: Are you trying to —

BO: I'm not trying to do anything. I just want you to see him. I'm asking you to. Will you go see Champ?

SUNNY: [*Pause.*] Yeah. I will.

BO: Thank you.

[*Taking pill bottle from his shirt pocket.*]

Sunny, will you take the top off this pill bottle? I can't with these hands.

SUNNY: [*Takes pill bottle and looks at label.*] They just give you these?

BO: No. These are for my back. Doctor wanted to give me painkillers but I told him I was already taking these and he said they'd do.

SUNNY: You told him you were taking these?

BO: Yes.

SUNNY: Did you take one of these before work?

BO: I did.

SUNNY: You tell him that too?

BO: He didn't ask.

SUNNY: Well thank God for that.

BO: Sunny —

SUNNY: You know OSHA's going to be all over that mill. And here you are on the job taking fucking horse tranquilizers.

BO: Muscle relaxers.

SUNNY: They won't see any difference.

BO: I was nowhere near that furnace when it blew.

SUNNY: How'd you get burned, then?

BO: Pulling them out of there after.

[MARLENE *stirs*. BO *quiets her*. SUNNY *hands him the pills*.]

I need something to take these pills with.

SUNNY: I'll get you some water.

BO: Give me the bottle in your bag.

SUNNY: Bo. I don't —

BO: Sunny, you know it's in there and I know it's in there.

[SUNNY *reaches in her bag and pulls out a pint of whiskey*.]

Take off the cap.

[*She does, and hands him the bottle. He takes the pills, takes another shot. She reaches for the bottle to put the cap back on.*]

No, I'll just hang on to this for a while. Why don't you run on and see Champ now? Last room on the left.

SUNNY: [*Hands him the bottle cap*.] I heard you the first time.

[*Exits*.]

[*The* WIDOWS *stand above, facing out, each holding a funeral urn full of ashes. As they speak they will scatter ashes on the ground in front of them*.]

WIDOW 2: For weeks it seemed it was sunny, bright.

WIDOW 1: Relentlessly cheerful.

WIDOW 3: I kept the venetian blinds cracked, and the air conditioner on.

WIDOW 1: And in the chill and the patterned light.

WIDOW 2: Watched the dust settle on the furniture.

WIDOW 3: And did not polish it once.

WIDOW 3: Toward September, when the tropical depressions

develop on the Gulf.

WIDOW 1: And hit the coast named as hurricanes.

WIDOW 3: [MARLENE *rises and joins them, going first to the bed, then coming downstage at the end of this section.*] It stormed for three days straight.

WIDOW 1: Knocking out the power.

WIDOW 2: Scaring the kids.

WIDOW 3: I pulled up the blinds and threw open all the windows.

WIDOW 1: Let the rain blow through the house, clearing away the dust.

MARLENE: Clearing my head.

WIDOW 1: A slight scent of salt on the wind.

WIDOW 2: I put fresh sheets on the bed.

WIDOW 3: White sheets. Linen.

WIDOW 1: A wedding gift used only for company.

MARLENE: I stripped slowly. So slowly.

WIDOW 2: Rubbed oil into my skin. All over myself.

WIDOW 3: Spread ashes on those clean white sheets.

WIDOW 2: And got into bed with my husband.

MARLENE: And when I was covered, I wrapped myself in the sheets, went outside and let the downpour wash me clean.

WIDOW 3: In the backyard on the patio he built.

WIDOW 1: I let the rain wash me clean.

[MARLENE *drops to all fours, heaving.* BO *comes up to her and rubs her between the shoulders.*]

BO: Marlene, Marlene honey, you all right? Marlene?

MARLENE: [*Heaving.*] I'm just sick.

BO: You want a nurse? I'll get you a nurse.

MARLENE: I'm just sick.

BO: You think it's what they gave you? Do you want some water?

[MARLENE *waves him away.*]

I'll get you some.

[*Starts off. The* MINISTER *and* SUNNY *approach.*]

SUNNY: Bo, wait.

BO: I'm just getting —

SUNNY: Wait.

[*She goes to* MARLENE *and holds her.*]

MINISTER: Mrs. Hotchkiss, Mrs. Hotchkiss. I'm sorry.

MARLENE: Oh, Jesus. [*Still heaving.*] Oh, Jesus. Goddamn.

SUNNY: [*Squatting down.*] He passed quiet, Marlene.

MARLENE: You were there?

SUNNY: Yes.

MARLENE: You were with him when he died?

SUNNY: I was with him.

MARLENE: Goddamn it. Goddamn you all.

[MARLENE *runs off,* SUNNY *follows.*]

SUNNY: Marlene!

[BO *exits.* JEMISON *enters and brings a chair downstage center. The* MINISTER *goes above and is helped on with a jacket as he passes the first* WIDOW, *handed a clipboard and glasses as he passes the next two.* JEMISON *should begin to speak as this is taking place. The* MINISTER *as the OSHA investigator should be different in tone and bearing.*]

JEMISON: I gave Bo a call and he came in early. He was at the mill by nine-thirty and we discussed everything — which furnace was out, how high the creek was, how much dry scrap he had to work with.

MINISTER: And he understood all of this.

JEMISON: Every bit. There was plenty of dry scrap left.

MINISTER: Uh-huh. You said that the shift was short-handed.

JEMISON: Yes, sir.

MINISTER: And you had to stay until Mr. Hotchkiss arrived.

JEMISON: Champ.

MINISTER: Yes.

JEMISON: Yes, sir.

MINISTER: When he arrived did he seem to you to be impaired in any way?

JEMISON: Impaired?

MINISTER: Under the influence of alcohol or drugs.

JEMISON: No, he was not impaired, sir.

MINISTER: Now, you left before the actual explosion — is that right?

JEMISON: Well before it.

MINISTER: You left the mill at twelve-thirty, according to the guard at the plant gate, and the explosion was around 2 A.M.

JEMISON: That's what I hear.

MINISTER: Yes.

[*Pause.*]

Mr. Jemison, in your opinion, what caused the explosion?

JEMISON: It could have been wet scrap. It could have been a gas tank in the scrap. It could have been a weak spot in the lining of the furnace wall. It could have been a lot of things. But I think it was just one of those things that happen. You know what I mean?

MINISTER: I'm afraid that I don't. Thank you, Mr. Jemison.

[*He exits.*]

JEMISON: The pleasure was mine.

[JEMISON *and the* WIDOWS *exit.* BO *enters, looking beat.* SUNNY *comes down the stairs and into the kitchen.*]

SUNNY: How did it go?

BO: It went.

SUNNY: What did they ask you?

BO: Everything.

SUNNY: Like?

BO: Like what kind of scrap did we use to charge the heats, how high was the creek exactly, what time I got there, why Champ was late.

SUNNY: Did they ask about your medication?

BO: Company doctor told them.

SUNNY: And —

BO: I told them I was taking the medication as directed. Exactly.

SUNNY: They believe you?

BO: Why shouldn't they?

SUNNY: Because it's not true.

BO: I've told you already, Sunny — I was nowhere near the furnace. The medication has no bearing.

SUNNY: That's the way you see it, maybe, but these guys are trying to get the mill off the hook. These guys want to be able to pass it off on human error.

BO: Sunny — these guys want to find out what happened. Period.

[BO *puts the phone on the hook.*]

Did you talk to Marlene today?

SUNNY: I tried.

BO: What did she say?

SUNNY: She said to tell the mill to shove their money.

BO: They want to settle.

SUNNY: Well, apparently she doesn't.

BO: They told me that they want to settle out of court with everyone, and if any one of the women takes them to court, they'll settle with no one.

SUNNY: That's kind of them.

BO: It's just the way it's done, I guess.

SUNNY: I think they're just trying to scare them.

BO: Well, I got to stay out of it. Let Marlene settle on her own. I can't get in the middle any more than I am already.

SUNNY: I don't think Marlene wants to settle at all. I think she meant just what she said.

BO: She's not thinking straight.

SUNNY: Thinking straight or not, she's made up her mind.

BO: I'll talk to her.

SUNNY: I don't think she'll talk to you.

BO: She'll talk to you.

SUNNY: I don't matter.

BO: Oh, man.

[*Reaches to get pills from his jacket pocket.*]

SUNNY: Does your back hurt?

BO: It's killing me.

SUNNY: Want me to rub it?

BO: No. I just need my pills.

[*Looks at bottle.*]

I'm almost out of these.

SUNNY: You can't refill the prescription. You got to have the doctor write you another.

BO: Well, I'm not going to do that.

SUNNY: Why not? The OSHA thing is over.

BO: You know what they asked me?

SUNNY: What?

BO: They asked me to describe it all in detail. What I heard, what I saw. What I did.

SUNNY: Well, of course they asked that.

BO: It was the way they asked it. Like they wished they'd been there to see it. To see the spectacular mill fire. Like when people ask me what the war was like.

SUNNY: What did you tell them?

BO: I told them it was like nothing they'd ever seen. Like nothing they'd ever want to see.

[BO *exits up the stairs.* SUNNY *watches him go, then exits. The* WIDOWS *enter with a set of sheets and pillows and make the bed as they speak.*]

WIDOW 1:   After a time I stopped waking in the middle of the night.

WIDOW 3:   Stopped feeling him lift the sheets and get into bed with me.

WIDOW 2:   Stopped seeing him sitting at the kitchen table.

WIDOW 1:   Drinking a beer, eating a sandwich.

WIDOW 2:   While I had my morning coffee.

WIDOW 1:   I can't say how long it took for that to happen.

WIDOW 3:   Because time was a funny thing then.

WIDOW 2:   Maybe before Chistmas.

WIDOW 1:   Maybe at the start of the Little League season.

WIDOW 2:   I just can't say.

WIDOW 3:   But all of a sudden, he wasn't there anymore.

WIDOW 2:   My life went on at my own rhythm.

WIDOW 3:   Not from eight to four, from four to twelve.

WIDOW 1:   From twelve to eight.

WIDOW 2:   There was day and there was night.

WIDOW 3:   And I started to sleep well, for the first time in my adult life.

WIDOW 1:   Because the call had come.

WIDOW 2:   And I was still in one piece.

[MARLENE *gets into bed, the radio blaring. She brings with her a mess of newspapers and mail.* BO *pounds on the door.*]

MARLENE: Come on in.

BO: [*Entering wearing mill clothes, he goes to the radio and switches it off.*] How you doing?

MARLENE: Ok.

BO: I called over to your office but they said you were sick.

MARLENE: I guess I am.

BO: You need anything?

MARLENE: No. I just couldn't sit there and look at a little green screen all day. I couldn't sit there all day.

BO: You called in sick all last week too.

MARLENE: You checking up on me?

BO: They volunteered that information.

MARLENE: They shouldn't have done that.

BO: Marlene — you're going to lose that job.

MARLENE: Am I?

BO: You keep up like this.

MARLENE: Like what?

BO: Girl, you know what I'm talking about.

MARLENE: Well, Bo, if I lose the job, I lose it. There are plenty of shitty jobs to be had in this world.

BO: May not be.

MARLENE: There always are.

BO: U. S. Steel laid off half their plant. More to come.

MARLENE: So?

BO: All those people with no money to spend. This town's going to look very different in a couple months.

MARLENE: They'll hire back.

BO: Not this time.

MARLENE: They're just trying to scare the union.

BO: Not this time.

MARLENE: Well, if there's not a shitty job to be had here, there's one somewhere else.

BO: You've never lived anywhere else.

MARLENE: Maybe it's time, then.

BO: Marlene — people been asking about you.

MARLENE: People?

BO: Yeah.

MARLENE: And what do these people want to know?

BO: They want to know why you're holding up the settlement to the other women.

MARLENE: Why I'm holding it up.

BO: You each got a letter from the mill. A release.

MARLENE: Saying I won't take the mill to court.

BO: Yeah.

MARLENE: [*Holds up letter.*] You mean this?

BO: [*Takes it and looks at it.*] How long you had this?

MARLENE: A while.

BO: How long is that?

MARLENE: I don't know. A while.

BO: Mill's not paying out until all of you sign this. I don't know what you're doing, but it ain't right.

MARLENE: Plenty of things ain't right with this world, Bo.

BO: [*Looking at letter.*] This letter says you turned down the money.

MARLENE: That's right.

BO: You turned it down.

MARLENE: Turned it down and in the future will not take the mill to court.

BO: You haven't signed it.

MARLENE: I will.

BO: I don't believe this.

MARLENE: You want to see me do it?

BO: No, I don't. I want you to listen to me.

MARLENE: I know what you got to say.

BO: Take the money.

MARLENE: I don't want it.

BO: You stop this shit. Stop it. You call the mill. You tell them you're taking the settlement and you tell them you want a straight release, same as everyone else.

MARLENE: I told the mill that this is what I wanted.

BO: And I'm telling you —

MARLENE: Don't you tell me what to do.

BO: You need to be told.

MARLENE: Don't.

BO: You might not want the money now —

MARLENE: I don't want it now.

BO: But in a couple years down the line —

MARLENE: I won't want it then, either.

BO: How can you know that?

MARLENE: I know it.

[*Snatches pen from his pocket and signs the letter.*]

BO: I don't believe you're doing this.

MARLENE: Believe it.

[*Holds letter out to him.*]

Why don't you drop this off at the front office on your way in to work?

BO: [*Crumples letter and throws it at her.*] You take it to them yourself.

[*Turns to head out, turns back.*]

You know, Marlene, if you change your mind —

MARLENE: I won't.

BO: If you change your mind, a letter like that will never stand up in a court of law.

MARLENE: It won't have to.

[*He heads out.*]

Hey, Bo —

[*He turns back.*]

How's your back?

[*He exits, she smooths the letter and puts it in an envelope. She exits. Shift over to* JEMISON. *Loud music is playing and he is drinking beer.* BO *approaches him.*]

JEMISON: Hey, buddy.

BO: Hey.

JEMISON: You want one of these?

BO: No.

JEMISON: Sure?

BO: Just give me a hit of yours.

JEMISON: I'll get you one of your very own.

BO: No, no, no.

JEMISON: [*Hollers.*] Hey! Janelle! Bring Bo here a Pabst.

BO: All right.

JEMISON: What time you got to be there?

BO: Sunny said around seven.

JEMISON: Plenty of time.

    [*Hollers.*]

    Janelle! Cup of gumbo, too!

    [*To* BO:] You want one?

BO: No.

JEMISON: Just one! One gumbo, two beers!

    [*To* BO:] So how you doing, man?

BO: Me? I'm fine.

JEMISON: How'd your shift run?

BO: It ran.

JEMISON: Yeah.

BO: You going?

JEMISON: Yeah, I am. I'm not on until midnight.

BO: That's right.

JEMISON: Any of your shift coming?

BO: Most of it. Yours?

JEMISON: Some. Mill should have closed down for it.

BO: Never happen.

JEMISON: Just saying they should. Would have been decent.

BO: They're not in the business of being decent.

JEMISON: Come again?

BO: You heard me.

JEMISON: Man, I never thought I'd hear you badmouth your employer.

BO: I'd hardly call that badmouth.

JEMISON: For you, it is.

BO: Well, maybe it is.

JEMISON: I'm not saying you —

BO: What you saying?

JEMISON: It's about damn time, is all.

BO: Yeah.

JEMISON: They danced on your ass for quite some time.

BO: Don't I know it.

JEMISON: And Marlene —

BO: Marlene called her own shots.

JEMISON: It still sucks.

BO: Yeah, it does.

JEMISON: Just covering their own ass, is all.

BO: They do it well.

JEMISON: Too well. This memorial service thing is the best part.

BO: What?

JEMISON: Memorial service. The mill put it together.

BO: Where'd you hear that?

JEMISON: Everybody knows.

BO: How come I don't?

JEMISON: I don't know. I mean, what did you think, Bo? Did you think First Baptist came up with it all by their selves?

BO: I don't — yeah. Yeah, that's what I thought. Why not?

JEMISON: Why? Why should they do something like that? Do

they need to look good?

BO: I guess not.

JEMISON: How much P.R. do the Baptists need in Alabama?

BO: I'm so fucking stupid.

JEMISON: No.

BO: I am.

JEMISON: No, man, you just got other things on your mind.

[BO *exits.* JEMISON *hollers out:*]

Janelle — hey — I don't want no cold gumbo and warm beer!

[*He exits. The* WIDOWS *enter.*]

WIDOW 1:   At first the checks came weekly. There it was every Friday.

WIDOW 2:   Just like he was still on payroll.

WIDOW 3:   Not as much as when he was on payroll. But just like.

WIDOW 1:   Not as much. I'd get to Friday and there'd be nothing.

WIDOW 3:   There'd be food in the fridge for the next day or so. But nothing beyond that.

WIDOW 2:   Then it was one of those holiday weekends. Lincoln or Washington or something. And the check didn't come.

WIDOW 1:   Monday came and it still was not there.

WIDOW 3:   Tuesday, Wednesday.

WIDOW 2:   I borrowed from my sister.

WIDOW 3:   And gave the mill a call.

WIDOW 1:   Got passed from office to office. Forwarded down the line to pension and benefits.

WIDOW 2:   The pension and benefits lady says all benefits are paid monthly.

WIDOW 3:   Once a month, around the first.

WIDOW 1:   It had come to her attention that checks were coming to me weekly.

WIDOW 2:   And that was not the way things were done.

[*The* WIDOWS *exit. Shift to* BO *coming downstairs, half dressed and in pain.* SUNNY *waits for him in the kitchen.*]

SUNNY: I called the mill.

BO: What for?

SUNNY: You're not going in.

BO: Sunny —

SUNNY: Bo, where's your brains? You can't hardly walk.

BO: I can walk.

SUNNY: Yeah, and does it feel good? Does it feel fine? No, it doesn't.

BO: All right, all right.

SUNNY: I want to call the doctor, too.

BO: Don't call the doctor.

SUNNY: Why not?

BO: I don't need to see him.

SUNNY: Why not?

BO: I'll be fine. I just strained it, is all.

SUNNY: Strained it? You're having back spasms. You didn't fucking strain your back.

BO: No.

SUNNY: So can I call the doctor?

BO: Call your doctor.

SUNNY: My doctor?

BO: Yeah, your doctor.

SUNNY: I don't know if he can prescribe —

BO: Your doctor or no doctor at all.

SUNNY: Hey, Bo, what's going on?

BO: Same shit that's been going on.

SUNNY: I thought OSHA was through.

BO: They finished with me a couple weeks ago. Then there was the mill management and the insurance company and even the fucking union had to jump in on it.

SUNNY: You're a foreman. You're not union.

BO: Champ and the other guys were.

SUNNY: I'm sorry.

BO: Yeah.

SUNNY: Why didn't you say anything?

BO: Say what?

SUNNY: Say they're putting you through hell. Tell me these things.

BO: Just out of practice, I guess.

SUNNY: Out of practice.

BO: You understand?

SUNNY: Yeah. I do.

[*They exit together,* SUNNY *supporting him and rubbing his lower back. The* WIDOWS *enter above, holding their coffee cups.*]

WIDOW 3: I've heard that when a person's soul leaves his body, there's a moment.

WIDOW 2: A moment of decision.

WIDOW 1: The soul looks back on the body.

[MARLENE *enters, smoking a cigarette, and stands downstage center.* CHAMP *enters from behind her, dressed again in the full reflective suit and hardhat, as at the top of the play.*]

WIDOW 3: Wracked with disease, age, or injury.

WIDOW 2: And decides either to return to the body.

WIDOW 3: Or to pass beyond. Leave it behind.

[CHAMP *brushes a hand through* MARLENE's *hair, then stands aside, on the periphery.*]

WIDOW 1: I don't know if that's true.

WIDOW 2: If that really happens.

WIDOW 3: But I like to think so.

[SUNNY *approaches* MARLENE, *dressed as at the top of the play.*]

MARLENE: You've been scarce.

SUNNY: I've been down in the parish hall.

MARLENE: Doing what?

SUNNY: Watching church women make coffee and finger sandwiches.

MARLENE: I'm not staying to make nice at some shitty little reception.

SUNNY: No one's asking you to.

MARLENE: Bo will.

SUNNY: No, he won't.

MARLENE: Yes he will.

SUNNY: Marlene — what can you be thinking?

MARLENE: What do you mean?

SUNNY: What can you be thinking about Bo?

MARLENE: He's the best company man I know.

SUNNY: Girl, you got your head right up your own ass.

MARLENE: Do I, Sunny? Do I really?

SUNNY: Without a doubt.

MARLENE: Well, I think he's been looking pretty good through this whole thing.

SUNNY: Any reason why he shouldn't?

MARLENE: You tell me.

SUNNY: You know as well as I do.

MARLENE: You tell me.

SUNNY: I'll tell you what you already know because you seem to need to hear it. Bo had nothing to do with it. You know it, OSHA knows it, the company, the union, everybody knows it. So whatever you got going on in your head about Bo — you got to let it go. Because it's not about anything he did or did not do. It's you. That's all it is. It's just you.

[*At some point during this speech,* BO *enters, unnoticed by either of the women, and stands back from them.*]

MARLENE: He held me down.

SUNNY: What?

MARLENE: Held me down. Did not ask me what was going on. Did not try to find out. Held me down and let them sedate me.

SUNNY: You're talking about the hospital?

MARLENE: It was right here.

[*Strokes the hollow of her throat.*]

Right here. I thought how strange that was. Right where his shirt collar would have been open his skin was untouched. Unburned. They let me into the room after they'd shot him full of morphine and left him to die.

BO: Marlene.

[*He approaches them.*]

MARLENE: What, Bo.

BO: No one left Champ to die. They did everything —

MARLENE: Yeah. They did everything. And then left him to die. I wanted him to die. Once I saw him, I knew. He was so — raw looking. His eyes were way deep inside him. Nothing coming in or out. I talked to him but there was nothing coming in or out. So I touched him. Here, right here.

[*Strokes the hollow of her throat.*]

The one place I could. Ran my fingers back and forth, light as air. His eyes came forward from back out of his head. Came to me. Locked in, focused. He said, clear as day he said, "Come to bed. It's time to go to bed." And I was so afraid. His arms and legs placed apart so they wouldn't touch each other. Spread across the bed. A small strip of space along side him. I made myself as narrow as I could on that strip. Lay down next to him and felt the heat rise off his burned skin. Saw it. I ran my fingers along his throat. And he said, "That's good. That feels so good."

WIDOW 1: [*Calling down from above.*] What the hell are you doing?

MARLENE: I'm just —

WIDOW 1: Do you realize —

MARLENE: I'm trying to tell —

WIDOW 1: I think you ought to—

MARLENE: Let go of me.

[BO *takes hold of her from behind.* MARLENE *struggles with him.*]

WIDOW 1: Help me! Orderly! I need some help here!

MARLENE: Get off of me!

WIDOW 1: Calm down! Calm down! I need some help here!

MARLENE: Get this bitch off of me! Get off of me! Let me go! Let me go!

[*She is suddenly quiet.* CHAMP *turns and walks slowly off.*]

It wouldn't have made any difference to him. But to me. It would have been all the difference in the world.

[BO *and* MARLENE *stand for a moment,* BO *still holding her. Then they move apart mutually.*]

BO: Marlene.

MARLENE: Yeah.

BO: Let's get out of here.

MARLENE: You want to go?

BO: I don't want to be here. Do you?

MARLENE: I never wanted to be here.

BO: Sunny?

SUNNY: Whatever.

BO: You don't mind.

SUNNY: Got no reason to.

BO: All right.

SUNNY: I'll get my car. It's out back.

MARLENE: I'm walking out the front.

SUNNY: Church is full of people.

MARLENE: That's even better. You going to come with me?

BO: Yeah, I'll come with you.

SUNNY: I'll bring my car around front.

BO: I got mine here.

SUNNY: Well.

BO: Come on, Sunny, what's your worry? People have always talked about you.

SUNNY: Bo!

BO: Well, you gave them something to talk about.

SUNNY: Somebody's got to.

[*Pause.*]

Ok. Let's go.

BO: [*Puts his arm lightly around* MARLENE'*s shoulder. They walk slightly ahead of* SUNNY.] You look good, Marlene. That's a pretty dress.

MARLENE: Thanks. Sunny helped me pick it out.

WIDOW 3: So why are you here?

WIDOW 2: I'm here to heal. How about you?

[*Fade, blackout, end.*]

THE END

ABOUT THE PLAYWRIGHTS

MARIA IRENE FORNES is the author of more than two dozen works for the stage. Among her best known are *Fefu and Her Friends*, *The Danube*, *Mud*, *The Conduct of Life*, *Sarita* and the musical *Promenade*. She has been awarded a total of six Obies, among which was the Obie for Sustained Achievement in Theatre in 1982. In 1985, she received an award from the American Academy and Institute of Arts and Letters. She directs at regional theatres and in New York and teaches playwriting at INTAR, Padua Hills and NYU.

CASSANDRA MEDLEY is the author of "Ms. Mae," the one-act monologue included in the hit revue, *A ... My Name Is Alice*, first produced by The Women's Project, recipient of the 1984 Outer Drama Critics Circle Award and currently touring regional theatres throughout the United States. Other plays include *Waking Women*, produced by Ensemble Studio Theatre in Marathon '87 and *Terrain*, produced by Ensemble Studio Theatre in the New Voices Series. This version of *Ma Rose* is the result of a commission by the Women's Project to develop *Ma Rose* from a one-act into a full-length play. It was a finalist for the Susan Smith Blackburn Award.

MARLANE MEYER won the Joseph Kesselring Award for *Etta Jenks* and was a finalist for the Susan Smith Blackburn Award. Other plays include *Kingfish*, produced at the Los Angeles Theatre Center in the 1988-89 season and slated for production by the New York Shakespeare Festival in 1989-90 and *Geography of Luck*, produced by the South Coast Rep and LATC, 1989. Formerly, playwright-in-residence at LATC, Marlene now lives in New York City.

LAVONNE MUELLER received the 1986 Drama League Award for *Five in the Killing Zone* and it was a Sundance Institute selection. She has had six plays produced off-Broadway: *Warriors from a Long Childhood* at Theatre Four and *Killings on the Last Line*, *Little Victories*, *The Only Women General*, *Breaking the Prairie Wolf Code* and *Colette* at The Women's Project and productions. Her play *Letters to a Daughter from Prison* was produced in India in spring 1989.

SALLY NEMETH received a first production of *Mill Fire* at Chicago's Goodman Theatre. Her play *Holy Days* premiered in London in 1988 and was produced subsequently in Dublin, Ireland, and New Zealand. Other plays include *Modern Lit*, commissioned by the Actors Theatre of Louisville and *Farther Than the Eye Can See*, produced at the Commons Theatre, Chicago. A new play, *Spinning into Blue*, was recently commissioned by the South Coast Repertory. Born in Chicago, Sally lived for a while in Birmingham where her father managed a steel mill. She now resides in New York.